Basic Design Theory
& Methods

PEARSON

Custom
Publishing

PEARSON

Education

Cover image: Courtesy of Photodisc/Getty Images

Taken from:

Graphic Design Portfolio-Builder: Adobe Photoshop and Adobe Illustrator Projects
by Sessions.edu Online School of Design
Copyright © 2006 by Sessions.edu Online School of Design
Published by Peachpit Press
A Pearson Education Company
Berkeley, California 94710

Product Design and Manufacture
by John R. Lindbeck
Copyright © 1995 by Prentice Hall, Inc.
A Pearson Education Company
Upper Saddle River, New Jersey 07458

Graphic Design: Vision, Process, Product
by Louis D. Ocepek
Copyright © 2003 by Pearson Education, Inc.
Published by Prentice Hall

This special edition published in cooperation with Pearson Custom Publishing.

All trademarks, service marks, registered trademarks, and registered service marks are the property of their respective owners and are used herein for identification purposes only.

Printed in the United States of America

     17 18 19 20

ISBN 0-536-08745-8

2007120062

KL

Please visit our web site at *www.pearsoncustom.com*

PEARSON CUSTOM PUBLISHING
501 Boylston Street, Suite 900, Boston, MA 02116
A Pearson Education Company

Contents

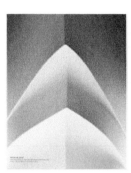

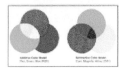

6 Color 210

Taken from *Graphic Design: Vision, Process, Product* by Louis D. Ocepek

7 Digital Illustration 224

Chapters 7–12 taken from *Graphic Design Portfolio-Builder* by Sessions.edu Online School of Design

8 Poster Design 270

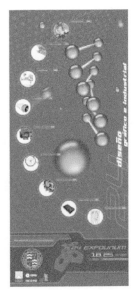

9 Logo Design 302

10 Advertising Design

11 Magazine Design 360

Art Credits and Contributions

CHAPTER 2

Bond Bath and Home Gallery
Paulina Margolies, owner
Designer: Patricio Sarzosa
www.psarzosa.com

War/Terror poster
Designer: Marty Neumeier
www.neutronllc.com

Maxwell's Apothecary product line
Laura Schwamb
STEAM Design Group
www.steam-design.com

**Wick Fowler's 2-Alarm Chili
    poster series**
Brock Davis art director, Tom Kelly
    creative director
Martin/Williams
www.martinwilliams.com

**Thoughts on Leaves & Letters: a Leaflet
    from Vangool Design & Typography**
Janine Vangool
Calgary, Alberta, Canada
www.vangooldesign.com

Project: Curious: The Pin-Up Collection
Design/Writer: Frank Viva
Studio: Viva Dolan Communications &
    Design Inc.
Photography: Ron Baxter Smith
Garments: Dean Horn
Client: Arjo Wiggins
Printing: Hemlock Printers Ltd.
www.vivadolan.com

**Ford Detroit International Jazz
    Festival poster**
Felix Sockwell, illustrator
www.felixsockwell.com

Lava Life poster ads
Marcos Chin, designer
www.marcoshin.com

Car wash logo and Green Tea package
Designer: Patricio Sarzosa
www.psarzosa.com

Outdoor ad
Target Corporation
1000 Nicollet Mall
Minneapolis, MN 55403
www.target.com

One Step Contact Solution
Williams Murray Hamm
www.creatingdifference.com

Gabriela Monroy
YWEML cover
www.m-o-s-t-r-a.com

**Azure Magazine
    "New Directions in Portugal"**
Concrete Media
http://concrete.ca

Consumer Explorers logo
Nin Glaister, designer
www.98pt6.com

Champion Athletic Apparel ad
Billy Hackley,/Kris Hendershott, art directors
Billy Hackley, designer, Hayes Henderson,
    creative director
Lee Reunion, photographer
Henderson/BromsteadArtCo.
http://hendersonbromsteadart.com

"A Delicate Balance,"
Developed for Seattle Repertory Theater
Designer/Illustrator: Dennis Clouse
Design firm: Cyclone Design
www.cyclone-design.com

Cascade Festival of Music Poster
tbd advertising, Bend, Oregon
www.tbdadvertising.com

CHAPTER 3

Photoshop User cover
Designer: Felix Nelson
www.photoshopuser.com

Chapter photographs
Donald Gambino

Room makeover projects
Adam Benefield
Melinda Langevin
John Messinger

CHAPTER 4

Spacehogboy illustration
John Schwegel
www.johnschwegel.com
john@johnschwegel.com

Chapter art
Michael Hamm, illustrator
www.pointsandpaths.com

Editorial illustrations
Sonoma Joe
Heidi Schmidt
www.heidischmidt.com

Rose and Bubble – Self portrait
Rose Nuñez
www.lifeinvector.com

"New" billboard
Leo Espinosa
www.leoespinosa.com

Bus ad projects
Jeff Weiner
Patricia Baumberger
Stephanie Adams

CHAPTER 5

Spenger's and Late Afternoon images
Artist: Bert Monroy
www.bertmonroy.com

Car composite
Photographer: Ken Milburn
www.kenmilburn.com

Guitar and 3D images
Designer: Colin Smith
www.photoshopcafe.com

Golf ball projects
Mareile Paley
Don Noray
Sabine Welte

CHAPTER 7

Georgia watch illustration
Joshua Hood
www.joshuahood.com

California illustration
© Chris Varricchione
cvarric@verizon.net

Chapter art
Young Mo Yoon, illustrator

Woman's face illustration
Todd Macadangdang, illustrator
Founder of Illustratorworld.com

Illustration projects
Brent Brooks
Jane Boss
Jonathan Swihart

CHAPTER 8

UNUMposter
Design by MOIMO
Mariana Monroy and Gabriela Monroy

Chapter illustrations
Lara Kohl

Lincoln Center for the Performing Arts
www.lincolncenter.org

INNU Hair Salon poster
Lyon Advertising
Austin, TX
www.lyonadvertising.com

Stop & Shop ad
Artist: Maranda Maberry
Design Firm: Mullen
www.mullen.com

Peace Begin With U poster
Glenn Sakamoto, designer
www.glennsakamoto.com
glenn@thinkboom.com

Red Poster
Designer/Illustrator: Dennis Clouse
Design firm: Cyclone Design
www.cyclone-design.com

Champion Athletic Apparel poster
Billy Hackley,/Kris Hendershott, art directors
Billy Hackley, designer, Hayes Henderson,
    creative director
Lee Reunion, photographer
Henderson/BromsteadArtCo.
http://hendersonbromsteadart.com

Trackstar Motorsports poster
Ann Taylor, art director, Tom Kelly creative
    director
Martin/Williams
www.martinwilliams.com

Vitra Poster
Designer: Patricio Sarzosa
www.psarzosa.com

Cub Scouts event poster
Design: Hunt Adkins
www.huntadkins.com

Steve Madden poster
Chameleon-USA
www.chameleon-usa.com

Turnaround and Cul-De-Sac posters
Design and Illustration: David Plunkert/Spur
www.spurdesign.com

Professional Bull Riders poster
Courtesy R + R Partners
www.rrpartners.com

NYC2012 logo and outdoor posters
Images courtesy NYC2012
www.nyc2012.com

Cascade Festival of Music Poster
tbd advertising, Bend, Oregon
www.tbdadvertising.com

Concert series projects
Hammad Iqbal
Wilbert Reddit
Ulf Finndahl

CHAPTER 9

Menu Pages identity
Slick City Media, Inc.
Designer: Thomas McKenna, Flatiron
    Industries
www.flatironworks.com

Fat Pipe, Inc.
Salt Lake City, Utah
www.fatpipeinc.com

Flatiron Industries logos
Designer: Thomas McKenna
www.flatironworks.com

**Cadbury Schweppes Americas
    Beverages**
Plano, TX
www.dpsu.com

Packiderm logo
DesignKitchen, Inc.
www.designkitchen.com

ANGEL LMS logo
ANGEL Learning, Inc.
Indianapolis, IN
www.angellearning.com

MultiMed Solutions
Courtesy of Yigal Ron
Designer: Thomas McKenna
www.multimedsolutions.com

CareText logo
Courtesy of Steven Merahn
www.caretext.com

WorldWide Studios logo
Designer: Thomas McKenna

i-silver logo
Courtesy of Nathan Scott Chappell
Designer: Thomas McKenna

Shawnimals logo
Shawn Smith, designer
www.shawnimals.com

Sewing Stars
Teresa Levy, designer
www.sewingstars.com

Bretford furniture logo
Planet Propaganda
www.planetpropaganda.com

Dinny Bin Records logo
Courtesy of Eddie Elliott
Designer: Thomas McKenna

Logo projects
Sean Lynde
Asa Iversen
Jeff Jenkins, www.quirkdesign.com

CHAPTER 10

The Diamond Trading Company ad
Designed by JWT U.S.A, Inc

Oregon Chai ad
tbd advertising, Bend, Oregon
www.tbdadvertising.com

Museum of Latin American Art and City Place Farmer's Market ads
Design by Nostrum, Inc.
www.nostruminc.com

Got Milk ad
Photography by Jack Andersen
Design by Goodby, Silverstein, and Partners
www.goodbysilverstein.com

Steve Madden and Gelati posters
Chameleon-USA
www.chameleon-usa.com

Playland poster
DDB Canada
Creative Director: Chris Staples
Copywriter: Ian Grais, Andy Linardatos
Art Director: Ian Grais
Photographer: Hans Sipma
Print Producer: Betty Anne Yuill

Wick Fowler's 2-Alarm Chili poster series
Brock Davis art director, Tom Kelly creative director
Martin/Williams
www.martinwilliams.com

Shelti Pool Table ad
Agency: MOVE advertising
Copywriter: Richard Verne
Art Director: Marco Morales
Client: Shelti Inc.
www.moveadv.com

Syngenta ad
Martin/Williams
www.martinwilliams.com
Art director: Bryan Michurski
Copywriter: Linda Birkenstock
Photographer/illustrator: Chris Sheehan
Print Production: Sandra Stish
Separator: Vertis
Retoucher: Chris Sheehan
Art Buyer: Doreen Holt
Account Manager: Leigh Theil
Project Manager: Kathleen Flanders
EKG: Meg Rice
www.martinwilliams.com

New York City photos
Dr. Jörg Heieck, photographer
© www.heieck.net

Ad design projects
Dominic Guadiz
Krista Olsen
Michael Wrigley

CHAPTER 11

**Zoetrope All-Story cover design
and spreads**
Eric Baker Design Associates, Inc.
www.ericbakerdesign.com

Seattle Weekly 25th anniversary covers
Designers/Illustrators: Dennis Clouse,
    Traci Daberko
Design firm: Cyclone Design
www.cyclone-design.com

SalterBaxter editorial spread
Designer: Alan Delgado
www.salterbaxter.com

Real Simple cover and spreads
Anita Calero, photographer
Reprinted with the permission of Real
    Simple Magazine © Time Inc.

Magnet Magazine spreads
With permission of publisher Eric T. Miller
Art Director: Kimberly Merritt
www.magnetmagazine.com

BUST Magazine cover
Reprinted with permission
www.bust.com

Azure Magazine spread "Z House"
Concrete Media
http://concrete.ca

**University of Missouri-Columbia spread
"Amphibian Advocate"**
Art direction and design: Blake Dinsdale
Photography © Getty Images/Tim Flach

ReadyMade Magazine spread
Reprinted with permission
www.readymademag.com

Venus magazine cover
Art direction: Laura Strom, Lauren
    Kessinger, Amy Schroeder
www.venuszine.com

Budget Living magazine cover
Reprinted with permission
www.budgetlivingmedia.com

Magazine design projects
Rollo Girando
Lauren Bzdak
Geordie McKernan

CHAPTER 12

Laura Schwamb
STEAM Design Group
www.steam-design.com

Coleman Exponent Package
Landor Associates
www.landorassociates.com

Anaf Spa and Nail Salon package
Designer: Sabine Welty

Candidas Chocolatier package
Planet Propaganda
www.planetpropaganda.com

Screaming Yellow Zonkers package
Reproduced with permission
Ubiquity Brands, Chicago, Il

Archer Farms packages
Templin Brink Design
www.templinbrinkdesign.com

**Clean & Co/Mrs. Mayer's Clean Day
Carry All Cleaning Kit**
Werner Design Works
Art Director: Sharon Werner
www.wdw.com

Maybelline Garnier Hair Color package
Reprinted with permission
www.maybelline.com

MarieBelle Hot Chocolate package
Reprinted with permission
Maribel Lieberman
www.mariebelle.com

Packaging design projects
Sahar O. Shawa
Erin Dorholt
Sabine Welte

1 **Design Theory**

Humankind always has been involved with fashioning artifacts to improve life and to ensure its continued progression. Remarkable as they were, these early works generally lacked an analytical dimension because to the primitive, design was essentially a matter of trial and error.

At some further period in history, humans began to direct this process of designing as they observed and experienced the requirements of a tool. For example, an implement to fell a tree had to have a sharpened edge in order to slice through the wood fibers. Field use led to the addition of a handle to this blow-of-the-fist stone ax because its superior performance was experienced, although its physics probably was not known. Thus, people continued for eons inventing baskets, pottery, wheels, and bow drills, finally discovering fire and metals and using this new technology in the further improvement of their artifacts.

It would appear that the first notable effort at systematizing the design process came from Aristotle and the important theories he established in his writings on metaphysics. (Adler, 1978.) Aristotle, the philosopher of Periclean Athens, was searching for answers to the fundamental questions of the causes and the principles of the known universe. He rejected the prevailing theories of leading thinkers because none was sufficiently analytical and none came to grips with the question of the existence of things everywhere. He theorized that for every artifact there were four reasons or causes that gave rise to its existence. Take, for example, a wine jug made of clay. The exemplification of these causes would run as follows:

1. The *material cause* refers to the substance of which the object is made. One reason for the jug's existence is the clay from which it is fashioned. It answers the question, What is it going to be made of?

2. The *formal cause* refers to the shape or configuration assumed by the object material. This particular container is distinguished from any other, or from a shapeless lump of clay, because of its form or shape. The question answered is, What is it that is being made?

3. The *efficient cause* refers to the maker or prime mover whose skills caused the object to be produced. The efficient cause of the jug is the potter who transformed a mental image of a jug into a physical reality—in this instance, one made of clay. This answers the question, Who made it and how?

4. Finally, and most important perhaps, is the *final cause*, the purpose, end, or function to which the object was brought into existence, answering the question, What is it being made for?

The final cause of the wine jug was the potter's desire to create a container to hold wine. The functional requirement of the end product is significant because it determines the form the jug will take in order to contain wine. Furthermore, there is a significant relationship between material and form because clay can be easily fashioned in a manner to strongly suggest a containment form to meet a specific function. Clay could be worked in this way; stone could not.

Since Aristotle first proposed this theory some 2,500 years ago, there have been many occasions for designers to develop and refine theories and give them currency. Obviously, the kinds of products humans came to know and the methods by which they were made have been changing constantly, but the basic theory underlying their existence has changed little. The scheme developed by Robert Scott relates to Aristotle's. (Scott, 1951.)

Scott also used the term *cause,* except that his list included the *first cause* (need or purpose); the *formal cause* (shape or contour); the *material cause* (substance); and the *technical cause* (methods employed to shape the substance)—quite similar to Aristotle, but different. Other theorists have offered schemes for examining product requirements, as well as providing methods that would guide their development. This appears to be the significant feature of all these systems, as they contrast with Aristotle's. Whereas his was concerned primarily with providing a rational explanation for objective existence, theorists subsequently have been concerned with perfecting schemes that would direct human effort in designing things efficiently in light of current technology. Designers may use different terminologies, but their intent is clearly the same—namely, to provide a set of considerations to guide the systematic process of creating new products and artifacts.

Design Defined

One of the most difficult tasks in any treatment of design theory is to arrive at a clear, workable, and acceptable definition of the term. A review of past and current literature reveals a plethora of suggested descriptions:

- Design is the quest for simplicity and order.

- Explicit in the term *design* are the concepts of order and organization.

- Design is the process of inventing artifacts that display a new physical order, organization, and form in response to function.

- Design if a conscious and intuitive effort directed toward the ordering of the functional, material, and visual requirements of a problem.

- Design is a statement of order and organization. Its goal is unity. It must hold together. It is an expression of the human ubiquitous quest for order.

- Design implies intention, meaning, and purpose.

- The planning and patterning of any act toward a desired, foreseeable end constitutes the design process.

- Designing is creative problem solving.

The common thread that connects these definitions is the assumption and expectation of order and organization. Further, these thoughts suggest that the predisposing factor in all design is an expressed human need for some product, and that the effort results in something useful. Consequently, the working definition to be employed in this book is that *design is the conscious, human process of planning physical things that display a new form in response to some predetermined need*. Further, this activity implies a creative, purposeful, systematic, innovative, and analytical approach to a problem—key events that distinguish serious design from mere idle speculation.

Guiding the Design Process

In the act of designing, primary consideration must be given to the needs of the user, involving the special functional, material, and visual requirements of the problem. These human factor needs translate as a series of subsets pertaining to purpose or use, physical substance, and appearance. Human factors are important in designing. The obvious aim is to create a product that not only works and is durable but also looks nice. Good design demands this attention to the several aspects of the problem at hand.

As an example, see Figure 1.1. Industrial casters are rolling supports for furniture or equipment that is frequently moved from place to place. Many are rather dull visually, even though they may work well. However, the wheel material so often is wood, brittle plastic, or hard rubber, which wears and flattens in time so that the caster is inoperable. Others are so slick and slippery that they slide aimlessly rather than rolling smoothly and providing convenient movement without scratching the floor. The example shown is a chrome-plated, twin-wheel model that offers increased mobility on both hard and carpeted floors in medical facilities, for instance. The soft plastic tires move over moderate obstacles and into elevators quietly and with ease. The unit has a safety brake and also features a ball-bearing support to permit easy and sure swiveling to change travel direction. The gently sloping hood protects the axle from hair, string, and other debris.

This caster also is a classic formal display of unity and variety, where the smooth transition from one visual element to another is quite remarkable. For example, the eye moves very gently from the threaded stem to the hooded fender and then to the wheel. There is no rough transition between the hub of this wheel and the firm, skid-proof plastic that form the tire. The elements are well balanced and form a visually satisfactory whole by appearing that they do, in fact, belong together. Functionally and aesthetically, this is an excellent example

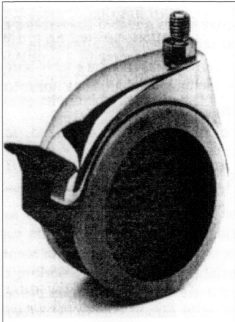

FIGURE 1.1 This elegant and functional industrial caster displays a sensitive organization of visual elements. Note the nice contrast of material tones and the smooth tire and hub interface. Courtesy of Jilson Casters, Incorporated.

of integrity in modern product design. It looks like it belongs in a hospital. It also serves to introduce the ramifications of the three design requirements, as developed more fully in the following paragraphs.

Functional Requirements

A product must fit the purpose or need for which it is intended. In other words, the well-designed article works as it is supposed to work. It functions. It is usable. The appliance that is difficult and awkward to use, the tool that fails to perform as intended, and the chair that neither adequately nor comfortably supports the human frame, are examples of poor design.

One of the better examples of a functional product is the common, homely little punch-type can opener seen in Figure 1.2. The tool was developed to cut a safe opening (one that would not sliver the lips) in the top of the flat top steel drink can (before the days of pull-tabs), and to be effective, reliable, and inexpensive. Manufactured by a simple two-step shearing and bending operation, it will open cans forever, even when it is rusted and worn. Tool convenience is extended by including a bottle-cap lifter opposite from the cutting end.

Considerable attention must be given to this matter of functionality. When planning a desk chair, for instance, the designer must either consult a reference containing anthropometric data or otherwise secure the bodily dimensions of those for whom the chair is intended, and analyze its purpose. For the chair to be functionally correct, it must fit the human frame and permit proper use.

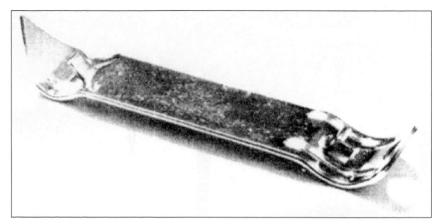

FIGURE 1.2 The familiar flat-top can opener is the penultimate utilitarian tool— inexpensive, durable, easy to use, easy to make, and very reliable.

FIGURE 1.3 Bent metal and bent wood are thoughtfully combined to create this pleasant side chair. Courtesy of Casala-Werke, Germany.

The gentle forms of the side chair in Figure 1.3, sensitively created by a clever combination of bent wood and steel rod, support the human frame comfortably and safely. Other chairs have other functions and must be designed for their special uses, such as those of typists, dentists, drafters, and milkers. Those readers who have ever hand-milked a cow in a rural barn will appreciate the efficiency of the three-legged milking stool. Barn floors are uneven and often dung-encrusted, and such a tri-structure stool will always be planted securely without wobbling. This barn stool always works, and exemplifies an approach to structural stability worthy of consideration in all design problems.

Tools must be usable. A good example is the hacksaw, shown in Figure 1.4. This saw has a number of features that make it work better than others. For one, the blade is positioned so that cuts can be made flush to a surface—a boon to a plumber who has to saw a rusty pipe that lies flat against a wall. Provision is also made for storing extra blades in the tubular handle. Note that the front grip and handle provide a safe, comfortable, and convenient shape for holding the instrument in use. These attributes, coupled with an obvious attention to appearance, make it an ideal metalworking tool.

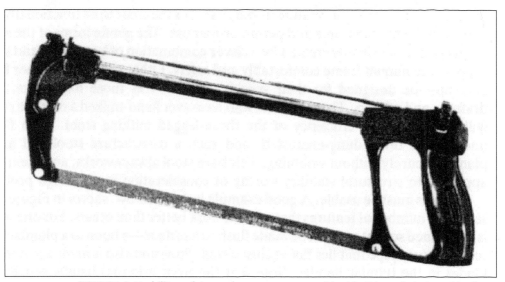

FIGURE 1.4 Usability, safety, and appearance are evident in this well-designed hack-saw.

The clever L-clamp lends itself to efficient and positive workpiece holding. (See Figure 1.5.) An easy push on the tough, forged clamping arm forces the jaws into contact with the work, friction locks them in place, and a few turns on the screw completes the holding operation. It is interesting to note the good design of many hand tools. Through hundreds of years of use and modification, these vernacular artifacts have been perfected for convenient and effective operation. Their shortcomings generally lie with an imprudent use of materials, and perhaps faulty fabrication, all to the end of reducing costs. Someone once wrote, appropriately, that the bitterness of poor design remains long after the sweetness of cheapness has passed.

Medical devices (another class of tools) also are planned with considerable attention to functional needs. The elegantly simple stapler (Figure 1.6) is in general use to join flaps of human skin following surgery. It is easy to hold and

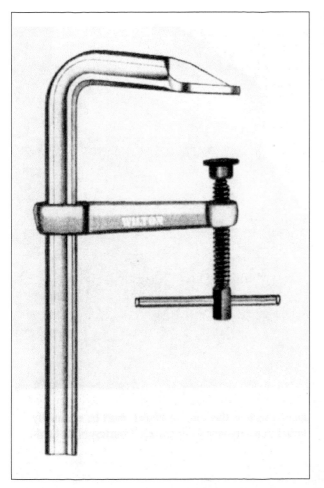

FIGURE 1.5 This rapid-acting clamp is durable, reliable, effective, and easy to use. Courtesy of Wilton Corporation.

direct the staple tip to the incision area, and a gentle squeeze of the handle cleverly bends the staple to effect the fastening. A clearly visible staple counter constantly alerts the surgeon to the number of fasteners remaining in the instrument. Form has followed function to the creation of a usable and attractive tool. The sad part is that it is a throw-away item for hygienic reasons, but perhaps for good cause.

Designers can be guilty of allowing aesthetics to interfere with function. The two nutcrackers in Figure 1.7 are a case in point. One is an elegant piece of metal sculpture, formally sensitive but lacking in the ability to crack nuts. It does not work very well. The other common shape is designed primarily to shell nuts,

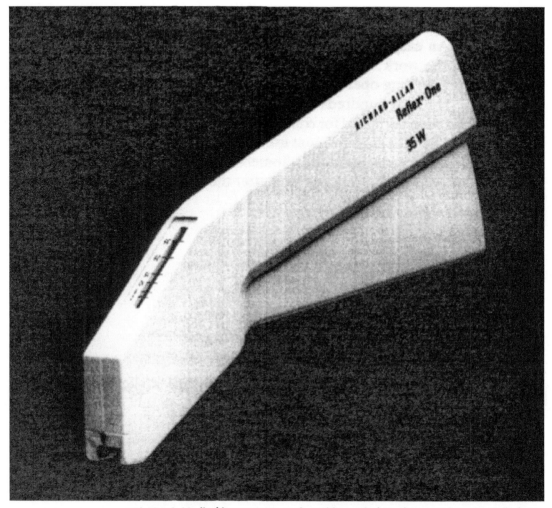

FIGURE 1.6 Medical instruments, such as this surgical stapler, must be essentially functional tools. This one is visually and ergonomically correct. Courtesy of Richard-Allan Medical Industries.

and is a very efficient tool. The message is to let function guide the design effort. The term, *form follows function,* has become a verbal icon for designers over the years, and while it may be creatively stifling if embraced too fervently, it does have some merit.

However, there lies a certain danger in oversimplifying or overemphasizing the role of function in design. As a response to a given need, an article may be perfectly adequate from the functional standpoint, but fail to be appealing to

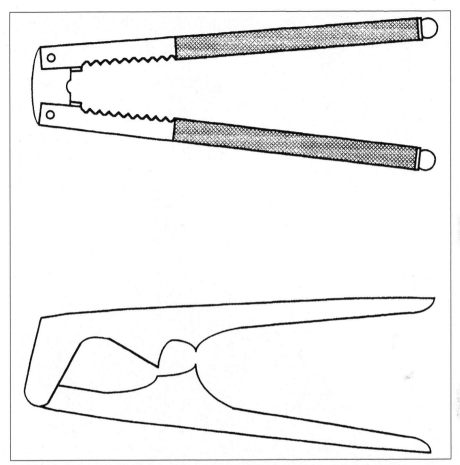

FIGURE 1.7 The nutcracker at the bottom is gracefully suggestive of function but is nonperforming. The one at the top is plain and uninspiring, but extremely functional.

the senses. For example, a can or a drinking glass may work perfectly well as a container for flowers, but neither is hardly suitable for the dining room table. A fine ceramic vase or a brass holder (Figure 1.8) would be far more visually pleasing. This is simply to say that functional sufficiency is no guarantee of good or appropriate design.

In any number of useful products, function does not dictate form, it merely indicates form in a general, logical way. The designer must select from a variety of possible solutions, each of which may be functionally and materially correct, that form that is aesthetically most satisfactory. That person does not unnecessarily embellish, elaborate, imitate, or enrich, but instead refines, simplifies,

FIGURE 1.8 This deep-etched brass vase is a very appropriate flower holder, visually as well as functionally. Design by the author.

and perfects. The key to the wise and proper employment of this element of function is in recognizing that the question, What is it to be used for? must be coupled with, Where and how is it to be used? Significantly, this leads directly back to the necessity of clearly defining the design problem.

Material Requirements

The project or product should reflect a simple, direct, and practical use of the substance of which it is made. The designer should achieve maximum benefit from a minimum amount of judiciously selected materials. If this element of wise utilization is present, the structure of the product will be sound and will be as strong as necessary without any waste of materials or excess bulk.

The creators of products must select from woods, metals, plastics, and ceramics in order to cause their artifacts to assume some shape and to work as they should. Wood is warm, pleasing, soft, insulating, easily worked, and combustible, but not as strong as most metals and plastics. Metal is durable, fire proof, tough, harder to work than wood, and can be fabricated by a broad range of processes, but it rusts and corrodes and is noisy. Plastic is easily formed, insulating, subject to temperature limitations, quiet, break resistant, and can be compounded to meet almost any product requirement. Ceramic materials are noisy, brittle, good insulators, easy to form while in a plastic state, and can withstand high temperatures, but difficult to form or modify after they have been fired or set.

A shortcoming often leveled at industrial designers is that they are insufficiently schooled in the science of materials and their processes. This can be remedied by the curriculum directors of design schools so that design education can be complete. Barring this, designers should include materials technologists on their design teams and consult them frequently. The bedside table shown in Figure 1.9 is a type commonly found in motels and hotels. This particular piece is an example of the work of a poorly prepared vernacular designer who lacked a knowledge of materials. It is misconstructed of a poor-quality particle board covered with an inexpensive, thin, simulated-wood, plastic-coated paper never intended to withstand the normal wear and abuse it will experience at the hands of room cleaners and guests. Note that the corner has eroded through repeated knocks and bumps and is unsightly. A competent, well-educated industrial designer would not make such a mistake. A more durable construction material is solid wood or particle board covered with a tough, high-quality plastic laminate sheet, preferably a solid color and not a simulated grain pattern. Such cost-cutting measures are uneconomical in the long run, for such tables soon must be discarded and replaced at a higher cost.

Questions of integrity and respect for materials might well be raised when a softwood is stained to imitate hardwood, or when plastic is finished to simulate wood or marble. In like manner, applying unnecessary

FIGURE 1.9 **A designer more knowledgeable in material science would not have miscast cheap wood fiberboard, covered with flimsy wood-grain plastic paper, as the material of choice for commercial furniture such as this side table.**

decorations or enrichment to alter the appearance of a material is in most cases questionable. Each of the many materials, both new and old, has some inherent qualities that should be exploited to the fullest. Only through a mature attitude toward them can one discover what they can be properly made to do. Metals can be bent, folded, and formed, as can plywood, plastic, and some other materials. Some can be soldered, welded, riveted, and glued, while others cannot. A working knowledge of material limitations manifests itself in many ways. Because of the softness of pewter, surface ornamentation is kept at a minimum or disregarded completely. Because a plastic becomes pliable when heated, the compression, vacuum, or manual forming methods are far preferable to cutting, squaring, and cementing methods. Materials should not be subjected to wild experimentation; they should be studied and tried, and they should be used for their own intrinsic qualities.

A designer beginning to visualize the form of an artifact also should understand the relationships between material, process, and structure. A common lever-action corkscrew used to remove the corks from wine bottles is a good illustration. (See Figure 1.10.) The device as shown on the left reveals the front and side views of the die-cast zinc remover housing. Note that the legs are properly straight, heavy, and durable. Shown in the inset is a lesser model, where the designer attempted to make the legs more visually pleasing by tapering them to reduce the mass. This aesthetic venture also reduced the strength of the legs at the point of highest stress, as can be seen, with the result that the tool broke at that point. Product failure was caused by a designer not knowing that narrow die-cast parts can be very brittle in section, and that the product form must account for this. The visualized form must be right for the purpose of the object and must grow out of the qualities of the material and its process. Form and material and process always have this interdependence. When in doubt, consult with a manufacturing engineer.

This interdependence also is illustrated by examining the article in Figure 1.11, a container for watering plants. The light, easily formed plastic material ends the problem of breakage and rusting. The handle is functional in that it fits the hand comfortably, makes carrying and pouring easier by offering alternative holding positions, and is easy to fill. This graceful container is a great improvement over its traditional metal counterpart.

A piece of heavy equipment has numerous special materials requirements. The plan for a dump box and its mechanisms require the particular qualifications of a design engineer. The model shown in Figure 1.12 demands that tough, durable, reliable steels be used in its construction. The box must bear heavy loads, is subjected to considerable field abuse, and must withstand high stresses. The hydraulic hoisting mechanism must be capable of lifting the box and its load

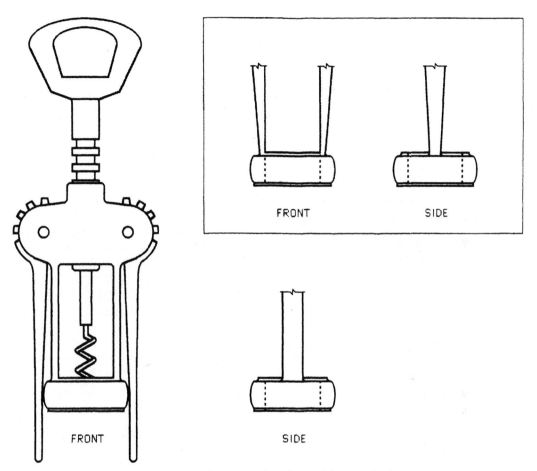

FRONT   SIDE

FRONT   SIDE

FIGURE 1.10 The corkscrew above is much stronger than the model shown in the inset, where the strength of the die-cast section was sacrificed for style.

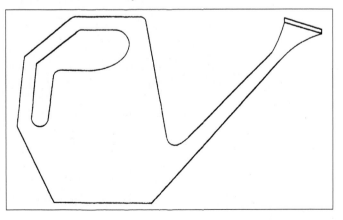

FIGURE 1.11 Easily formed and durable plastic is the proper material for this convenient and attractive watering can.

FIGURE 1.12 The structure and mechanisms for this heavy duty dump box require tough, durable steels. Material matches function in this engineering design example. Courtesy of Peterbilt Motors Co.

reliably and safely. Knowing the peculiar functions of a product and applying the necessary analyses will lead to some very logical materials choices.

Too many materials or contrasting forms employed in one object can result in a "busy" appearance. In such situations, the wide variety in form and material seriously impairs the unified appearance that must be present in objects. In short, the several elements of an article should appear to belong together, and not as exemplified in Figure 1.13. The somewhat bizarre lamp has too many conflicting formal, textural, and material elements for visual comfort. There is too much going on. The key point is to provide enough contrast to relieve monotony, but not enough to disturb unity.

Visual Requirements

A project or product should have a pleasing appearance to the beholder. Simply stated, this requirement translates as a concern for those factors that figure into the visual correctness of a thing. It deals with aesthetics, or the philosophic

FIGURE 1.13 Too many contrasting materials and forms can be visually disturbing, as is apparent in this odd lamp.

study dealing with the nature of the beautiful and with judgments concerning beauty, with showing good taste, and with a sensitivity to appearance. Humans respond more positively to pleasing rather than ugly objects. This is probably the most difficult of any of the design requirements, for what one person views as beautiful may be visually unacceptable to another. Some individuals like buildings that display a clean, crisp, rectangular organization of forms, while others prefer gently curving structures quite similar to what a sculptor would do. Taste, or a person's likes and dislikes, cannot be dictated. There is no mathematically positive right or wrong, inasmuch as human aesthetic responses emerge through nature, nurture, and experience. This elusive quality of taste may be expressed as: "For the sort of people who like this sort of thing, this is just the sort of thing that that sort of people like." While the formal aspect of an object is elusive, the designer must reckon with it in order to achieve product success. It should be pointed out here that engineering designers generally are less concerned with appearance than are industrial designers. This is not a criticism, but an observation. A technical person designing an automotive disc brake does not really care what it looks like. Appearance in this instance is not part of the product specifications. It must only work, and work perfectly.

Most design or art textbooks have a chapter or two devoted to the *elements and principles of design*. In six words, this sums up the context of the term *visual requirements*. It has to do with proper balance, correct proportion, compatible colors and textures, and structure. It means that through practice and the cultivation of a discriminating eye, the designer will be able to recognize what is worthwhile and what is not, and apply this attribute to creative tasks. A person's ability to use this knowledge rests with an understanding of the visual symbols with which one works in the process of designing.

Human beings are, by nature, creatures of organization, and as such find existence and progress difficult amidst chaos. Forward movement requires the measured step, the action based on logic and decision. People are creatures of order because they are surrounded by it. There is order in the measure of time that gives control to the day, to the rhythm of the seasons, and to work and play, all of which contribute to the human penchant for propriety and organization. This factor is both a plague and a source of immeasurable enjoyment.

Although there are few rigid rules regarding how one should respond to this matter of order, people still feel compelled to attend to it. It is no accident, therefore, that one's designs also reflect this feeling for order. The several definitions of design presented earlier generally reflect this concern for order. Each physical unit in the universe is comprised of lines and shapes, forms, colors, and textures organized in such a manner as to create functional and pleasing objects. Without some measure of organization or order, a contemporary living room would be nothing more than a jumbled tangle of shapes and forms. Instead, because of some indefinable law of order, design features can be arranged in such a manner as to build a visually pleasing totality. It is an examination of these arrangements and principles—*the visual organization theory*—that follows.

Design Elements

Designers communicate ideas by manipulating visual symbols in much the same fashion as they use letters in expressing a written language. This language of vision has four basic symbols that are used to graphically represent design ideas: lines, planes, forms, and surface qualities. These are quite properly called *elements of design* because they are the irreducible components of the more complex two- and three-dimensional design objects, and as such are the fundamental building blocks of all structures.

A *line* is the path generated by a point moving through space. Because it is unidimensional, direction is its most significant property. A line is an expression of continuity between two points. Lines carefully drawn and controlled are the connecting links between a mental image and a resultant physical shape. When properly spaced and joined, they establish surfaces and determine form. (See Figure 1.14.) Note that the several recurring lines give definition to the attractive and functional interchangeable garden rake and hoe parts. All outlines, contours, shapes, openings, appointments, and plane intersections are established by lines.

Whether lines are straight or curved, their role in directing attention and determining form is significant. Such lines serve to suggest emotional feelings. Vertical lines are strong, dignified, and aggressive. Horizontal lines are passive. Angular lines show motion. Each curved line expresses beauty in its grace and elegance, though the feeling it creates is not necessarily one of strength. Curved lines arcing outward produce a sense of fullness and charm, whereas those that curve inward create a feeling of poverty and emptiness. However, in combination, such curves can reflect the dignity of the candlestick in Figure 1.15, or of a lamp or a soaring arch. Straight lines, in turn, represent or suggest strength, vitality, stability, and security. Direction also plays a part here. A vertical line is noble and in balance, as suggested in the towering strength of a tall tree. Diagonals convey movement and, when used alone and unsupported, they convey a sense of falling. This becomes a challenge to one's sense of gravity, and from this emerges a feeling of lightning-like, or broken lines. In a sense, these lines lie in opposition to one another, and they tend to create discord or a harsh effect, as with the bandsaw blades in Figure 1.16. However, the dissonant lines of the blades are quite functional, for they provide sharp cutting edges that can tear through the fibers of a piece of pine or oak. Such an academic discussion of line work could continue, but the point has been made. Lines serve to convey feelings and to determine basic shapes, and an appreciation of this will contribute much to design success.

FIGURE 1.14 Repeated forms were used to create the rake structure, resulting in a pleasing rhythmic pattern. The parts are interchangeable. Courtesy of Design Forum Finland.

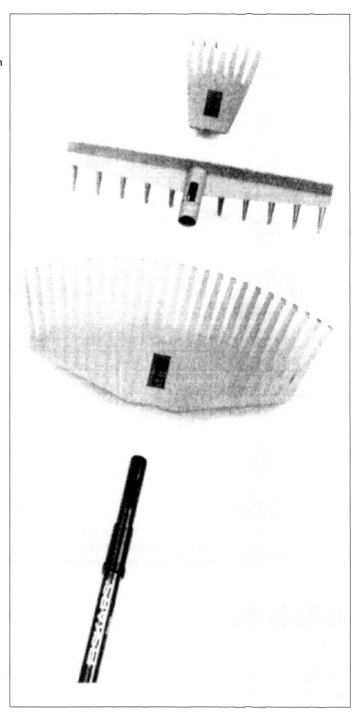

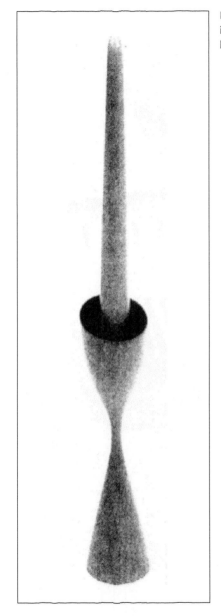

FIGURE 1.15 **This elegant teak candle-stick is comprised of graceful curved lines. Design by the author.**

FIGURE 1.16 **Jagged, coarse lines define the shapes and functions of these efficient bandsaw blades.**

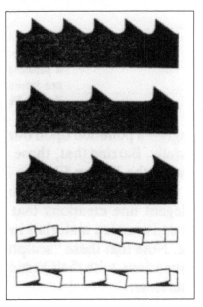

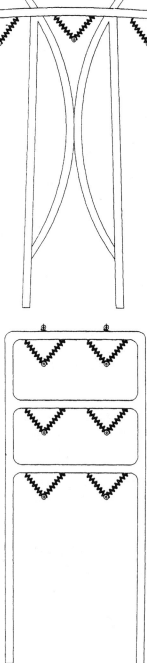

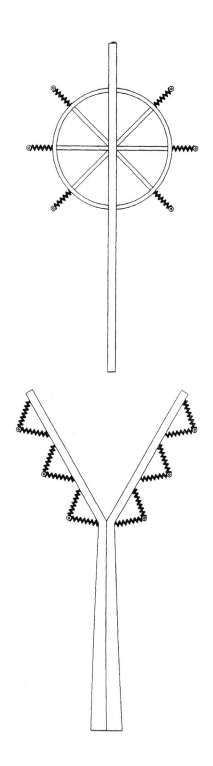

FIGURE 1.17 These striking power transmission poles are a dramatic departure from the less-attractive styles so familiar to both urban and rural dwellers—proof that attention to the aesthetics of the most mundane artifacts pays off. Courtesy of Edison Electric Institute.

The second class of design elements are *shapes, planes,* or *surfaces,* which are created when lines are joined, closed, or commingled. For example, the forests of wooden telephone poles add little to the appearance of urban America, although many of the rural electric power transmission structures are aesthetic marvels of engineering design. Those ungainly posts with timber cross-members, generally tilted and askew, are uniquely ugly—a pollution upon our cities—better they should be buried, and many are, thankfully. Barring that, those created some years ago by Henry Dreyfuss and Associates for the Edison Electric Institute demonstrate that above-ground utility poles can be as aesthetically pleasing as they are structurally sound. Note the simple yet elegant line creations that define the shapes of the structures in Figure 1.17. Their construction materials include wood, metal, plastic and concrete to good advantage. Note that these "sculptures" are quite adequately line-described visually in two dimensions, with their vertical members, arced trusses, circles, diagonals, and bold insulators.

Some configurations are dictated by prevailing standards. Tatami mats are made of straw covered with bound reeds. They measure about 3 feet by 6 feet and determine the size and shape of the rooms of Japanese homes. Instead of square feet, such a home is described as a 16 tatami structure. Similarly, 4 feet by 8 feet sheets of plywood dictate the modular size of U.S. homes. Designers must work within the limitations of these and many other standards in their work, but must not permit this to unduly restrict creativity.

Forms are the three-dimensional constructions comprised of combinations of lines and planes, and are limitless in variety. They can be as simply geometrical as the office furniture in Figure 1.18, or more contrived in contour as the elegant plastic concept lawnmower in Figure 1.19. The furniture sketches depict a layout that would neatly fit into the work spaces of a functional office. The lawnmower is sculpted to contain the cutting and power mechanisms safely, and to create an efficient form that will repel any accumulation of dirt and grass clippings. The specifications for machine housings, for sporting goods, or for railroad cars can to a certain extent dictate the utilitarian forms for these diverse products. While such considerations can obviously influence structure, it must be remembered that the options for form are limitless. Only an imaginative attention to the potentials of lines, planes, and solids, to direct the senses of both art and propriety, can lead to visual satisfaction.

The faces of planes and solids can be enhanced, embellished, or modified by coloring and texturing. *Surface quality* then becomes the fourth design element. Such treatments or characteristics can add interest or emphasis to a design and thereby generally contribute to appearance. A side chair of pale bentwood and patterned upholstery (see Figure 1.20) exemplifies this

Creating space-efficient, elegant reception areas is made easier with Support Cabinets. They allow visibility while providing enclosure, storage, and work space.

THE TWO WORK CABINETS SERVE AS TRANSACTION COUNTERS AND PROVIDE MUCH NEEDED STORAGE SPACE.

BECAUSE RECEPTION AREAS ARE APPROACHED FROM THE SIDES AS WELL AS FROM THE FRONT, THESE 38" WORK CABINETS ARE POSITIONED FOR ENCLOSURE.

THE VIEW FROM BEHIND THIS RECEPTION STATION SHOWS PEDESTAL STORAGE BENEATH THE WORK SURFACE. TALL CABINETS DEFINE THE RECEPTION AREA AND PROVIDE COAT STORAGE.

RECEPTION AREAS CAN BE MADE MORE OR LESS FORMAL DEPENDING ON THE HEIGHT OF THE SUPPORT CABINETS USED.

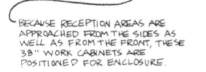

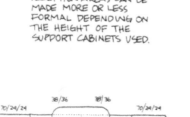

FIGURE 1.18 Rectilinear structures are ideal for office furniture because they fit the shape of room layouts and provide functional work surfaces. Courtesy of Herman Miller Inc.

FIGURE 1.19 Plastic materials were used in this functional and sensitive conceptual lawn mower. Courtesy of The Dow Chemical Company.

FIGURE 1.20 Textured and patterned upholstery material provides a gentle contrast to the smooth bentwood structure of this side chair. Courtesy of Kinnarps AB, Stockholm.

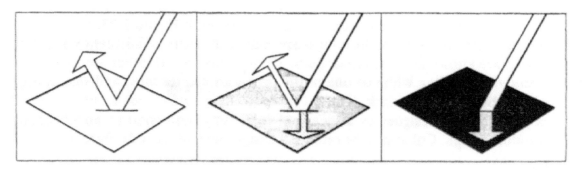

FIGURE 1.21 Relative absorption and reflection of light by white, gray, and black surfaces. Color and texture also affect the amount of reflected light.

treatment with woven and plain surfaces in contrast to each other. This serves to produce a very striking appearance that is obtained through varied yet compatible elements. The reason for this positive human reacton to surface quality is that product surfaces serve as light reflectors and absorbers. (See Figure 1.21.) The ability of a surface to reflect the light striking it is called *value*. White surfaces reflect all the light and lie at the top of a *value scale*. Black, with theoretically no light-reflectng ability, is at the bottom of the scale, with all colors and tones falling between. (See Figure 1.22.) Color becomes a significant part of all well-designed products.

Individual reactions to color are frequently based on past associations. By frequent identification with some idea, faith, or individual experience, color becomes symbolic. This explains why purple is so often associated with royalty, greenish-yellow with sickness and disease, blue with atmosphere or despair, green with freshness and youth, white with purity, and yellow with sunshine and happiness. Furthermore, associations with basic foods have so conditioned people that they could not enjoy a meal of purple bread, green milk, or black potatoes. Similarly, most Americans associate color and taste in some learned, cultural way. Green jelly beans should have a lime taste, yellow is lemon, black is licorice, orange is orange, red is cherry, white is peppermint, and purple is grape. Research also has led to the realization that color plays a role in the workplace.

In addition to its aesthetic appeal, color has a definite effect on other design elements. Certain combinations of color can change the relative size relationships of adjoining areas or masses. Though shapes may be exactly the same size, one can appear larger than another because of its color. Another type of illusion produced by color is an advancing and receding effect. When yellow, a warm advancing color, is used with violet, a cold receding color, a three-dimensional effect is produced. And so, as suggested in the discussion of lines, colors,

FIGURE 1.22 **This scale represents 10 different values ranging from white, limited by the integrity of the paper, to black, a characteristic of the ink. The grays in between are mixtures of black and white carefully controlled to vary the amount of reflected light.**

too, can produce certain emotional feelings and can, therefore be used in conjunction with line to produce a desired effect upon the beholder.

Specifically how is color experienced? First of all, the sun radiates energy in the form of wavelengths. Sunlight contains all the colors of the spectrum, and each is expressed by wavelengths within a certain range. When light sources such as the sun or artificial lamps reach an object, some light rays are absorbed and some reflected, depending on the colors in the light source and color of the object. Only the reflected light is seen by the eye. A painter mixes colors that will selectively absorb or reflect the specific hues to impart a desired color to an object. The eye defines the shape and color of the object by transforming the radiant energy into chemical energy, energizing nerve endings, and sending impulses to the optic nerve. The optic nerve registers the message and sends it to the sight center of the brain, at which point the individual becomes aware of the color of the object. This is a rather cursory explanation of what happens in color perception, but the point is that humans have succeeded in identifying and separating these spectrum colors, and reproducing them with great accuracy in order to color objects.

To guide this activity, a number of different color systems have evolved, one of the more usable of which is the Prang color wheel in Figure 1.23. Note that three primary and three secondary hues are indicated. Pairs of adjacent colors on this wheel are known as *harmonious* hues. Those opposite each other are called *complementaries*. Adding white to one of the primaries creates *tints*, and *shades* are produced by mixing a black. The art of controlling surface color must be carefully studied by the designer as a means of increasing both contrast and interest in a product design. Color must be rated as a design element second only to line and form.

A second reflective quality of a surface is obtained with the property of *texture*. Texture is actually a pattern of contrast in light reflection that identifies the surface rather than the form of an object. Natural textures are characteristic of many materials such as the smoothness of an egg or the roughness of burlap cloth, and it is understandable that people often identify texture with a sense of touch. Every material has a personal texture that can be described as fine or

FIGURE 1.23 **As shown in this chart, the Prang color system is comprised of three groups of hues. The** *primaries* **are connected with a heavy line, and the** *secondaries* **with a light line. The** *intermediaries* **lie between the primaries and secondaries. Primaries are those from which all other hues are made.**

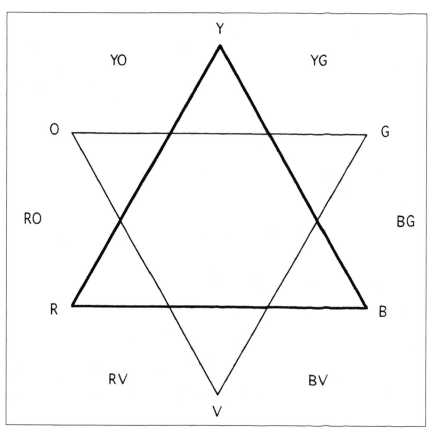

as coarse, and that perhaps is more indicative of the feel of the surface than of the visual impact. Not all textures are inherent or naturally occurring. Some result from a processing technique, such as embossing, which imparts visual as well as functional qualities. For instance, automobile tires have tread patterns cast into them during manufacture to provide a positive gripping action on wet or snowy highways. (See Figure 1.24.)

Textures provide for better hand purchase, as with a knurled metal or rubber tool handle, or a grooved control knob on a television set. A roughened wooden rod (or a light coat of mild adhesive) on a trouser hanger will prevent the garment from slipping to the closet floor. Textured patches applied to the floor of a shower stall will prevent falls while bathing. An embossed metal or plastic sheet on a gasoline dispensing pump will not readily show scratches. A soft fabric covering on an automobile instrument panel top will prevent sun glare in the eyes of the driver. In addition to the matter of visual enrichment, texture also has an important functional role.

FIGURE 1.24 The tread pattern on this automobile tire is both functional and visually pleasing. The designer used repetition of form to provide for good surface gripping and safety. Courtesy of The Goodyear Tire & Rubber Company.

Design Principles

It has been said that a beautiful painting is to be looked at but not talked about—an adage that reflects the difficulty of putting into words the emotions and feelings that exist in visual artistry. The professional designer is equally hard-pressed to describe the superior qualities of a well-designed industrial product. How can one remove a part from the whole and evaluate it as a separate entity? Although it is virtually impossible to thus break a design into components, or speak of the method of organization that gives it unity, one can generalize about some of the attributes common to well-designed things. Such characteristics are called *design principles* and they relate to the arrangement of the four elements of design into meaningful wholes. Authors and designers identify constituent principles according to what makes most sense to them. This author has selected *unity and variety*, and *balance and proportion* as the most representative of these principles.

Unity and Variety

Unity and balance are closely related, for within a design there must be a sense of belonging or similarity (unity) among the component parts to achieve order and wholeness. Concurrently, there must be sufficient diversity or contrast (variety) among the parts to display interest and to relieve monotony. This is well illustrated in the 1937 Elgin Skylark bicycle pictured on the cover of this book. It is a study in style with the teardrop pedals and sweeping fenders, and was marketed by Sears Roebuck as "the prettiest thing on wheels." The graceful arcs of the grilled skirt and front frame members contrast nicely with the linear struts to create a striking rhythmic pattern. It is an elegant machine. Unity and variety contribute to the means by which the overall effect of a design is analyzed. Unity is harmony, similarity, agreement, repetition, affirmation, and continuity. If a design has unity, it means that everything in it is woven together according to some well-developed scheme. Variety provides the aesthetic contrast.

Unity and variety relate to all art forms. For example, they are recognized as the essence of music, unity being achieved by the repetition of a basic theme, and variety by contrasting patterns on this theme. A unifying motif runs through the course of Beethoven's *Fifth Symphony*, which causes this musical piece to present a sensation of totality or wholeness; yet the monotony is relieved by contrasting musical structures. Compare this scheme with Figure 1.25. Note how the monotony is relieved in a brick structure by the random introduction of bricks of contrasting shades. The wall is an example of perfect unity achieved by the predictable pattern of bricks of identical size and shape as well as spacing.

FIGURE 1.25 Brick walls exemplify unity through repetition of similar shapes. This wall also displays variety by the random placement of contrasting-color bricks for emphasis and a nice visual effect.

Variety comes about with the inclusion of the shaded bricks to provide contrast and emphasis. Unfortunately, some architects specify distressed and malformed bricks to emphasize this contrast, as in Figure 1.26. The result is visual discordance and emotional chaos. This same concern holds true in poetry, where the countermotion of phrases provides a variation or contrast. Variety, then, implies the use of contrasting elements, so controlled and placed as to hold and retain attention. Variety means interest—the opposite of monotony.

Rhythm is the flow or movement of the viewing eye as controlled by the repetition of either similar or varying elements, and is therefore closely related to unity and variety. Familiar examples of rhythm are found in music as the listener senses the regular recurrence of beats that establish a definite pattern. The

FIGURE 1.26 Contrast in this wall is overdone by using rather grotesque distressed bricks with little thought. The wall is contrived and visually unpleasant.

listener learns to anticipate what is to come from what has occurred. Painting, too, concerns itself with a rhythmic pattern of identical forms, and rhythmic patterns can also be observed in architecture. Such terms have meaning, to be sure, in all art forms, and they have a similar meaning to the visual expression that lies in a product. For example, the Finnish hunting knife, or *puukko* (see Figure 1.27), is a vivid expression of unity and variety. Note the clean controlling line that gives shape to this piece. It can be experienced by tracing the outline of the knife with the finger. Another unifying line enters midway through the sculptured handle and is carried into the blade and continues to the point. Variety is achieved with two contrasting materials: the smooth, black nylon

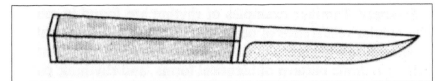

FIGURE 1.27 **This hunting and carving knife is a good illustration of unity and variety in product design. Notice how the outline is unbroken by any linear irregularities.**

hand and the brushed finish on the stainless steel blade. This is a nice harmonious blend of design elements and a very usable product.

Rhythm also has some interesting product safety and convenience relationships, as evidenced in the regular pattern of the steps in a stairway. A person descending a stairway exhibits a learned expectation that the step tread will have a depth of about 10 inches and the riser a height of about 7 inches. This is especially important in a poorly lighted stairway area. Random tread and riser sizes would be confusing and dangerous, and could result in a serious accident. (See Figure 1.28.) Similarly, the placement of light switches at a standard height of 42 inches above the floor is both a convenience and a visual feature. Such natural mappings are examples of applied rhythm and are quite important design considerations.

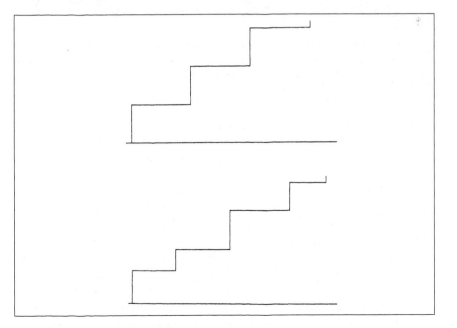

FIGURE 1.28 **The top stairway displays a functional rhythmic pattern. The lower example is erratic and confusing, and difficult to use.**

Balance and Proportion

Balance and proportion are two other familiar principles. The features of the wheelskate in Figure 1.29 are balanced both visually and physically. The horizontal row of identical wheels counterbalances the vertical structure of the shell and blade. Proportion, as a principle, deals with the relationship of the size of one part to the whole and is directly related to the concept of balance. Balance is the quality of equilibrium achieved and sustained through the proper proportioning of the parts of any whole. Ratios of approximately 1:3 or 2:3 are generally considered visually good.

FIGURE 1.29 An improved rollerblade, called the Metroblade, incorporates removable shoes to permit users to skate freely without excess baggage, and to walk safely when they reach their destinations. It is also a functionally attractive device, well proportioned and balanced. Photo courtesy of Rollerblade, Inc.

Geometric designs can be based on proportions derived from the *golden section,* a system attributed to the Greeks who devised it as a means of securing the pleasing proportions of their magnificent buildings, sculptures, and artifacts. The diagram is generated by starting with a square, and a radius is scribed about point (A) which bisects a side of the square. The sides of the newly formed rectangle have proportions of 1.618 to 1. By proceeding according to the drawing in Figure 1.30, the system can be repeated to secure a series of rectangles all having well-defined size relationships. The arrangement of these forms can result in pieces that reflect the pleasant space divisions shown in Figure 1.31. Such geometric spacings can become the bases for graphic layouts, wall cabinets, or tabletops. In design, proportion is one of the most effective means of creating unity among the various components. The use of proportionate elements—whether of lines, dimensions, areas, colors, or textures—helps to establish a feeling of fullness and unity, binding all elements

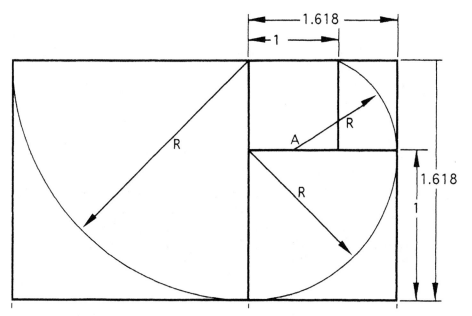

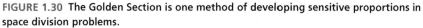

FIGURE 1.30 The Golden Section is one method of developing sensitive proportions in space division problems.

together so tightly that removing or altering a single element would disturb the whole design. Proportion also is an element of shape, as suggested earlier in the example of the tatami mats.

Balance relates to proportion in that it is not only a biological necessity in people's makeup but also something we look for in all visual objects. What's more, people seem to be able to recognize this property easily. Balance that can be seen in an object is known as *optical balance.* When the two halves of an

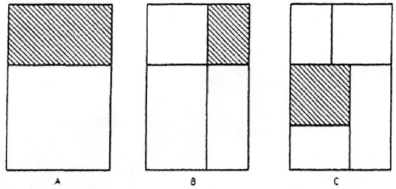

FIGURE 1.31 These geometric shapes are variations of the Golden Section, and are applicable to graphic design and storage shelving problems, for example.

object are exactly alike on either side of an axis, the relation is known as *formal symmetry*. A design can also be symmetrical when organized radially around a center point. Wheel discs in automobiles are good examples of radial symmetry. (See Figure 1.32.) However, as illustrated, balance need not be a strictly formal arrangement, for there is such a thing as *informal symmetry* in which balance is perceived just as surely as in the formal scheme.

FIGURE 1.32 Automobile wheel disc designs are typical creative applications of radial symmetry. Courtesy of Ford Motor Company.

The screwdriver in Figure 1.33 is an uncommonly attractive tool, the handle of which is composed of a linear body with half-circle ends capped with concentric circles, one a utilitarian hole for tool hanging, the other a shallow depression serving as a finger purchase to aid in turning the integral driver shaft and point. The rhythmic pattern of sturdy ridges presents a textured gripping surface, functional as well as visually satisfying. A satin black durable finish ends the composition.

Sensitive, well-designed objects are never achieved by memorizing a long list of design principles and a second list of rules or generalizations regarding their proper application. Designers do not set out to consciously create well-propor-

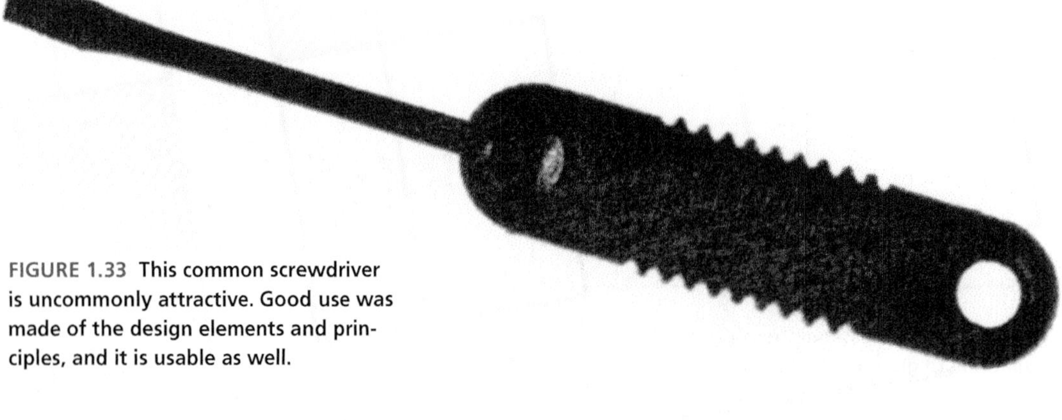

FIGURE 1.33 This common screwdriver is uncommonly attractive. Good use was made of the design elements and principles, and it is usable as well.

tioned, well-balanced lamps, or unified tables or chairs to exhibit variety. Instead, they embark on the design mission with open, creative minds, searching for form, experimenting with space combinations, sketching possible contours, and seeking solutions that reflect a good organization of elements. Experience, practice, study, intuition, and reflection will lead to the ability to discriminate among sensitive and awkward forms. When this feeling of "rightness" about an object is present, the parts of a lamp will be in proportion, the table will look as though all the parts belong together, and the chair will display an interesting structural variety. The absence of this feeling of rightness causes visual tension, or the sense of strained, pulling forces in a composition. The constructions in Figure 1.34 provide a summary of preferred spatial relationships.

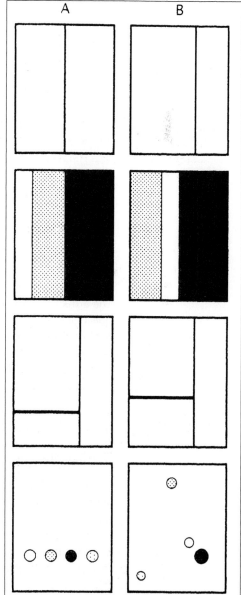

FIGURE 1.34 **Preferred spatial relationship examples are shown in Column B.**

Industrial Design

Industrial design is a term coined by Americans in 1913 as a synonym for "art in industry," which was to provide society with usable and visually pleasing artifacts. According to the Industrial Designers Society of America, it is the professional service of creating and developing concepts and specifications that optimize the function, value, and appearance of products and systems for the mutual benefit of both user and manufacturer. Industrial designers translate consumer needs into consumer products, ranging from chairs to toys to home appliances. Some develop functional and attractive product shells and machine coverings, such as automobile bodies, drill press housings, and typewriter cases. Others undertake the total design of an artifact, such as a coffee pot or a medical device. Manufacturers who are properly concerned with product quality will engage teams of engineering and industrial design people to create artifacts that work, look nice, and are easy to produce. This collaborative effort is of course the essence of the concept of design for manufacture.

Industrial designer are, by training and inclination, especially capable of working with the visual aspects of a design problem. They can examine the engineering specifications and details of the workings of an automatic washer, and provide for its cover and its ergonomics. An interaction with the technical specialists will ensure that it is producible, safe, easily maintained, and economical. Some examples and analyses of their work follow.

The attractive track light in Figure 1.35 is a pleasing example of the work of quality industrial designers. The light is usable and convenient, provides illumination where needed, is strong and durable, and features contours that will fit into any interior setting. One designer's narrative (which follows) provides insights into the industrial design process as it reveals the thinking and experimenting involved in creating a chair.

The Eli chair (named for the designer's son) was planned to provide comfort for dining and other short-period seating situations. In developing the piece, Bruce Sienkowski highlighted the beauty of the manufacturing processes used to transform the material from their raw state to the finished product.

By its very nature, a chair is in contact with its user at all times during seating. When creating Eli, the designer injected elements of form and material that add pleasantly to this use. An analysis of the chair reveals that its components contain some human-like characteristics. (See Figure 1.36.) From a straight frontal view, the taper of the chair legs relates to a trouser leg joined to the "belt" (front stretcher), creating a pleat at the joint. At the center of the belt is the buckle or "navel." The arms flair out from the seat as though the "hands" were

FIGURE 1.35 An attractive and usable track light. A good example of the work of an industrial designer. Courtesy of Lumiance, Haarlem, Holland.

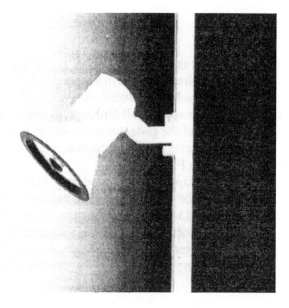

FIGURE 1.36 The Eli chair displays a good mix of wood and metal materials. Courtesy of Charlotte, Inc.

on the "waist," and the "elbows" are protruding strongly. The "back," attached at the waist, terminates at the top corners, representing the strength of the "shoulders." The holes make reference to buttons of a collar while offering an integrated handhold. At the base of the leg is the finishing touch—the "shoes."

During the development of the chair, a number of alternatives were considered, particularly in the glide (or "shoe"). The initial concept was much more literally a shoe. Although unique and in keeping with the theme, this concept was impractical in application. Each of the succeeding ideas became more refined and universal, as the same glide was used on all four legs, as shown in Figure 1.37. The familiar pediment or pad nature of the glide was maintained throughout the design process. Alternative arm arrangements were also studied, and each evaluated for the interplay of form and function. (See Figure 1.38.)

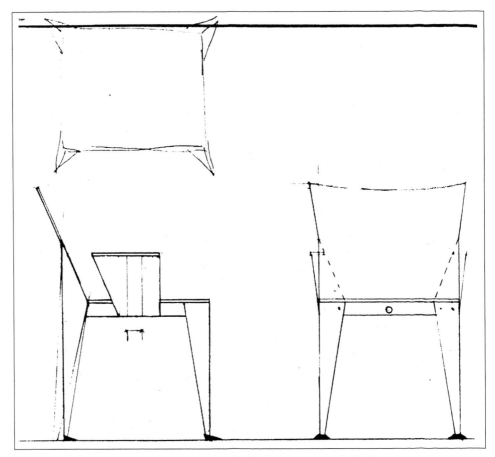

FIGURE 1.37 Foot pad design for the Eli chair. Courtesy of Charlotte, Inc

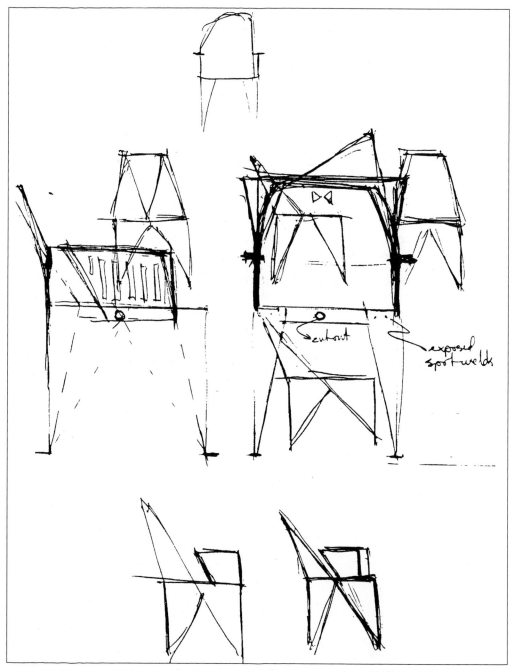

FIGURE 1.38 Designers typically study a number of arrangements for chair elements such as these arm structures. Courtesy of Charlotte, Inc.

The juxtaposition of wood and steel calls attention to each of the materials separately while at the same time highlighting their integration of form. The steel provides a rigid hard edge of strength, characteristic of a strong base, while the wood, molded with soft curves, provides support in all areas of user contact. The wood provides "warmth," both physically and mentally, essential to the comfort of the user. A working sketch of one of the chair impressions appears in Figure 1.39.

The available chair finishes accentuate the materials used in its construction. The tough protective clear coat on the steel base allows the inherent visual excitement of the manufacturing process to show through. The base is also available in opaque paint finishes, allowing an opportunity to be playful with color. The molded plywood seat, back, and arms are available in wood tones, maintaining the natural character of the wood. As his work progressed, the thoughts of Sienkowski reveal how ideas were generated, modified, rejected, and refined, leading to the ultimate Eli chair.

Industrial designers also play an important role in creating sensitive housings or shells for production equipment. The design of the industrial sanding machine in Figure 1.40 was cited as "a successful response to a complex design problem that was very well thought out and executed." The team of industrial and engineering designers created a new model of an old machine, which displays greatly improved ergonomics, safety, and visual features, and consumes less energy in its operation as well.

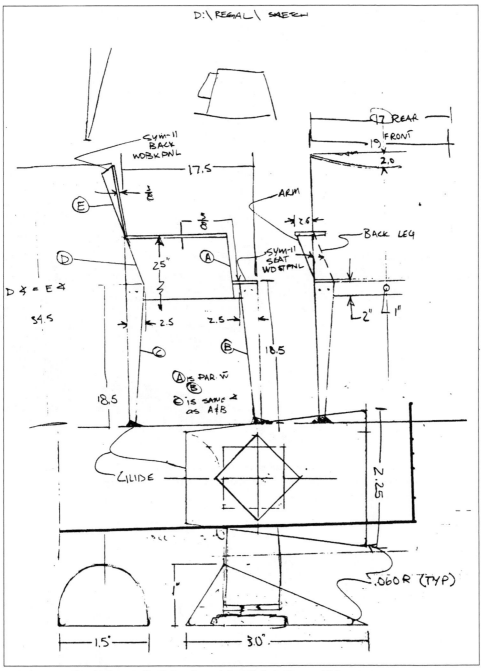

FIGURE 1.39 The designer's final sketches of the Eli chair, from which a prototype was made for analysis and modification. Courtesy of Charlotte, Inc.

FIGURE 1.40 A team comprised of industrial and engineering designers guided the planning for this efficient and dynamic industrial sanding machine. Courtesy of Timesavers, Inc.

Engineering Design

Engineering design may be defined as the process by which a need is transformed into an actuality. It should be noted that achieving this actuality may involve any or all of the disciplines of engineering, and that the need itself may be very specific or general. The activities of inventing, drafting, analyzing, synthesizing and shaping all may be contributors to the design process individually or in groups. It seems that through the design process a need is met by creating something real. The something created may be an electronic circuit, the apparatus for lowering a wheelchair from a van, a machine, a chemical, or any of a myriad of other things generally defined as useful. The designer's attention is somehow drawn to a need that requires satisfaction. Engineering design requires that engineering principles involving analysis be involved in the process. The air-powered angle drill in Figure 1.41 illustrates this. The turbine and power mechanism design had to be based on principles of pneumatics and gearing to match the product specifications. An industrial designer-ergonomist would provide input regarding the requirements of a tool such as this used in manual parts assembly.

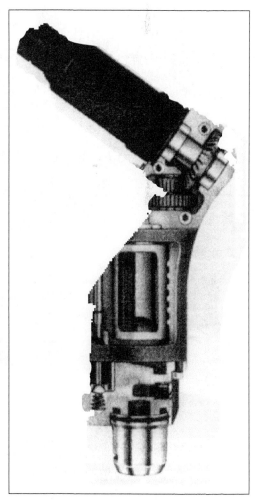

FIGURE 1.41 Mechanisms for products such as this angle drill are good examples of engineering design tasks. Courtesy of Sioux Tools, Inc.

Design engineers are responsible for large vehicles such as powerful commercial trucks. These engineers create cleverly functional automatic production machinery, the bottle filler and capper in Figure 1.42 being a classic example. They also invent special apparatus for lifting a wheelchair into a van to simplify in some small measure the life of a person who has a disability. They design engines, bridges, airplanes, space vehicles, telephones, and off-road construction equipment. Material scientists were responsible for the new extended mobility automotive tire that can

FIGURE 1.42 Equipment for bottle filling and capping is complex and requires a broad knowledge of machine design. The functional and material requirements must be carefully analyzed to assure product success. Courtesy of Cozzoli Machine Company.

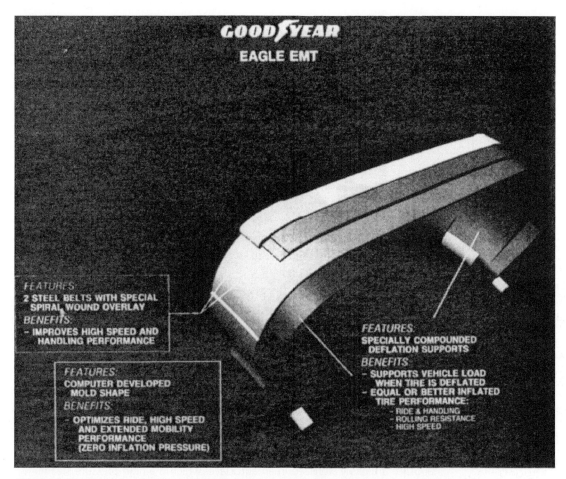

FIGURE 1.43 Materials scientists and tire performance specialists collaborated on the design of this extended mobility tire, which will support a vehicle load when deflated. Courtesy of The Goodyear Tire & Rubber Company.

perform at zero pressure. (See Figure 1.43.) In short, engineering designers concern themselves primarily with technical devices and systems, many but not all of which also require the services of industrial designers.

According to another definition, engineering design is an activity where scientific techniques are employed to make decisions regarding the selection and use of materials to create a system or device that satisfies a set of specifications. Furthermore, engineering design by both definition and implication concerns itself with solutions that diminish the significance of aesthetics or visual order in the problem solution. Function is supreme, as indicated in the engineering design problem narrative that follows.

Every engineering designer has some personal design problem format that seems to work. In general, the steps include defining the need clearly; examining strategies used by others; defining constraints such as weight, size, and cost; weighing alternatives; and then considering how to synthesize available technology to meet the product needs. If the specifics of the problem are not fully understood, it is unlikely that the attempts to meet them will be successful. By examining the best works of other manufacturers and by identifying common product faults, the designer can avoid having to retrace old steps or repeating old mistakes. This does not mean that new mistakes will not be discovered, such as errors that are not always the result of poor judgment or analysis. It is almost axiomatic that new designs require some degree of testing. When new or different arrangements of elements are advanced, unforeseen or unpredictable behavior may result. Safety, reliability, or function may be compromised because constraints or needs have been met. Testing is usually the only way to approach this problem.

Many design project proposals originate from criticisms identified by users of other products. The salespeople of a manufacturing company are in a particularly good position to refer product ideas from their customers. Of course, not every such idea will become a marketable product, nor does every design proposal come through the sales department. The example described next did not quite follow this path, but it serves to illustrate the initiation process. The following was a problem used by a university professor in his engineering design class, and is typical of such academic activities.

Dentists and other heal-care providers are properly concerned with HIV and other infectious diseases, and so it is important that they maintain their equipment in a sterile condition. Most of the tools and appliances found in a dental office are easily sterilized in an autoclave, which is a high-pressure steam chamber. The major exception is the dental handpiece, or drill. Generically, a handpiece consists of an air turbine that rotates at over 200,000 revolutions per minute. It has two or three small tubes entering the handle, at least one of which is for air and one for a water coolant. The turbine is about 6 or 7 mm in diameter, with notches around the periphery to produce the turbine effect. At either end of a hollow turbine shaft there are two tiny ball-bearing assemblies. (See Figure 1.44.) These bearings are a problem source during sterilization, for heat and moisture in the autoclave tend to damage them, or at least make disassembly and relubrication necessary. Because of the small size and complexity of the bearing assembly, the task is time consuming and costly.

One concerned dentist decided that a disposable handpiece would solve the problem, and figured that the drill would be cost effective if it could be sold for under $15. It was also determined that the drill would have to work with

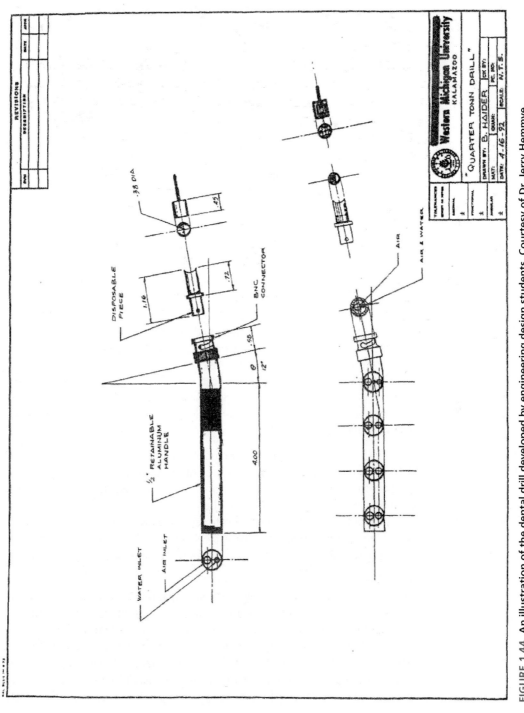

FIGURE 1.44 An illustration of the dental drill developed by engineering design students. Courtesy of Dr. Jerry Hemmye.

a common office air and water supply, and would have to survive at least 30 minutes of use. Here, then, was a tentative product description along with some general specifications, gleaned from studies of handpieces and test data that had appeared in dental journals. The dentist then presented the problem to two student research teams in an engineering design class.

Following the discussion, the teams now knew what the product was, what performance was required, and what the cost limitations were. This design project did not involve inventing something that had never existed before, nor did it require the use of exotic materials. A number of similar disposable dental drills already were on the market. Aside from the high-speed operation and the small size of the components, the project did not seem to involve anything unconventional. A search of the literature and examination of a number of handpieces made by different manufacturers led the teams to believe that it would be possible to meet the tool requirements.

Further review led the students to the conclusion that there were only a few technologies involved, and that air turbines used in such drills appeared to be rather unsophisticated. They considered that a significant improvement in performance might be possible by doing a fluid dynamicis study of the turbine. However, they felt that such a study would be time consuming and inflate the product cost, so they agreed to postpone it unless it became a critical matter. The groups also learned that the expense of the miniature ball bearings was a major factor in the overall handpiece cost; they elected to investigate the use of sleeve (journal) type bearings using available food grade plastics; and they decided that a molded plastic handle would reduce product cost and make it more environmentally sound.

In this design problem, a number of crucial design decisions were made early, most of them driven by cost. From this point on, there were two design schemes followed. Had there been more teams, there would have been more schemes. One team chose to design a handpiece with hose attachments in the conventional fashion, with the complete assembly disposable. The other team chose to make the handle of stainless steel with just the turbine end detachable and disposable. Both teams worked on making turbines and bearings in the most economical manner.

The two teams succeeded in making turbines and bearings that met the specifications, but one turbine was measured at 420,000 revolutions per minute. Because of time constraints, neither team produced a finished handpiece, although all the elements necessary to its production were completed. It is interesting to note that handpiece manufacturers have not ignored the original problem. At least one supplier has redesigned the handpiece to allow for easy cleaning and relubrication of the bearings at no great increase in product cost.

At the moment, it appears that this tool is the market leader. If the disposable tool manufacturer had a product with a lower profit initially, perhaps the market would have been captured. Because of the conservative nature of the usual dentist, it is not likely that disposable handpieces will account for any sizable part of the market.

There are countless examples of such successful technical products. A unique engineering device has made available to the product design community a spring with many applications. (See Figure 1.45.) The spring is an integral unit consisting of an inner steel shaft surrounded by a molded rubber cylinder with

FIGURE 1.45 This rubber torsion spring was designed to create a durable, reliable spring with many applications. Courtesy of BFGoodrich Company, Engineered Polymer Products Division.

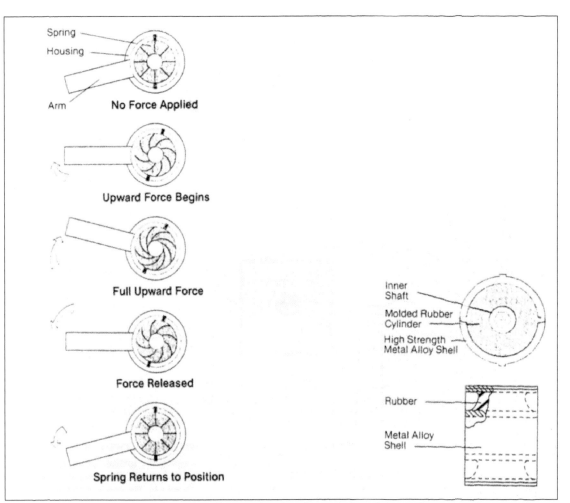

Spring
Housing
Arm
No Force Applied

Upward Force Begins

Full Upward Force

Force Released

Spring Returns to Position

Inner
Shaft
Molded Rubber
Cylinder
High Strength
Metal Alloy Shell

Rubber

Metal Alloy
Shell

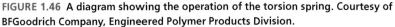

FIGURE 1.46 A diagram showing the operation of the torsion spring. Courtesy of BFGoodrich Company, Engineered Polymer Products Division.

outer half-shells to form a durable, compact, lightweight part. (See Figure 1.46.) The spring is designed to absorb impact through the rubber cylinder as it is twisted by the movement of the inner shaft. The unit replaces the conventional metal leaf or air spring for suspension applications in buses, heavy equipment, and military vehicles. Smaller, more compact configurations are available for the seating market. (See Figure 1.47.)

A good illustration of the proper mix of a technical product's functional, material, and visual requirements may be seen in the award-winning Crown FC Series electric forklift truck. (See Figure 1.48.) One's first impression is with the clean flowing lines and shapes organized to create a visually satisfying structure.

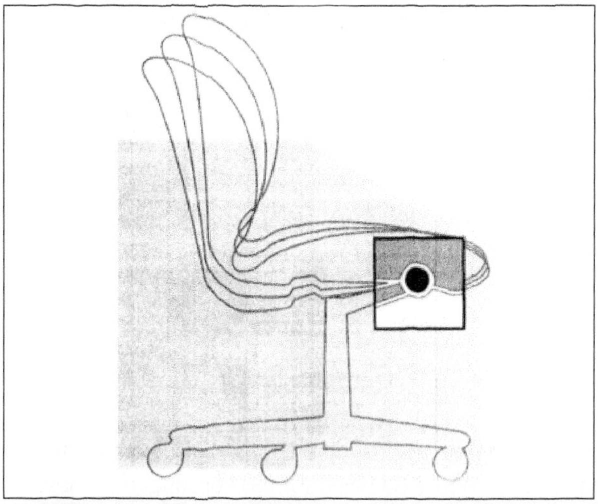

FIGURE 1.47 Office chairs such as this employ the torsion spring to self-adjust to body loads. Courtesy of BFGoodrich Company, Engineered Polymer Products Division.

FIGURE 1.48 This award-winning forklift truck is handsome and functional, and the result of a good collaborative effort by engineering and industrial designers. Courtesy of Crown Equipment Corporation.

The smooth wheels present a nice collage of color, texture, and form, and the clever placement of the wheel assembly hexagonal bolt-heads add pleasing contrast points. This material-handling vehicle looks functional and it is, and the attention to ergonomics results in good operator efficiency, safety, and comfort. There is a sensible selection of appropriate metals and plastics for strength, durability, and finish. This machine is a striking example of the collaborative efforts of engineering and industrial designers.

Craft Design

The tremendous range of sensitive craft pieces available today attests to both the skill and inventiveness of the designer-crafter. Pottery, glassware, jewelry, carved wood, furniture, and metal pieces all result from the basic premise that for some creations, little attention should be given to mass production. These are essentially hand-crafted, one-of-a-kind artifacts with a primary emphasis on blending the skills of the artist-crafter. Such products transcend the anonymity of the mass-manufactured article, fulfilling a basic human need of both maker and buyer. The delicate crystal glaze on a porcelain pot, the graceful form of a raised sterling bowl, or the delicate details of a jewelry piece exemplify the efforts born of reflective experimentation and a sensitive hand and eye. The inventor-maker satisfies a personal desire to create a unique article, such as the candlestick described earlier in Figure 2.15, where the subtleties of the craft are not compromised. The consumer experiences some vicarious thrill of the joy of creation by possessing an object that satisfies the human need for aesthetic pleasure. The bookend in Figure 2.49, for example, was created by a crafter with considerable metal machining skills. He experimented with a metal shaper to produce on a metal surface a series of gradually spaced intersecting lines, resulting in a pleasing visual effect.

It is difficult to differentiate sharply between the work of the designer-crafter and the industrial designer, for their paths cross, join, and then part at some point, as dictated by the demands of their respective tasks. It might be said that crafters generally possess the ability to invent unique forms and then to render these ideas into skillfully executed pieces. Designers for industry most frequently function as members of research and development teams, where they contribute their visual expertise. Essentially, their tasks are directed toward the design of quality goods for mass production. The fire tools in Figure 2.50 are a functional composition of teak wood and black conversion-finished mild steel structural members. The combination of round and rectangular shapes, harmonious materials, and nicely spaced handle screws provides for unity and variety. This craft product could be easily replicated, and many such craft examples end

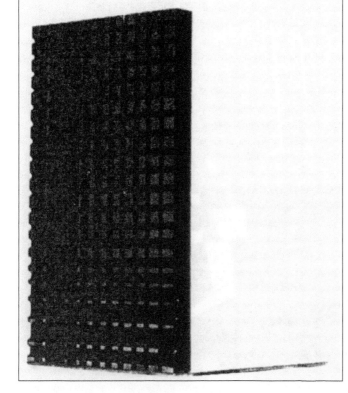

FIGURE 1.49 Craftwork is exemplified by its uniqueness. This bookend of 0.5-inch mild steel was created with a metal shaper. The problem involved a study of the visual effects possible using this machine.

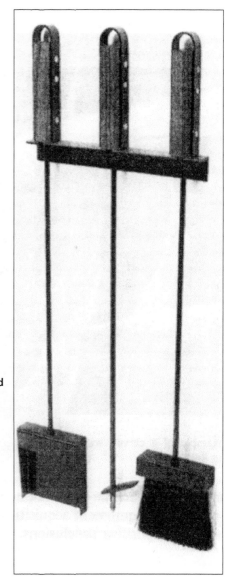

FIGURE 1.50 Fire tools lend themselves to any number of material and form combinations. This teakwood and blackened steel set is a good example. Design by the author.

up being mass-produced. Before this can happen, the fire tools would have to be analyzed by manufacturing engineers to determine their producibility and to recommend necessary modifications. The aim here would be to produce a marketable item without sacrificing the integrity of the original, unique artifact.

The attractive wood-carving against a flat-black background is a nice blend of textures. (See Figure 2.51.) This pleasant marine motif exemplifies the work of the skilled designer-crafter, a sensitive creation depicting fish suspended amongst sinuous weeds. This carver had an intimate understanding of the subject and executed it with graceful forms.

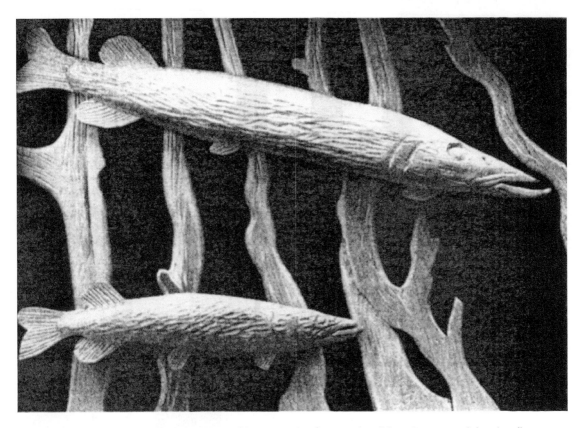

FIGURE 1.51 A striking example of a carved wall-hanging—graceful and well executed. Courtesy of Craig Spink.

The Design Process

Designing is properly considered to be a process because in order to achieve optimum problem solutions, several factors and subtasks must be undertaken in an orderly fashion. Different authors and practitioners may use different process formats, but the aim always is to provide an effective design system. A typical diagram of this process is shown in Figure 2.52, followed by brief descriptions of its constituent elements.

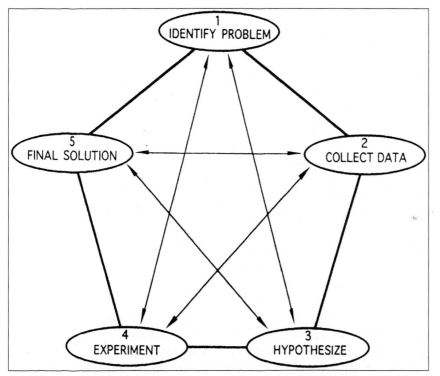

FIGURE 1.52 This chart depicting the stages of the product design process serves as a guide to creative design activities.

Phase 1: Identify Problem

A design task may emerge as a perceived need for an existing product, such as a better safety switch for a chainsaw, or as a new product, such as a high-performance engine on a concept automobile. Conversely, the task may be totally innovative and with greater visual requirements, as exemplified by a new line of furniture or the refitting of an aircraft interior. Whatever the source, such tasks must be carefully analyzed to ascertain their appropriateness for a specific company, and for their potential as successful products. Design is costly and time-consuming. As a new product is conceived or an existing one improved, the primary objective is to present a commodity that will meet a need or render a service in a manner superior to that of any former or similar product. This can result only from a judicious problem definition.

Phase 2: Collect Data

This is the research phase of product design. Once the problem has been defined and given focus, pertinent data must be gathered, information retrieved, benchmarks examined, market assessments made, and cost analyses undertaken. Any factors that bear on the problem must be studied, leading to the presentation of tentative product specifications. An evaluation of existing facilities may lead to the conclusion that such an undertaking is not cost effective because of possible extensive refitting or equipment acquisition. Data collection is equally valid for its negative as well as positive conclusions.

Phase 3: Hypothesize

This activity is the concept-development stage, where intuition and technical experience merge to produce a range of possible problem solutions. Pondering the task, considering alternatives, taking creative leaps, sketching possibilities, studying the visual requirements, weighing them against purpose and materials, modifying, and discussing are all necessary to this phase. Continual reference must be made to the original problem and its analyses. Hypothesis is the heart of the design process, the stage at which potential configurations emerge and are evaluated.

Phase 4: Experiment

At this point, the possible solutions are refined and tested, and the prototypes are built, evaluated, modified, and compared to earlier data and analyses. Is the product strong enough? Does it work? Is it visually correct?

Is it safe, easily maintained, producible, vandal-proof, and marketable? Experimentation is precisely what the term implies—the opportunity to critically examine the various problem solutions and to detect and correct errors before the article is put into production.

Phase 5: Final Solution

The logical result of the previous four phases of work is the ultimate problem solution. At this stage of the process, considerable attention must be given to those refinements needed to satisfy special methods of manufacture, to simplify the product so that it can be easily assembled, to modify it so that standard components may be used, or to improve its appearance, among others. Obviously, this is a final opportunity for all members of the design-for-manufacture group—the industrial designer, the engineering designer, the production engineer, the safety engineer, the product maintenance specialist, the ergonomist, and others—to meet and congratulate each other on the elegant product they have created.

Benchmarking

Special mention should be given to an important source of data to be used in the design process. This is an innovative technique called *benchmarking*. According to the dictionary, a benchmark is a land surveyor symbol cut into a bronze plate to serve as a reference point or standard by which something can be measured or judged. What this term implies in product design is an organized process of measuring a company's operations and products against those leading performers and competitors. The ultimate goal is to know the industry's best practices, and incorporate these into company operations in order to strengthen the market position. Although benchmarking is a relatively new practice (first surfacing in the early 1980s), its use is growing because of its obvious benefits.

In his very fine book on the subject (the book itself being something of a benchmark), Robert C. Camp (Camp, 1989) provides a working definition of the term: "Benchmarking is the search for industry best practices that lead to superior performance." Furthermore, he offers four basic philosophical steps of benchmarking as being fundamental to success: know your operation; know the industry leaders or competitors; incorporate the best; and gain superiority.

The process itself is straightforward and simple. A manager will generally begin by deciding which aspect of corporate management is in need of benchmarking, such as operations, product development, automation, service, or the like.

Next, specialists in that area determine which competitive company is the very best at that function, and then collect data to exchange and discuss with that company. This is followed by an analysis of the data, leading to the incorporation of the most effective approaches used by the benchmarked company. Product design and methodology are prime candidates for benchmarking, and designers would do well to adopt its principles.

It is interesting to speculate how a company might proceed when a specific product has been for benchmarking, for example, a refrigerator. A team assigned this problem would most likely identify the three best refrigerators on the market and analyze them to learn why they are the industry leaders. They could study such factors as energy efficiency, user-friendliness, silent operation, simple but effective door closing, size and shape, durability of finish, storage convenience, and the like. Assume that one negative feature is present in all three target models—that of automatic door closure. One person may then concentrate on determining the causes of door failure. Improper seal material may wear in time so that the door would not close completely. Is it a material fault, a door seal design error, a poor hinge mechanism, or a manufacturing error? Continued analysis would pinpoint the fault, which could then be corrected and incorporated into a new design concept. All such features could be systematically studied, leading to an optimum appliance design. The next step would be to perfect the manufacture of the product, so that it could be made better and at less cost and in turn emerge as the industry leader. This super-refrigerator would later be benchmarked by the competition.

Questions and Activities

1. Contrast and compare Aristotle's four causes, Scott's four causes, and the three design requirements described early in the chapter. Present your opinion as to their relevance as approaches to modern design.

2. Study the material on the definition of design and write one of your own.

3. In your own words, describe what is meant by the functional, material, and visual requirements and how they guide the design process.

4. Select three products and describe how they do or do not meet the aims of the three design requirements.

5. Cite some instances where you feel that materials simulation might be justified (e.g., when plastic laminate is finished to simulate wood or marble).

6. Do you feel that the author's comments on the nutcrackers in Figure 1.7 is justified? Explain your reasons.

7. Sketch some product examples that illustrate the meanings of the terms *unity, variety, proportion,* and *balance.*

8. Refer to Figure 1.17 and sketch some other impressions of telephone poles.

9. Define the terms *value, hue, shade,* and *tint.*

10. Give some examples of functional textures in product design.

11. Describe the differences between industrial design and engineering design by selecting and analyzing a product example of each.

12. Select a few examples of good crafts design and analyze them from the standpoint of producibility. How many design changes were necessary to improve their producibility? Did these changes affect the integrity on the original craft piece?

13. Write a short paragraph on how the five-step design process can aid in creating quality products.

14. Describe the benchmarking process, and search the literature on the subject to identify some examples of it.

Notes

Adler, Mortimer J. *Aristotle for Everybody.* New York: Macmillan, 1978.

Camp, Robert C. *Benchmarking: The Search for Industry Best Practices That Lead to Superior Performance.* Milwaukee: ASQC Quality Press, 1989.

Scott, Robert G. *Design Fundamentals.* New York: McGraw-Hill, 1951.

2 Intro to Graphic Design

It was in 1922 that book designer William A. Dwiggins first used the words graphic design to describe the emerging field of visual communication. Students at the Bauhaus art school in Germany were creating daring poster designs through the collage of photographic images and typography.

Fast-forward to today, and graphic design is over 80 years old but still lookin' good. Always a field in flux, graphic design has undergone a revolution in the last 20 years as production methods have moved from the pasteboard to the PC.

Has design itself changed? Yes and no. New media have emerged, but the basic principles of art and design are still required to create good work. In this first chapter, we will explore what graphic design is and discuss the important roles of imagery, color, typography, and composition.

FIGURE 2.1: Detail from a creative ad campaign by Viva Dolan Communications.

In this chapter you will:

- Learn some of the defining characteristics of graphic design.
- Get an overview of the professional graphic design process.
- Learn how design conveys a visual message.
- Explore how design can support a company brand.
- Learn how design communicates to an audience.
- Investigate the roles of imagery, color, typography, and composition in design.
- Critique two outstanding examples of visual design.

What Is Graphic Design?

Graphic design is often associated with images. Billboards and magazine ads show us that designers can speak volumes without using the written word. And yet, graphic design is not just about creating powerful pictures—that's what artists, photographers, and illustrators do. It's about communication. In fact, "visual communication" is the most accurate way to describe the purpose of graphic design.

Clients and employers approach the designer with some information that must be communicated to a wide audience. The designer's mission (should he or she choose to accept it) is to bring order and clarity to this information so that others may understand it. You might think of a designer as a special kind of translator who turns dreary old words into an inviting, accessible visual message.

In today's vast information jungle, this is no small challenge. Amid the neon blaze of Times Square or downtown Tokyo, or in the luxurious, glossy expanse of a fashion magazine, simply organizing information is no longer enough. Designers must discover clever metaphors and creative solutions to make their work stand out and grab the attention they are asked to grab.

FIGURE 2.2: New York's Times Square. In a world saturated with visual messages, designers must create messages that stand out and are memorable.

As you begin to study graphic design, you will find that inventive ideas are as important as artistic skill. Award-winning designs are never merely decorative. The best work commands your attention through the clever, artful visual communication of a concept. Visual design is just part of the equation; creative strategy and copywriting must work in concert with a mastery of graphic elements to carry the message.

Defining Graphic Design

What are some of the defining characteristics of graphic design? There's a lot more to design than the creative process. Let's begin by exploring its role in the world of business.

The Design Process

Message to all art school types: Graphic design is rarely created in a vacuum or through bursts of random creativity. Most graphic design jobs begin with a commercial objective established through a time-tested process.

A design firm or agency is typically hired by a client to create something: a logo, for example, or a CD cover, a magazine layout, or a Web site. Designers and project managers meet with the client and work collaboratively to define the purpose of the project: What is its message? Who is its target audience? The initial meeting generates a document that provides the client and design team with a written statement of the project's goals, often called a *project brief* or *design brief*.

FIGURE 2.3: **Visual identity developed for Bond Bath and Home Gallery, a Soho-based home furniture and accessory emporium. Designer Patricio Sarzosa was asked to create a visual identity that conveyed a luxury retail brand that was friendly and accessible.**

The project brief may contain abstract goals or statements that may not even be remotely visual. If you're hired to redesign the Coke can, for example, your objectives may include increasing a perception of quality, making the product seem to taste better, or attracting a specific group of consumers. The brief will also include all-important information on the project's budget, deadlines, and production requirements.

> ▼ note
>
> **The project brief is a formal document that is used as a benchmarking tool and often updated as a project unfolds.**

The design team uses the project brief as a guide through the creative phase. Depending on the size and requirements of the project, a team of *creatives*—designers, illustrators, photographers, copywriters—may be assembled to brainstorm ideas and develop a range of solutions for presentation to the client. In smaller agencies, a single designer may be asked to handle multiple facets of the creative task.

As a project evolves over weeks and months, critique of the work within the design agency and multiple rounds of feedback from the client will refine and polish the message. No designer ever gets it right the first time. Client meetings help make sure that the client (the design customer) is satisfied with the art direction and that the work is addressing his or her business needs.

FIGURE 2.4: Logo, colors, and icons were applied consistently to business collateral and the store frontage.

Graphic Design

visual communication

Defining charac...
--The Design process
- visual Message
-

Once every detail in the project is finalized—a decision that rests with the client—the design team is generally responsible for managing the printing and production of the work. This may involve working with the printer to finalize all specifications of the job, preparing digital files for printing, and monitoring print quality. A working knowledge of production techniques and a good relationship with a printer is important to getting the best results.

The Visual Message

Hang around designers long enough, and you'll get to hear the phrase "less is more," often accompanied by sage nodding of heads. That is because economy of expression is an essential characteristic of graphic design. Design must convey a visual message with minimum fuss and maximum clarity.

Consider the job of the outdoor ad designer. Her work must attract attention, be understood quickly—often literally at a glance—and communicate without any risk of ambiguity. This can be achieved only if every element of the design is harnessed to support the message, and all unnecessary, potentially distracting elements are removed.

FIGURE 2.5: This anti-war poster created by master designer Marty Neumeier conveys a complex idea through a deceptively simple visual message. Pure graphic design!

Nothing in a design is arbitrary nor should it be. From image treatment to color swatches to paper texture, every element in a well-executed design has a motive. A shrewd designer is continually asking himself how the various elements and techniques at his disposal, such as color, cropping, contrast—in fact, anything—can be better used in service of the message.

"Less is more" is a principle that all graphic designers learn to embrace, sooner or later. Simplicity and clarity are essential in any visual communication.

Designers spend an inordinate amount of time stripping out extraneous details and simplifying a design. Why does nearly every product photo in advertising have a white background? It's because any background detail would distract attention from the product, where the attention belongs. Why do designers mutter the words "busy layout" or "text heavy" with such disdain? Because they understand that removing clutter adds clarity.

A great design looks effortless, like it was just meant to be that way. But as with many things in life, achieving simplicity in your graphic design work is harder than it looks, and sometimes requires years of experience. Almost any piece of content can be too much information—the amount of text, the number of colors, the freckles on the model's nose. If it doesn't contribute to your message, consider editing it out.

Supporting the Brand

Here's a reality check: Even if you're a freelance designer, you're rarely working for yourself. Let's hope not, anyway. The vast majority of design jobs are commercial in nature; a designer is hired by a company or organization to produce items that will enhance its marketing, advertising, publishing, or promotional efforts. To put it another way, one major function of design is to support a brand.

When you work with clients as a designer, you are not working with a blank slate. Quite the opposite: The more important the job, the more likely you'll need to work creatively within constraints. You may be hired for your unmistakable artistic style, but ultimately you're working for the client, and your design work needs to support his brand, not yours.

FIGURE 2.6: **Most design projects begin with a specific audience in mind. Magazine designers, for example, cater to the interests of well-established groups of readers.**

Every large company has a visual identity system: a set of standards that dictate exactly how its logo, colors, and typography will appear in all its communications to customers. To build a brand, consistency in these elements is vital. Repeated exposure to a consistent message makes customers more and more familiar with a brand, because a brand that is easy to recognize is easy to remember. For companies that also deliver excellent products and services, repetition of a message leads to that magic phenomenon called brand recognition.

That brings us to the dilemma every designer faces: Be a genius, but do it in our house style. Packaging designers grapple with this constantly. Imagine you are hired to design a brand extension for a shampoo line. You may need to use that company's logo, signature colors, and carton dimensions to create a design that dovetails nicely with other company product packages on the store shelf. At the same time, however, you'll need to create some original, distinctive graphic feature that attracts shoppers' attention and says "This is new".

FIGURE 2.7: **A range of product packages developed for Maxwell's Apothecary. Consistency in typography and graphic elements makes each package part of the product line.**

That's branding, and designers play a huge role in making it happen. Brands are always evolving, as companies perpetually redefine their values, refresh tired products, and reach out to new audiences. If you want to connect to the next generation, you've got to have designers on board.

Communicating to an Audience

Are you talking to me? You'd better be if you're a designer; it's your job to communicate. A skilled designer knows how to create messages that are understood by everyone but also appeal very directly to a specific target audience.

The concept of designing for a target audience is a product of scientific marketing methods that emerged in the 1960s. Recognizing that they could profit by marketing directly to specific segments of the population—as opposed to the mass market—companies began to classify customers into groups based on geographic location, gender, age, income, and so on, and advertise accordingly.

FIGURE 2.8: **The Wick's Fowler Chili ad series packs a punch—and speaks to a very specific audience.**

Today, a design firm hired for a project is often supplied with a marketing brief on the company's target customers. Good designers zero in on this information and do their own research to get familiar with the customers' tastes: What brands do they buy? What fashions do they wear? What are their lifestyles? Understanding the customers helps you find a visual language to reach them.

> ▼ tip

Create a mood board for every design project. Do some research and gather some design pieces that will give you a sense of how to address the unique tastes of your target audience.

Of course, many companies want their message to reach everyone, not just the nice folks who are currently their customers. And so designers also look for ways to make a niche message understandable to the general public. A designer must be a scholar of how people read, how they consume images, and what they respond to.

One key consideration is the context in which the message will appear. Where will people see it? What will they be doing at the time? What other messages will appear alongside yours? A magazine cover needs to pop out on a crowded newsstand. An ad inside it needs to catch the attention of a reader casually flipping through. A billboard for the magazine may be viewed at a distance of hundreds of yards, by drivers idling at an intersection or flying past in a hurry.

Elements of Design

Every design we've looked at so far exhibits a skill in handling four elements: imagery, color, typography, and composition. Now we'll explore some basic principles for each area.

The Role of Imagery

The use of imagery—photographic images or illustrations—is the most direct way to communicate to a wide audience. There's a scientific reason for this: Our mind processes any kind of picture—a shape, a representation, even an outline of a figure—much more quickly than it does a word or sentence.

There's a commercial reason, too. Design must speak to a wide audience and speak quickly. This is partly because we are inundated with visual messages—we see graphic design everywhere. How much time do you devote to scanning a magazine ad, evaluating cereal boxes, or checking out someone's cool new sneakers? Not a lot. A design often has a fraction of a second to command attention and communicate. If the message is not compelling or clear, the opportunity is lost.

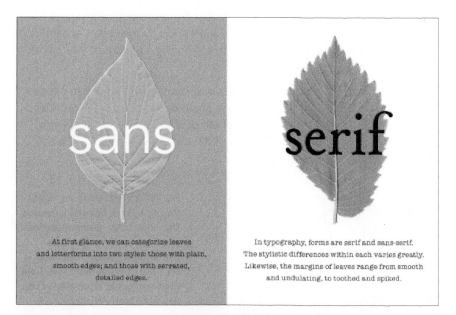

At first glance, we can categorize leaves and letterforms into two styles: those with plain, smooth edges; and those with serrated, detailed edges.

In typography, forms are serif and sans-serif. The stylistic differences within each varies greatly. Likewise, the margins of leaves range from smooth and undulating, to toothed and spiked.

FIGURE 2.9: In this promotional leaflet design, Canadian designer Janine Vangool uses a visual analogy to communicate what typography is all about.

▼ tip

If a professional photographer is not available (or affordable) designers often use stock photography for high profile jobs. The quality of the source image is a paramount consideration.

Read these words, then try to visualize them: Bowler hat. SUV. Convenient online services. Imagery is important in design because a picture (a cliché, but true) often conveys far more than mere words can. Almost any concept that you can imagine: a car, a refreshing taste, trust, fresh produce, retirement—is more quickly (and better) expressed through an image than the written word.

Simply showing a picture is not enough, however. Whether it's a photograph or an illustration, imagery must be expertly handled—cropped, edited, or simplified to bring out the essence of the message. The more economical the message, the better it communicates. A simple approach without distracting or irrelevant detail will determine whether the viewer grasps the concept or jumps to the wrong conclusion.

At a psychological level, the imagery in an ad or layout does much more than simply conveying a concept. It also communicates a general feeling, emotion, or mood that a viewer will associate with the product or publication. Tapping this intangible quality of imagery is essential to brand marketing. It is why designers, some of them, get paid the big bucks.

Photographic Images

To excel at design, it helps to immerse yourself in photography. The best designers understand the powerful qualities in the photographic image. A photograph catches the eye because it is understood by the viewer as capturing reality. The eye is immediately drawn to it, prompting questions of who, what, where, and why. It begs for interpretation.

Show me a photo of a person, and I will try to identify *who* it is. (Two people? I will try to figure out their relationship.) A photo of a product? I will wonder *what* it does or who made it. If I see a photo of a place: I will want to know *where* it is or what type of place it is. Or if it's a photo of an action or event, I will ask *why* it is happening.

FIGURE 2.10: Fashion ad, right? Wrong—closer inspection reveals that Viva Dolan Communications created this ad to showcase ArjoWiggins paper. The model is wearing clothing fabricated from high-end paper stock marketed to the fashion industry.

What makes a photographic image successful in a design context? The subject of each photograph is immediately clear and quite simple, and yet the image is rich in color or detail. The image is powerful enough that it attracts the eye and explains itself almost without the need for accompanying text. The designer has integrated the image with the other elements into a pleasing composition.

The designer has made sure the emotive qualities of the image that are most important to the message stand out: a smile, the eyes, the reflective surface of the car, the play of light on a diamond. The scaling and cropping of the image and its treatment (color, black and white, or duotone), together with its framing, help direct the viewer to the salient parts.

Of course, another compelling aspect of photographic imagery is that it can be altered, doctored, enhanced, or (to put it another way) Photoshopped. The digital image is so wonderfully malleable. Today, 90 percent of the photographic images we see in the media have been retouched: digitally altered, corrected for color, or otherwise made more appealing. This may include removing extraneous details, replacing backgrounds, and even creating whole new scenes with multiple images.

FIGURE 2.11: This background image for the Sessions.edu Web site was composited from a series of New York City photos. The result is a larger-than-life background that evokes the excitement of the big city.

And boy, do we love it. Such digital imagery is superbly evocative precisely because we interpret it as realistic, even when we realize that an image has been digitally altered. Many eye-catching ads introduce subtle, unnatural elements to an image, playing on the tension between artifice and reality. And we're fascinated. Our attention is drawn because we realize that something is not real and we want to figure out what it is.

Illustration

What role does the traditional art of illustration play today? One might think that as more people design on computers, drawing itself would begin to die out.

Not so. Digital photography is so prevalent now that anything drawn or otherwise crafted, sculpted, stitched, or fashioned by hand has a higher value. Line art and drawings suggest individuality, style, humanity, and a point of view. Illustrations are often used in fashion and publishing to create a nostalgic association with the past, when everything was made by hand.

Furthermore, you can draw on the computer. Digital illustrations—created in vector art programs such as Illustrator—evoke many of the same feelings traditional illustrations do. They look hand-drawn, but they fit neatly into any design context because they can be edited, replicated, and mass-produced at will.

FIGURE 2.12: Illustration is inherently creative, and so this wonderfully free Felix Sockwell illustration is a great choice for the Ford Detroit International Jazz Festival poster.

Digital illustrations have an inherent association with creativity. Illustrations are used when a designer must communicate artistic, editorial, or business flair. The creative spark of the illustrator, his or her skill in handling the art of representation, can be associated in the viewer's mind with the company or organization that is delivering the message.

Digital illustration also is a crucial component of visual identity design. Since the first companies began, illustrators have created symbols or marks that worked along with typography to convey the identity of a company or organization. And further back in time, artists created flags and crests for kings and nobles. Unlike photographs—which we interpret as slices of reality—an illustrator's drawings are understood as symbolic representations of a person, company, or concept.

FIGURE 2.13: Logo design is a natural application for illustration. This playful Ecuadorean car wash logo was designed for a woman-owned business.

Zoinks! Let's not forget that illustration can impart a tone that is playful, imaginative, or downright fun. Illustrations and sketches resonate with the universal experience of our childhood attempts to represent the world through pictures. They remind us of newspaper cartoon strips and animated movies. They are often associated with products or messages that evoke a playful experience or provide a relief from the ennui of adult life.

FIGURE 2.14: Designer Marcos Chin's marvelous ads for online dating site Lava Life create an appealing image that refreshes the sometimes uncertain realm of dating. Stylish young singles are depicted in the process of becoming attracted to each other.

As you can see, the choice of imagery—photo or illustration—is important for a designer. Who would want a photo of a scaly fish on their can of tuna? Conversely, who would want to see a fun illustration used in a serious context like an insurance ad? It's a choice between realism and representation. One compromise is to use photos and illustrations together in a project; one is usually the focus while the others play a supporting role.

Color

Color is the graphic designer's best friend and most powerful weapon. In the digital era, color is chosen and deployed with a few clicks or keystrokes. The use of color can bring an immediate, emotive quality to visual communication. Color can help establish the overall genre and mood of a piece as well as the relative importance of the different elements within it.

Good designers understand how to tap our universal associations with color. When we see green, we think "healthy" or "natural"; when we see red, we think "dangerous" or "important." Blue is often used to evoke calm, purple to convey luxury. While these underlying qualities of color vary from country to country, they are surprisingly consistent in the West.

FIGURE 2.15: Color is particularly important in food packaging. This Green Tea package design uses colors that are very appropriate for a Japanese audience.

In addition to inspiring moods, colors are associated with brand identities—political parties, nationalities, sports teams, and companies, to name just a few. Subtle variations of red could bring to mind associations as diverse as the Republican party, the country of China, the San Francisco 49ers, or Coca-Cola. Being aware of existing color associations will help you avoid sending the wrong message.

Based on how they reach the eye, colors, also known as *hues*, can be perceived as warm or cool, light or dark, active or calm. Some colors pop out, others recede. Designers can adjust the tone and intensity of a color (its brightness and saturation) to tailor how it is perceived.

FIGURE 2.16: Notice the use of color to both excite the eye and reinforce a brand in these billboard ads for fashionable retailer Target. The company's visual identity is both vivid and unmistakable.

Complicating the issue further is the fact that color is relative. The perception of any color varies depending on what other colors it is combined with. Designers must use great care to select color schemes, or sets of colors, that are appropriate for a project and convey the right message. A tool called a color wheel is used to select harmonious color schemes. Designers must also consider the lighting and environment in which the piece will be displayed.

tip

Colors in design are never purely decorative; they are chosen for a reason. It's good practice for a designer to explain his or her color choices to clients.

Every designer should take some time to learn color theory: the principles that explain how and why color interactions produce pleasing effects and desired emotions. Deploying color appropriately—often by using it sparingly—is key to the success of visual communication.

Typography

Typography—broadly defined as the art of type design and text layout—is essential to graphic design. Text and image must work together to create a message. Most design projects actually begin with some poor, bare information that needs a designer's touch. And without text, if you think about it, a design project would simply be art, photography, or illustration.

Like every other element in a design project, the written component, often called the *copy*, must be honed to capture the viewer's attention. No use in creating a razor-sharp image to accompany some flabby prose! The field of advertising illustrates just how intelligently and creatively text and image can be combined. In ad agencies, copywriters work with visual designers to make sure that both visuals and copy work in perfect sync.

FIGURE 2.17: Beautiful design concepts can emerge from the imaginative use of typography, as witnessed in this packaging design for a lens cleaner.

To tap the power of type, a designer must understand how letterforms and typefaces are constructed. The fonts that we so casually access from our drop-down menus are the product of centuries of evolution in printing, having been originally hammered out in hot metal (and before that, chiseled into stone). A typeface is still defined by certain distinct visual components.

One fundamental is the vertical proportion of the typeface: the distance between the baseline, upon which a row of letters sits, and the x-height, ascender line, and descender line. These points of reference—the height of lowercase letters, and the length of their upstrokes and downstrokes—are generally consistent within a typeface.

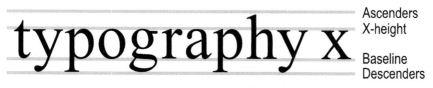

Ascenders
X-height
Baseline
Descenders

FIGURE 2.18: **The heights and proportions of x-heights, ascenders, and descenders are among the major features that distinguish typefaces.**

Why should a designer care about such minutiae? The more you get to know typography, the more you realize that a typeface is just like a color—it has a very specific language and the ability to convey specific emotions or moods. In high-level design projects, typography is handled with as much care as imagery or color.

Any graphic design begins with the important choice of typeface or font. Unless the typeface is already dictated by the client or publisher, a designer must choose between serif and sans-serif fonts (with and without ledges on the ends of letters, respectively) and drill deeper into finer distinctions between type families: Times, Palatino, Garamond, or Bodoni? Or perhaps a custom, avant-garde solution from a type foundry—a type design firm—will provide the required edge?

Equally important to the layout of type are decisions about the hierarchy of information. The size, weight, proportions, and placement of text on the page are critical to helping the reader's eye navigate through the layout and intuit the importance and purpose of each piece of content.

FIGURE 2.19: The choice of typeface—traditional, austere, or playful—is an important design decision.

Prominent text (titles, headlines, and company logos) may need fine-tuning for coherence and impact, in which case the designer will adjust the *kerning* or spacing between pairs of letters. In blocks of text (*body copy*), margins and justification (line length and left/right alignment) and tracking and line spacing (spaces between letters and lines) may all be tweaked to promote readability and enhance the overall composition.

Studying typography can yield enormous dividends. The more you immerse yourself, the more you will discover that type itself is a graphic element. The shapes of letterforms—their distinctive contours and the negative spaces they create—are powerful tools in your work. A mastery of typography is the mark of a designer.

FIGURE 2.20: Expressive use of type is the hallmark of a designer, shown here in Gabriela Monroy's work.

Composition

Now that we've explored how imagery, color, and typography each play a role in a design, let's look at the big picture: composition. Composition is the art of layout or placement of all those elements on a page. It's the heart of graphic design, and yet when done well, it is invisible—the feature a viewer will be least conscious of.

Most design projects begin with the arrangement of elements on a page: a two-dimensional surface or screen with defined boundaries. The page is a blank slate. You can place elements anywhere on it, and divide the space any way you like. Careful, though—proportion and balance will play an enormous role in the psychological impact of your message.

Emphasis is a critical element in composition. It's particularly important in editorial design, in which the size, color, and grouping of elements are used to establish a visual hierarchy. In a magazine article, for example, the relative importance of different blocks of text or images helps the reader quickly scan and grasp the purpose of each item: headline, byline, body text, pull quote, and so on.

FIGURE 2.21: This two-page spread for architecture magazine *Azure* does a wonderful job of creatively interpreting the article title to pull the reader into the story.

Depending on how you place objects on the page, you can attract the eye to a place of rest or lead it in a merry dance by suggesting movement. A single, centered object or set of objects will evoke calm, stillness, and equilibrium. Objects sitting to the left or right may connote movement or draw attention in that direction. Objects positioned toward the top or bottom of the page will pull the eye up or down.

When you place any object in a two-dimensional space, part of your image will be interpreted as positive space (the subject of the piece) while other parts will be seen as negative space (the background). Using contrast will give due emphasis to the subject of the piece. But this doesn't mean to ignore the background. The form of the background plays a strong role in the viewer's perception of the overall composition. Smart designers are often able to exploit the shape of negative space and the ambiguity between what is foreground and what is background to add intrigue and impact to a piece.

FIGURE 2.22: A half-munched apple or a marketing company that understands its customers? This identity developed by 98pt6 plays a clever game with negative space.

The balance of your composition must complement the message too. Designs with elements proportioned equally on a central axis (visible or implicit) are said to be *symmetrical*. Symmetrical compositions suggest calm, order, and rationality. Everything has been neatly arranged for you. Compositions that distribute elements unevenly, by weighting the page mostly to the left or right, are said to be *asymmetrical*. These can feel unbalanced, energetic, and edgy—which could be the right direction for a certain kind of project.

FIGURE 2.23: This ad for a new product line of Champion Athletic apparel exhibits masterful composition and use of negative space. Strong lines pull the eye to the top of the page, reinforcing a sense of the athlete's poise and well-being.

Critique the Design

In this project, you'll develop your critiquing skills by comparing and contrasting two excellent professional designs. Learning to evaluate how and why a design works (or doesn't work) is a critical step in any designer's development.

This chapter has given you a foundation in essential aspects of graphic design work and the roles of imagery, color, typography, and composition. This written assignment will challenge you to assess how these elements are handled by the pros.

Project Brief: The Big Crit

A major design and advertising magazine is preparing for its annual award ceremony. You are a lucky design journalist employed to help the magazine critique hundreds of cutting-edge designs to identify this year's winners.

To help the panel, you need to put together an intelligent critique that addresses not just the details of the visual design but also how creatively the designers addressed the client's overall business challenge. Critical questions are provided to guide your thinking (**FIGURES 2.23** and **2.24**).

FIGURE 2.24: "A Delicate Balance," a poster developed for Seattle Repertory Theater by Cyclone Design.

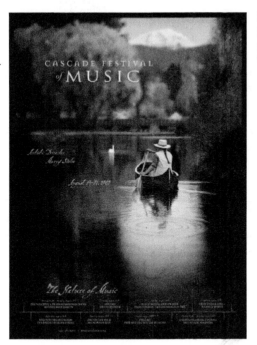

FIGURE 2.25: Poster for the Cascade Festival of Music in Bend, Oregon, developed by TBD Advertising.

Project Summary

Write down your initial emotional (noncritical) reaction to each piece. Try to see the designs through the eyes of an average person, not a designer.

Critique each piece in terms of imagery, color, typography, and composition.

Think about the project brief for each work, and critique how each piece addressed the company's business challenge.

Project Steps

1. First Impressions

Put aside everything you know about design, and write down your raw first impressions:

1. What is the first visual element that you noticed in each piece?

2. What was your initial emotional response? Write down the first ten words (adjectives, nouns, or verbs) that popped into your head.

3. Look at each piece out of the corner of your eye, with other pieces, and from a distance. How eye-catching is it?

4. How easy is it to figure out the message of the each piece? Is the point immediately apparent, or does it take a few moments to click? Why?

2. Design Critique

Now put on your designer hat and think about how each element in the design contributes to the overall message:

1. Summarize what you think the purpose or message of the piece is.

2. Comment on the designer's choice of imagery. Why do you think the designer chose a photograph as opposed to an illustration, or vice versa?

3. Photographs—Did the designer do anything with the scaling, cropping, framing, or treatment of the photograph to bring out its emotional message?

4. Illustrations—Did the use of illustration contribute to a sense of creativity, a symbolic message, or a sense of play?

5. Color—Did the choice of colors evoke any strong emotional associations? How would you describe the mood evoked?

6. Typography—What emotions are evoked by the typefaces used? Did the designer do anything unusual with the text layout? What is the information hierarchy—in what order is the text intended be read?

7. Composition—How does the placement of lines, points, or objects guide your eyes through the page? Which elements are the subject (positive space) and which are background (negative space)? Does the composition feel balanced or unbalanced?

8. Does the design (your answers to questions 2–8) support the apparent purpose of the piece (your answer to question 1)?

THE BIG PICTURE

Now try to think about the designer's project brief. Considering the project's likely goals, think about how well each piece meets these business objectives:

1. Does the design communicate a specific message quickly and memorably? How?

2. Does the design support the brand of the company or organization? How?

3. Does the design try to connect to a target audience? Can you guess what the target audience is, and will the piece also be understandable by the general public? Why or why not?

Photoshop Essentials

Adobe Photoshop, the professional painting and photo-retouching tool, is fast becoming a cultural icon. The product is now a household word and even a verb: "Let me Photoshop it to fix the color" or "Why did you Photoshop Donald Trump's head on Grandma's body?"

The secret to Photoshop's success is simply its ability to manipulate the photographic image: perfecting, enhancing, or reinventing bitmap-based (raster) files for maximum effect. It's by far the industry-standard bitmap image manipulation tool, and a must-know for every graphic designer.

In this chapter, we'll explore the fundamentals of Photoshop—concepts like layers, selections, masks, and using type—to build a foundation in techniques for editing photographic images. At the end of the chapter, you'll tackle a fun and challenging photo compositing project.

FIGURE 3.1: With Photoshop, you can turn a digital image into a tasty treat.

In this chapter you will:

- Learn about the role of Photoshop in design projects.

- Learn how bitmap images are edited.

- Learn to use layers to manage complex artwork in Photoshop.

- Learn to select areas of an image using basic selection tools.

- Learn to perform basic modifications on selected areas of an image.

- Learn to select complex areas using Quick Mask mode.

- Learn to input and format text using the Type tool, the Character palette, and the Paragraph palette.

- Learn to adjust lighting in a photo using an adjustment layer.

- Create a composite from a variety of images.

Photoshop and Graphic Design

Adobe Photoshop is all about image manipulation—starting with raw photographic material (or even from scratch) and creating something unique. Artists often use Photoshop as a sort of digital brush that can be used for photo-realistic images—images that look real but aren't—or fantastic, surreal digital effects.

For graphic and Web designers, it is even more indispensable. The odd thing is that when Photoshop is handled by a professional, its use goes mostly undetected. Think about every photographic image you encounter in your busy day: in catalogs and glossy magazine ads, on Web sites and book covers. If those images grabbed your attention and enhanced the message, they most likely had work done on them in Photoshop.

FIGURE 3.2: High-impact graphic concepts are the hallmark of Photoshop, as shown on the cover of *Photoshop User* magazine.

How does Photoshop fit into the graphic design process? In a design agency, conceptual development comes first, digital imaging second. On an ad campaign, a creative director will meet with designers and copywriters and brainstorm a strong visual idea. If a photographic image is required, the designer may obtain images from a stock photography company, hire a photographer, or even conduct the shoot herself. Only afterward will the image be imported into Photoshop for editing.

FIGURE 3.3 Photoshop projects start with a concept—what if your instructor were an appetizer?

And then what? Well, the sky's the limit. Sheer flexibility as a photo-retouching tool is what gave Photoshop its name. You can change the lighting in an image, adjust its sharpness, modify colors, change backgrounds, and even compile multiple photos into a single, seamless image via a process called *compositing*. Then, embellish to your heart's content, using a variety of painting and drawing tools, effects, and filters.

One caution: Just because you can doesn't mean that you should. It's important for design students to realize that endless tweaking in Photoshop does not equal good design. In fact, Photoshop is used mostly to eliminate distracting detail—to produce a simpler, clearer, more powerful, or more appropriate visual. Less is more, remember?

High design. Low financing.

Come see our full line of new and pre-owned cars today.

FIGURE 3.4: Less is more. Most projects are about clarifying a message by bringing out essentials and removing unnecessary detail.

Proficiency in Photoshop should be an essential goal for any design student. So many computer users are familiar with Photoshop to some degree that graphic designers must attain a high level of expertise to stand out professionally. A fluent designer can recognize the graphic potential in any bitmap image (or part of an image), manipulate it at will, and take care of the details so that the viewer is convinced or even fooled.

Editing and Organizing Images

In this section, we'll work on the essentials of Photoshop—the ability to organize artwork into layers, to select parts of an image for editing, to use silhouettes and masks, and to add and format text. This will build a foundation for later work. Basic ads and posters (good ones, too) can be created using just these tools.

About Bitmap Art

To understand how Photoshop works, it's helpful to know how bitmap art is put together. When an image is referred to as a bitmap (or "raster"), it simply means that it's made up of lots of tiny squares of color called *pixels*. Pixels are generally so small that they are not individually visible in a final, published image. Combinations of pixels are perceived as a continuous tone rather than a grid of squares.

With a painting application such as Photoshop, you can create brushstrokes on any bitmap image just as you would on a traditional canvas, by changing the color information in a group of pixels. To the naked eye, these brushstrokes will look smooth and painted, but zooming in will reveal that any edits to an image are indeed made up of changes to tiny dots.

FIGURE 3.5: Pixels make up every bitmap image on your computer screen and every image taken by your digital camera.

Bitmap art is "resolution dependent," which means that the number of pixels per inch (onscreen) or dots per inch (in print) determines the image's size. High-resolution images have many pixels, resulting in rich detail and fine print quality. Low-resolution images (typically used onscreen, such as for the Web) have fewer pixels and are therefore less detailed.

If you try to change a low-resolution image to high, or even try to enlarge any bitmap image, you will see a loss of detail, so it's important to always work at your intended size and resolution from the beginning of a project.

Using Layers

Getting comfortable with layers is an important skill for designers. Using layers, you can isolate any part of an image for editing, and stack different elements in an image on top of each other. Computer artists often use as many as 20 different layers to achieve subtle effects in a digital image.

CREATING LAYERS

Managing your artwork using layers requires some effort, it's true, but Photoshop creates most layers for you. Any time you copy and paste an image or drag a layer between documents, Photoshop will create a new layer. Thanks, Photoshop!

To create your own layers, use the Create New Layer button at the bottom of the Layers palette. If you're a shortcut junkie, Shift+Ctrl+N (PC) or Command+N (Mac) will create a new layer for you by opening the New Layer dialog box. Add the Alt/Option key into the shortcut, and Photoshop will automatically create a new layer for you with a default name (such as "Layer 1").

What if you want to create layers from an existing image? Photoshop allows you to create a new layer from a current selection. This is a powerful shortcut, as it saves you the time it would take you to copy a selection, create a new layer, and paste it into the new layer.

To create a new layer from a current selection, simply select something on a layer with one of the Marquee tools. Then choose Layer > New > Layer via Copy or Layer > New > Layer via Cut. The first option copies the contents of the current selection onto a new layer but leaves the original layer intact. The second option cuts the contents of the current selection and places it on a new layer. The shortcuts for these commands are Ctrl+J/Command+J and Ctrl+Shift+J/Command+Shift+J, respectively. Memorize them well; they'll undoubtedly save you time.

FIGURE 3.6: This image contains several different layers. You can have thousands if you're so inclined, but the more layers you add, the slower Photoshop will run.

ACTIVE AND HIDDEN LAYERS

To develop flexibility with layers, you must keep close tabs on which layers are active and which are hidden. An active layer is the one that is currently selected for editing. Hidden layers aren't editable, poor things, until you make them active.

You can determine which layer is active by looking at the Layers palette. The active layer will be highlighted. It will also contain a small paintbrush icon located just to the right of the visibility icon (more on this next) in the Layers palette. To make a layer active, just click the name of the layer. Remember, you can only have one layer active at a time.

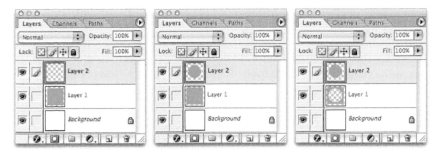

FIGURE 3.7: Three types of new layers you can create. Left to right: new blank layer, new layer via copy, and new layer via cut.

Note the distinction here between selecting a layer and making a selection with one of the Marquee tools.

Layers can be hidden or shown very easily. The leftmost icon on a layer in the Layers palette, represented by an eyeball, toggles the visibility of a layer. Hiding a layer doesn't remove it from your document—it just makes it invisible until you're ready to see it again.

LINKED LAYERS

If you need to move or transform more than one layer at a time, then you'll need to link layers together. A designer might use this technique to apply a color or effect to specific layers within an image.

To link multiple layers together, click to the left of one of the preview thumb- nails in the Layers palette. This will display a link symbol that indicates that the active layer (the one with the small paintbrush icon) is now linked to it.

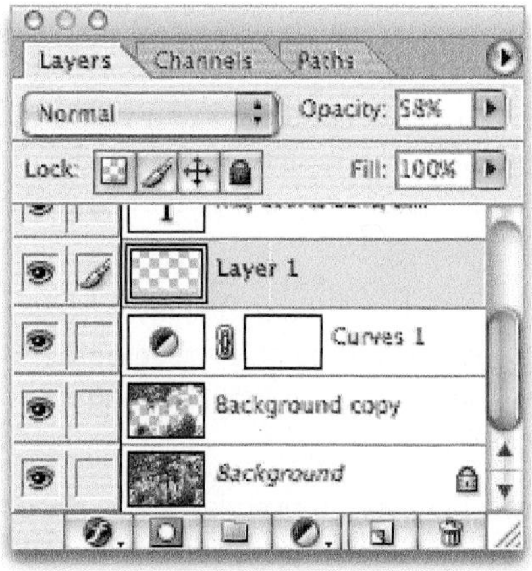

FIGURE 3.8: The active layer is highlighted and has a paintbrush icon next to the thumbnail.

Now you can move layers, transform them, or align them with each other. To move layers, select the Move tool and move them just as you would a single layer. To transform them, select any of the options from the Edit > Transform menu. To align layers, first select the Move tool. Then pick any of the alignment choices that are displayed in the Options bar.

THE BACKGROUND LAYER

The background layer is like the cardboard backing of a drawing pad. It is added automatically when you create a new canvas in Photoshop; it's locked, and no other layers can be dragged beneath it. The first thing I do when opening a new canvas in Photoshop is to create a normal layer from the background layer. To me, the background layer has so many restrictions that it usually becomes more of an inconvenience than anything else.

To convert the background layer to a normal layer, just Alt-double-click/Option-double-click the layer and it will become Layer 0—unlocked and ready to be used, moved, or discarded. If you like to be more in control, then leave out the Alt/Option key and just double-click the layer. The New Layer dialog will display and you'll be able to name the layer whatever you please.

MOVING AND DUPLICATING LAYERS

To move a layer within a Photoshop document, just drag it up or down in the layer stacking order. To duplicate a layer, select Duplicate Layer from the Layers palette options menu, and the active layer will be duplicated.

Alternatively, you can drag the layer to New Layer icon at the bottom of the Layers palette. Also, if you don't have a current marquee selection, then just press Ctrl+J/Command+J. This will create a new layer from the current selection (which is nothing) and is a great time saver.

To move a layer to another (open) Photoshop canvas, just drag the layer from the Layers palette to the new document. You'll need to be able to see both canvases to do this, however. You can also select the Move tool and drag the contents of a layer from one canvas to another.

Often, moving a layer can leave you unsure where your moved layer was placed in the new document. To prevent this problem, hold down the Shift key when dragging the layer to the new document, and Photoshop will place the contents of the layer in the center of the canvas.

Making Selections

Now that we've got our layers under control, let's start having fun with an imaging project. We will start with a picture of a Volkswagen Beetle (fabulous lime green, of course) that I took at dawn one morning when I couldn't sleep but had the urge to take pictures with my new digital camera. Here it is, parked in the driveway. Shhhh! It's still asleep.

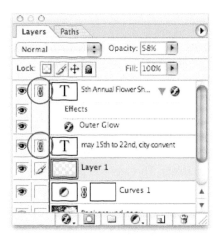

FIGURE 3.9: Linked layers will move together, helping keep your image consistent while leaving the contents of each layer separate.

FIGURE 3.10: This Beetle photo will need some work before it's ready for a slick, professional ad.

Nice, but we have to do a few things to this picture. We want to give it a professional look for an advertisement, so the background must be eliminated (which means we have to silhouette the Beetle first). Then we will make the car face the other way, and finally, we'll give the windows a sleek reflection and touch up the wheels.

Each of these three tools has various options and settings that can be changed in the Options bar when the tool is active.

THE SELECTION TOOLS

The selection process reigns in Photoshop. Selecting an item or area enables you to perform an action upon it. A selected item can be cut, copy, pasted, deleted, distorted, blurred, feathered, scale down, rotated, duplicated, or made negative. To edit, first select. Let's examine the tools that do it:

Lasso tool:
Pressing L on your keyboard or clicking the Lasso icon in your toolbox will activate the Lasso tool. The Lasso allows you to draw a freehand shape around the area you want to select. This lets you precisely select only the parts you really want.

Rectangular/Elliptical Marquee tool:
The Marquee (press M on your keyboard) lets you select a rectangular or elliptical shape in your image. You can drag the rectangle or ellipse to any size you like.

Magic Wand tool:
Clicking just once with your Magic Wand (press W) will select all of the pixels whose color is similar to the one you clicked. If you click a white pixel, for example, it will "look for" all of the other white (and near-white) pixels and select them.

MAKING A SILHOUETTE

Like many design projects, this one begins with isolating the subject of the piece. We want to make the background disappear to white, silhouetting the car. We will do that by selecting the car first, then inverting the selection so that everything except the car is selected. Then we will clear the inverted part so nothing's left but our shiny new Beetle. Let's do it!

In Photoshop, open the image VW_photo.jpg from your Images CD. Start by selecting the car with the Lasso tool .
If the Lasso you see is shaped differently than the one in this icon, click Shift+L until the right one appears in the toolbox, or hold down the button in the tool-box and grab the Lasso from the flyout menu that appears.

Click and hold your mouse button and carefully drag along the rear of the car (I started with the back bumper) to the top, down over the front, back around the front wheel, under the shadow, and under the rear wheel, finishing at the back bumper again. Don't worry if your selection isn't perfect.

FIGURE 3.11: Keep an eye on the "marching ants" that show you the selected area.

If some parts did not get selected that should have been, do this: With the dashed selection outline still active (the "marching ants" crawling around the Beetle), hold the Shift key and add to your selection simply by lassoing those little parts you missed the first time. You can do this any number of times.

If you selected areas that you did not want to select, just hold the Alt/Option key and use the Lasso to similarly subtract the offending areas. You can do this any number of times until you've selected just the parts of the image you want.

Now that you've selected the car, you must silhouette it by deleting the background and making it white. Do this by choosing Select > Inverse. You have now selected everything except the car. Press the Delete key, and the background should change to white. If it is a different color, choose Edit > Undo, then press the D key (setting white as the background color), and press the Delete key again. Save this file as VWSilo.psd.

With the selected area still on the screen, reselect just the car by choosing Select > Inverse. Good! Now that you've got just the car on a white background, we must make the car face the other direction. Choose Edit > Transform > Flip Horizontal. If you see a trace of the green outline of the car after you have flipped it, don't worry; you can clean that up by choosing Select > Inverse, then pressing the Delete key. Finally, choose Select > Deselect.

ADDITIONAL SELECTIONS

Nice job—but we aren't done yet. Let's clean up our act. We must select the windows and delete the grass and dirt showing through them, replacing them with a sleek, showroom-type gradient blend since we are creating an ad. Do

▼ tip

The Shift key plus any selection tool (Lasso, Rectangular/ Elliptical Marquee, Magic Wand) will add to your selection. The Alt/Option key plus any selection tool will subtract from your selection. To select all of your image, choose Select > All (or Ctrl+A/ Command+A). To deselect areas of your image, choose Select > Deselect (Ctrl+D/ Command+D).

▼ note

This icon, near the bottom of your toolbox, allows you to change your foreground and background colors to the default Photoshop choices, which are black for the foreground and white for the background. You can either click the icon or press D on your keyboard to switch your current colors to the default.

this by first carefully selecting the front window with the Lasso tool. Then, hold Shift to add the rear passenger window to your selection with the Lasso tool. Now, delete to make selected areas white by pressing the Delete key, or using a slower way, Edit > Clear.

FIGURE 3.12: Deleting your selection will show the background color in its place.

OK, now we'll fill the windows with a black-to-white (foreground to background) gradient from the top of the window to the bottom, using the Gradient tool. To fill with the gradient, make sure you have the default colors in your toolbox (black as the foreground color and white as the background) by pressing the D key or by clicking the ▣ icon in the toolbar.

Now press G for Gradient tool ▣, or select it from your toolbox. Click within your car window near the top, and drag your mouse straight down to the bottom of the window and let go. Adjust the gradient as necessary by undoing and trying the gradient again. Remember: To undo your most recent step, go to Edit > Undo or Ctrl+Z/Command+Z.

▼ note

Gradient tool: This tool allows you to paint a gradient, a blending of two colors into each other. You can create a black-to-white gradient (or vice versa) to fill your selection, or blend any other colors of the rainbow.

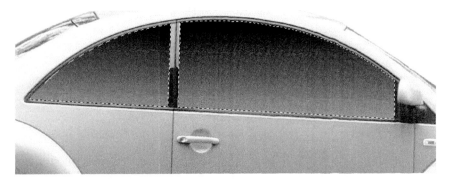

FIGURE 3.13: Get that showroom-sleek look with a swipe of your Gradient tool.

Great! What's next? We must zoom in and select the VW logos on the wheels and make them upright. (After all, that's what the client would want, right?)

Do this by selecting the Zoom tool  and then clicking in the center of the front wheel logo until it is a good size for you to work with.

Now, choose the Elliptical Marquee tool ⬭, and select the circular VW logo from the center. Do this by holding down Alt/Option when you click and start dragging the marquee, and hold down the Shift key to make a perfect circle.

Try it until you have it. If it's not right, just undo or deselect to start afresh.

Now, rotate your selection by choosing Edit > Free Transform. You will see a bounding box with corner handles (little boxes) around your selected region. Position your mouse just outside of a corner until you see a curved, double-ended arrow, then move and rotate it until the VW logo is upright. If you grab and move a straight arrow instead of a curved arrow, you will change the size of your selection—we don't want to do that now. Press the Enter/Return key to accept that choice. Now do the same steps for the other wheel's logo, and then deselect and save.

FIGURE 3.14: **Attention to the details is important for a designer.**

note

Zoom tool: Zooming allows you to move closer to or further from the actual size of your image to focus in on details or to fit something giant on your screen. Clicking the Zoom tool over your image will "zoom in" and center on the area you clicked. Holding down the Alt/Option key will zoom back out when you click. The percentage of your image's size is noted at the top of your image window—100 percent is actual size.

Great! Now we've got an advertising-ready image of the car. Who would believe what it once looked like? To finish off the ad, I threw in some clean and simple advertising text.

High design. Low financing.

Come see our full line of new and pre-owned cars today.

FIGURE 3.15: After that hard work, our photo is ready for center stage.

Selecting with Quick Masks

What's the big deal about masks? They asked Zorro the same thing. Masks are often brushed off by design students as another advanced topic they'll get to someday. I'll admit that it sounds difficult. But in essence, a mask is just a selection.

If I leave you with one concept from this mask discussion (other than how to use them) it would be this motto: "Black conceals, white reveals." As you learn about masks and start to use them, this little saying may come in quite handy.

QUICK MASK MODE

Quick Mask mode is another way to view a selection that you've made using one of the selection tools. Once you've created a selection, you can use this method of masking to view that selection, or add or subtract areas in it.

To use Quick Mask mode, first create a selection. Press Q or click the Quick Mask Mode button ▣ in the toolbox. At this point, you'll see everything but the area you selected covered by a red tinted overlay.

FIGURE 3.16: In Standard mode (left), the selected area is represented by the "marching ants." In Quick Mask mode (right), the selected area is the portion without the red overlay.

The red overlay covers and protects the area outside the active selection. Currently selected areas are left unprotected by this mask. By default, Quick Mask mode colors the protected area using a red, 50 percent opaque overlay, but you can change this by double-clicking the Quick Mask Mode icon in the toolbox.

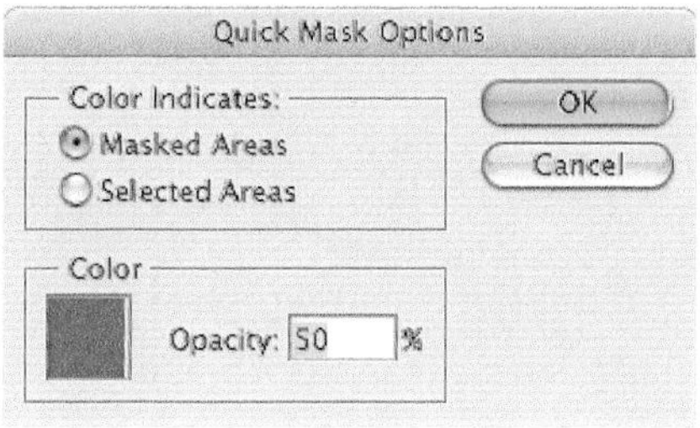

FIGURE 3.17: In some images, it's easier to differentiate the masked and unmasked areas if you choose a different overlay color.

Now you can edit the mask by using the normal painting tools, thus editing your selection. Use black to add to the overlay or white to take away from it. You'll notice that once you select the Brush tool, for example, the swatches in the toolbox automatically turn black and white. This is because only black, white, and shades of gray can be used on masks. So if you were to try to select a color, say blue, the swatch would turn to a dark gray color instead.

▼ tip

I've found that round brushes, either soft or hard, work best when in Quick Mask mode. Use a hard-edged brush for areas with a noticeable contrast between the selection and its background. Use soft-edged brushes for areas that you'd like to appear more blurred or subtle.

Once you're done manipulating your mask, click the Standard Mode button ▣ in the toolbox to turn off the mask and return to your original image. You'll see that the "marching ants" that indicate selection surround what was the unprotected area of the mask. Now you're free to perform any needed modifications to this selection.

FIGURE 3.18: In Quick Mask mode, I made my overlay color blue, then used black and white paint to mask everything but the leaf. When I switch back to Standard mode, the selection will be perfect.

Using Type

Most graphic design projects require you to combine images with some text, as we did with the Beetle retouching project. Simple text treatments, such as for posters or Web site mockups, can be easily accomplished in Photoshop.

THE TYPE TOOL

Using the Type tool is simple. Photoshop creates type on a new layer each time you choose the Type tool and click in your image area. You simply type your text, and then choose a color, size, justification, and so forth. Pressing the Enter/Return key puts your type on a layer above the layer that was previously active.

As with other layers, you can duplicate, delete, show/hide, and change the stacking order of Type layers. However, what is special is that Type layers give you "live" or "editable" text. You can double-click the T icon in the Layers palette at any time and edit your text, its size, the font, or other characteristics. Neat, huh?

However, you can't paint (or anything else) on that Type layer until you rasterize the layer and make it a "nonlive" or "noneditable" layer. Then the type becomes an image—just an array of pixels.

Create a new Photoshop file (File > New) that is 5 inches by 5 inches, in RGB color mode, at 72 dpi resolution, and with a white background.

Now choose the Type tool 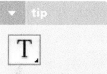. Click your cursor anywhere on your image area and type anything you like, such as a company name. I used the name Greenwood Farms because I'm going to design a package for a fictional food company. The back of a food product package usually has a lot of text on it: introductory copy, ingredients, nutritional info, and so on—so this project will be perfect for exploring the Type tool.

The letters go directly on your image area, and you can change format settings like font, size, and color in your Options bar. Be sure to highlight the text you've typed before changing settings so that the changes will be made to the selected area. When you're done, press Enter/Return.

FIGURE 3.19: I set my text's anti-aliasing to Sharp, giving the letters clean, smooth edges rather than jagged ones.

In your Layers palette, you should now see your Type layer (with the T icon) above your original, white background layer. Double-click the T in the Layers palette and edit your text. Make sure your text is highlighted to edit it. Choose a different font and size. Make it a different color by clicking the rectangular color box, and press Enter/Return. Easy, right?

tip

Type tool: This tool gives you the ability to place type directly on your document as a new layer. After selecting the Type tool and clicking the cursor anywhere on your document, a new layer is created to house your text, and you're ready to start typing and formatting your text—almost like you would with a word-processing application.

Now create another Type layer by clicking below your name in the image area with the Type tool. Type something else (I used the product name), make it a different font, size, and color, and press Enter/Return. Nice! You see another layer. You can do this again and again if you want. Or, you can go back and edit any layer by double-clicking the T in the Layers palette. Remember, this is "live" or "editable" text.

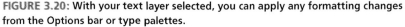

FIGURE 3.20: With your text layer selected, you can apply any formatting changes from the Options bar or type palettes.

THE CHARACTER PALETTE

When you're setting the text in a small area like the back of a package, precision counts. How close are the letters to one another? How close are the lines? Flush left or flush right?

These characteristics of your typography can easily be manipulated in Photoshop with two palettes in particular—the Character palette and the Paragraph palette. We'll discuss the most useful components of each palette, but you should experiment further on your own.

If you don't already see the Character palette on your screen, go to Window > Character to pop it up. As you can see if you have your Type tool selected, many of the options on the palette are mirrored in the Options bar (the color box, font selection menu, font size area, and anti-aliasing). But others aren't as common, so they're found only in this palette.

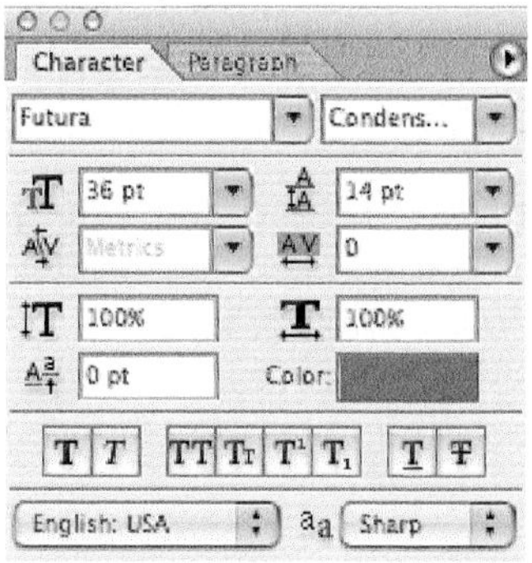

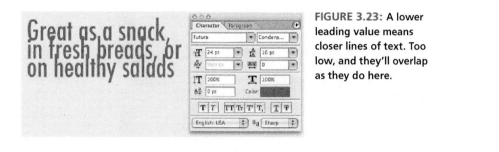

FIGURE 3.21: The Character palette is full of options—some of which you have already used and some you haven't.

On a new document, with your Type tool, type up a few lines, separated by paragraph returns. Pick any font, size, and color you like.

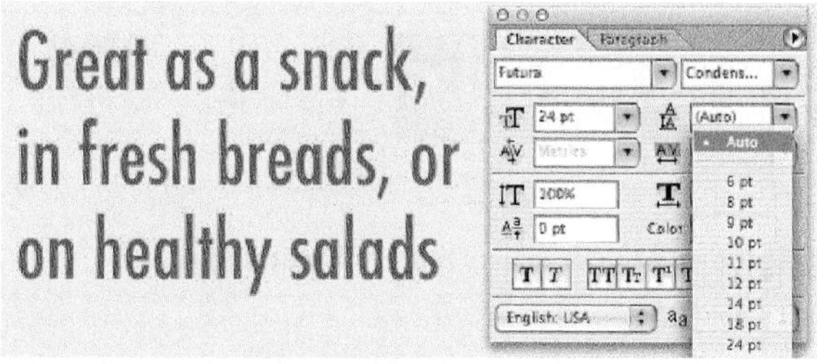

Great as a snack, in fresh breads, or on healthy salads

FIGURE 3.22: The default leading is fine for most purposes.

Notice the drop-down menu on the Character palette, which by default says (Auto). This is the Leading setting. *Leading* is the distance between lines of text. If you don't like the default point value, you can set it manually with the menu or by specifying a new value. A smaller value will bring the lines closer, and a higher value will draw them apart.

Great as a snack, in fresh breads, or on healthy salads

FIGURE 3.23: A lower leading value means closer lines of text. Too low, and they'll overlap as they do here.

Now let's check out the next row of drop-down menus. The first is Kerning and the second is Tracking, and they have similar jobs. Both affect the spacing between letters, but they work a little differently.

To use kerning, place your cursor between two letters, and change the Kerning value in the Character palette to move those two characters closer together (a negative value) or farther apart (a positive value). To use tracking, select all of the characters you wish to modify, and change the Tracking value in the same manner. This will move all of the selected characters closer together or farther apart, rather than modifying just two.

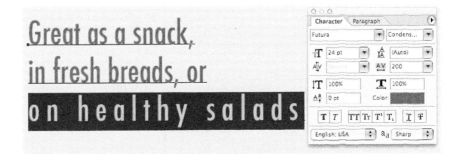

FIGURE 3.24: A high tracking value gives your letters a lot of breathing room.

Let's wrap up our look at this palette with the T buttons at the bottom. These are handy styles you can add to your selected text.

The first two are Faux Bold and Faux Italic. Sometimes the font you're using won't have its own bold or italic set (which you can select in the drop-down menu next to the typeface name), so Photoshop can simulate one for you.

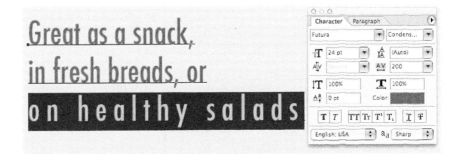

FIGURE 3.25: Use the faux settings only when your font doesn't come with its own bold or italic set. (I'm using Faux Italic here.) The versions supplied with a font are usually best.

The remaining "T" buttons give you styles like small caps, superscript, underlining, and strikethrough. Hover your mouse over the button on the palette for a pop-up explanation if you're not sure what it does—and just experiment.

THE PARAGRAPH PALETTE

The Paragraph palette is usually found tabbed right next to the Character palette—click the Paragraph tab to display it. If you can't find it, go to Window > Paragraph to pop it up.

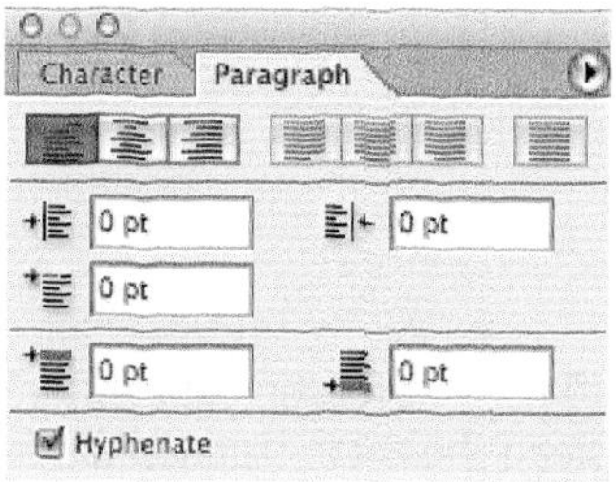
Character
Paragraph
0 pt
0 pt
0 pt
0 pt
0 pt
Hyphenate

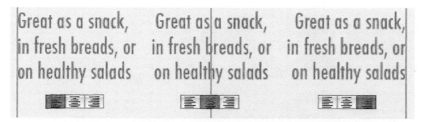

FIGURE 3.26: The most common Paragraph palette buttons, the alignment settings, are also found in the Options bar.

The Paragraph palette is most useful when dealing with lengthy passages of body text, though you can use its Left, Center, and Right buttons (also found in the Options bar) on text of any size.

Great as a snack,
in fresh breads, or
on healthy salads
Great as a snack,
in fresh breads, or
on healthy salads
Great as a snack,
in fresh breads, or
on healthy salads

FIGURE 3.27: The alignment settings work just like the ones you're used to in a word-processing program.

To use the remaining features, you'll need to create a text area with your Type tool and fill it with text. This defines a rectangle for the text to fit in; your Paragraph palette settings will influence how the text in the box is displayed.

Click and drag a large rectangle on your document with the Type tool. You'll see that you have created a box with handles, much like a transformation bounding box. Copy some text from another document, and paste it in the text area you just created.

Now you can experiment with the other tools in the Paragraph palette. Try the justification buttons on the top bar, indentation effects, and other settings.

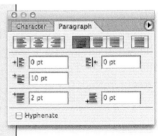

FIGURE 3.28: To alleviate text overload in a text box, I justified the lines, added indents, and changed the spacing between paragraphs.

By modifying my type settings in a number of different ways, I've set up a hierarchy of information on the food package. Notice that to keep it simple I did this with just a limited number of fonts, varying instead the color, sizing, and other settings.

FIGURE 3.29: Here's my finished package with all of my text set in a clear hierarchy.

Adjustment Layers

As a designer, you'll frequently be asked to work with images that require some global correction, such as lighting or color balance. Let's explore that now. In Photoshop, open the image Lowlight_dish.jpg from your Images CD, and make sure the Layers palette is showing. We will adjust the lighting of the photo using an adjustment layer. An adjustment layer allows you to make and edit global changes to an image on a separate layer, so you don't mess up your original.

FIGURE 3.30: You'll use adjustment layers to give this dark photo more attractive lighting.

Go to the bottom of the Layers palette and click the half-black/half-white circle icon ⬤. This will pop open a menu allowing you to choose from a range of possible adjustments to your image. Choose Levels.

▼ note

Clicking the little black-and-white circle on the bottom of your Layers palette will open a menu allowing you to create various types of adjustment layers. For now, we'll stick with a Levels adjustment layer to adjust lighting, but you can also change color, saturation, and other options.

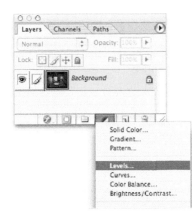

FIGURE 3.31: **Choose Levels from the adjustment layer menu, but take note of the many other options.**

See the black mountain of data? That is a histogram, which shows the balance of information on the dark areas (blacks), the middle-toned areas (grays), and light areas (whites) of your image. As you can see from the Levels dialog, the image has too much histogram information to the left side of the chart, or toward the dark areas (blacks), and hardly any toward the light areas (whites). We need to fix that.

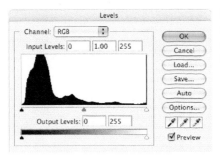

FIGURE 3.32: **The Levels histogram shows you information on the amounts of dark, medium-light, and bright areas of your image.**

After a Levels adjustment layer has been made, it will sit above your main layer and the histogram/slider icon will be visible. Double-clicking this icon will allow you to tweak your existing adjustments.

Make sure the Preview box is checked so that you can see the changes to your image as you make them. Now click the little white triangle on the right side of the chart and slide it over to the left until the Input Levels value says 168. Grab the little gray triangle and slide it until the Input Levels value in the middle says 1.15. Your rates may vary due to your monitor's brightness—feel free to use different values than these if you need to. Press Enter/Return or click OK to accept your choices.

Very good—you just created an adjustment layer in the Layers palette. It has this icon ▦ indicating that it is a lighting control or setting, but no real pixels are on that layer. The adjustment layer is visually blank—no pixels, just data—

so make sure you are not in that layer whenever you actually want to select or edit pixels. At any time, you can go back and edit your adjustment layer to your liking. Simply double-click the Levels icon on the layer to reedit your Levels.

We did as much as we could for the overall picture, without "blowing out" the items on the place mat. Now we will selectively choose other areas and lighten them. First make sure you click the Background layer of the Layers palette to target your pixel info, not your levels info.

FIGURE 3.33: Here's what we've got so far, but some areas still need work.

Select the place mat and everything that's on it with the Lasso tool. When you get to a straight edge on the place mat, use this neat trick: Hold down the Alt/Option key and click (but do not drag) the Lasso at one corner of the place mat, then move to the next corner and click (without dragging). Then you can release Alt/Option and continue with free-form selecting.

Because the place mat is selected, and we really want to edit everything except that, we must choose Select > Inverse. Now, make a Levels adjustment layer for that area. Move the white slider to the left until the levels are how you like them. You may need to move the gray slider slightly as well. Press Enter/Return or click OK to accept your choices.

FIGURE 3.34: The finished photo is lighter in all the right spots.

The lower adjustment layer is the "everything except the place mat" layer, because you inverted your selection before you made that layer. The layer above it is the adjustment for the whole image. See the before-and-after effects of your adjustment levels by clicking on and off the eye icon next to each adjustment layer. Additionally, you can change the opacity of those adjustment layers by sliding the Opacity slider in the Layers palette for each adjustment layer.

Once you're done, you can incorporate all those adjustment settings into the final photo by choosing Flatten Image from the Layers palette's options menu or going to Layer > Flatten Image.

Photo Compositing Project

In this project, you'll explore the challenge of photo compositing—compiling a variety of photos into a single, convincing image. This technique is used often in professional graphic design projects, though you might not realize it since the results can appear seamless.

The photo compositing requires a variety of Photoshop features including precision selecting, pattern definition, "pasting into," and lighting effects. We'll walk through these features as you work on creating a detailed and persuasive image of a room from an empty shell.

Project Brief: Interior Decorating

We're moving to the city and our bleak, empty new apartment needs life—fast! The outside looks nice, but the inside looks bare. Can you turn this room into a place that people will want to hang out in and invite friends to visit?

FIGURE 3.35: Where will the guests sit? It's your job to make this room more comfortable.

FIGURE 3.36: The room I made in Photoshop—casual and cozy.

Starting with the empty room image, your job is to create a fully decorated room using Photoshop techniques, your own creativity, and a variety of furniture and accessory images of your choice.

There are just a few requirements for this exercise:

- "Paint" all of the walls.

- Add "wallpaper" to at least one wall.

- Modify the windows in a major way—for example, add curtains, or change the outside view, maybe even change the style or placement of the windows.

- Change the carpet. You can repair it and change its color, or change the floor covering altogether with a new rug or style.

- Include at least three large pieces of furniture or appliances (for example, couch, chair, and TV; or couch, bookshelf, and coffee table).

- Place a piece of artwork on at least one of the walls.

Project Summary

- **Plan your room design and find appropriate working images.**
- **Use selections and transformations to add furniture and accessories to the room.**
- **Apply lighting and shading techniques to add realism to the components of the image.**
- **Create a convincing photo composite incorporating all of the required elements.**

Project Steps

You are free to use any methods in Photoshop to create your room redesign, as long as the requirements are met, but I'll walk you through how I created my version and give you some tips and ideas to guide you along.

1. Obtaining the Empty Room File and Component Images

First, in Photoshop, open the originalroom.jpg image from your Images CD. This will be your starting point, and all work should be done on this file.

Looking at the empty room as well as the project requirements, think about what you'd like to do to this space. What feeling and attitude should it have? What colors and textures will give it this feeling? What kinds of furniture and accessories would look best in the room?

You can use any furniture and accessory images to decorate the given room and give it character. Consider taking your own photos of these pieces, or visit home decor Web sites for images and inspiration. Don't bring these images into the room just yet—hang on to them, and bring them in as needed.

2. Selecting and Modifying the Carpet

The carpet is a good starting place for this project. Decide what you want to do with it, then make a selection of the entire carpet. Remember that you can make straight-edged selections by holding down the Alt/Option key and clicking with the Lasso tool, or you can use any other selection method you prefer. Save your selection in case you decide to go back to the floor later in the project—just go to Select > Save Selection.

To change the color of the rug, you can first clean it up using the Clone Stamp tool 📥. Alt/Option-click with the tool on a clean area of the carpet, then click a dirty area to "stamp" the clean selection you made. It takes practice, so Edit > Undo as needed and keep trying. With the rug clean, click the half-black/half-white circle icon on the Layers palette to make an adjustment layer and choose Hue/Saturation. With the Hue/Saturation sliders, you can pick any color you like. Remember, because it's an adjustment layer, you can always change it later.

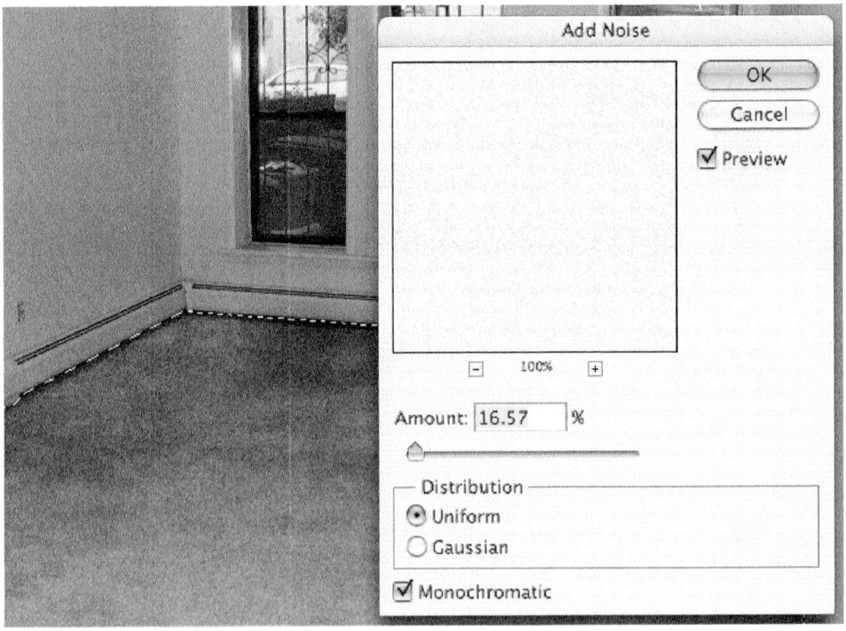

FIGURE 3.37: I made the rug plusher using the Add Noise filter (Filter > Noise > Add Noise).

If you'd rather change the texture of the rug, try a filter in the Filters menu. You may need to go to Edit > Fade after you add the filter to make the effect a bit more subtle. Alternatively, you could fill your rug selection with a new pattern altogether, perhaps giving the room a tiled or wood floor.

3. Revamping the Walls

Time for a fresh coat of paint. Selecting the walls will take some time and some care—it looks simple on the surface, but you may want to zoom in on some areas like the baseboard heaters and windowsills. Remember to subtract (Alt-click/Option-click) the windows from your selection. Save your selection to use later if needed.

Clean up the rough or dirty spots of the walls, then use any method you prefer to color the walls—for example a Hue/Saturation adjustment layer, or Edit > Fill > Foreground Color. If using a fill, do it on a new layer so you can adjust the opacity (using the slider on the Layers palette) or other features independently of the room layer. For an added decorative touch, you can paint the ceiling or paint different walls different colors, but try to keep it tasteful. We do want a realistic room!

FIGURE 3.38: I filled my wall selection with blue, reduced the opacity, and chose Multiply in the Layers palette menu so the color blended with the shading of the original walls.

Now for some wallpaper. Pick a wall and select it carefully—the back one is best because of its angles. Save the selection in case you need it later. (You should do this with all the selections you make throughout the project.)

Find a pattern from another document to use as wallpaper. If you find a good pattern on the Web or from your own photos, open the file in Photoshop, select the area you want as your pattern (it can be very small, just one piece of the repeating pattern), and go to Edit > Define Pattern to save it as a Photoshop pattern.

With the pattern defined, the wall selected, and a new layer in your room document created, fill the selection with the pattern by going to Edit > Fill and choosing your pattern in the Fill dialog. Lower the opacity or use another technique (such as a Blend mode in the menu on the Layers palette) to make it more subtle and shaded properly. It may take some tinkering before you've got the perfect wall covering.

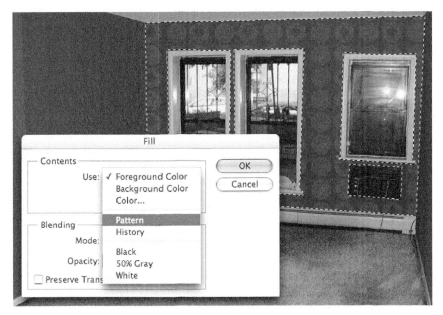

FIGURE 3.39: I defined a couple of dots on a fabric image as my pattern, and let it repeat throughout the back wall selection.

4. Changing the View

In our final step before moving furniture into the room, let's make this a room with a view. First, do a repair job with your Clone Stamp tool to clean up the second windowsill, or use another method to repair it if you prefer.

Then pick an image to place in the windows, giving the room a more exciting view than cars and garbage cans. Try some greenery, a skyline, or even some clouds if this apartment is on a high floor.

Select the glass of the windows carefully. To place your chosen background image, use the Paste Into technique. Open your scenery image and select it all (Select > All), then go to Edit > Copy. Now, return to your room document and choose Edit > Paste Into, which will insert the copied scenery into the window selection.

FIGURE 3.40: A prettier view, don't you think?

Alternatively, if you'd like to keep the current view, find or take a picture of curtains or other window treatments, and add them to these windows using the techniques you'll use shortly for furniture and accessories.

Pause here and give your room a thorough look-over. Make sure that you are happy with everything, and make changes now if you feel you need to.

5. Furnishing the Room

Find images online or take some photos of furnishings.

Begin by choosing all of the large pieces you wish to have in your room and opening the images in Photoshop. Remember that you must have at least three large pieces of furniture or appliances. You don't have to use the pieces exactly as you see them—if you want to change their color, place an image on a TV screen, or make any other changes, go for it.

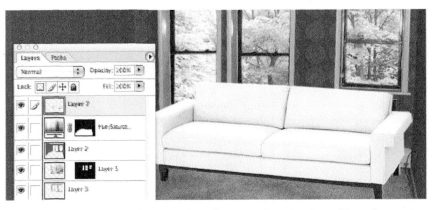

FIGURE 3.41: I found a sleek photo of a sofa, then selected it, flipped it, and transformed it to make a perfect fit in my room.

Next, very carefully select each one in its respective document and drag it using the Move tool onto your room. Use any of the selection techniques you learned in the warm-ups. The Lasso tool will be particularly useful, and you can refine the Lasso selections using Quick Mask mode.

With your pieces in the room, all on separate layers, you can use Edit > Free Transform to shrink, rotate, and otherwise shape them as needed to conform to the room. Remember that you'll need to make active the layer you wish to change by clicking it in the Layers palette.

Also try Edit > Transform > Flip Horizontal to get the mirror image of your piece if needed.

Place all three of your major pieces, but don't worry yet about the lighting and shading, which we'll tackle shortly; just make sure that their edges are clean with no excess bits and pieces. If they're not, you can use your Eraser tool to clean them up, but remember that precise selection should avert the need to do this.

6. Accessorizing

With the three major pieces placed exactly how you like, you can now add the accessories to the room. Have some fun decorating—place items on tables, add some cozy throw pillows, small furnishings or lamps, a few shelves (with more accessories!), and so on. Use the same process that you did with the furniture until you have your room decorated to your liking.

FIGURE 3.42: The bowl of green apples and some throw pillows made the place feel like a real home.

Next, let's get some art on those walls. Grab anything you like from the Web that goes with your room—sites that sell posters are a great place to look. You can even "frame" your favorite digital photos by placing a border around them (Edit > Stroke).

So you've got your artwork. You've selected it and dragged it into the room with the Move tool. You've scaled it to the size you like with Edit > Free Transform. But what's wrong with this picture?

The art won't look realistic until its perspective has been manipulated to match the angle of the wall. The best way to address this, although challenging, is with Edit > Transform > Distort.

Drag the corner handles of the distort bounding box carefully, making the vertical sides parallel to the walls, and the horizontal sides in the same direction as the floor and ceiling lines. Try to imagine the floor and ceiling lines extended as far as they need to be until they meet, then aim the top and bottom borders of your art toward this "vanishing point."

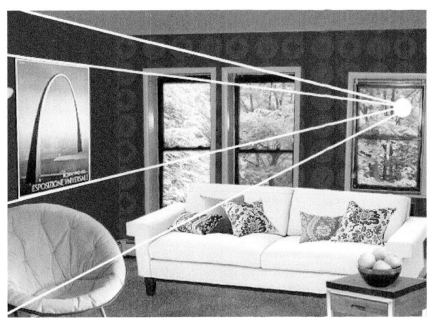

FIGURE 3.43: You could eyeball the vanishing point or make some lines on a new layer to act as guides. Then delete the line layer when you're done.

7. Lighting and Shading

At this stage, all of the items in your room should be placed and styled exactly how you want them. But there's something else keeping your room from looking realistic—shadows. To begin working on these, let's improve the lighting on all of the pieces in the room using Levels adjustment layers. This will give us a good starting point before we make more detailed lighting and shadow tweaks.

Do a Levels adjustment layer for the main room layer, just as you did for the warm-up earlier. Use your best judgment on the settings. Then, for the pieces in the room, you'll first need to load a selection before applying an adjustment layer—otherwise the levels you adjust will affect all the layers below as well. If you didn't save selections of everything, it's OK. Go to Select > Load Selection, and in the Channel menu, choose Transparency for the layer you wish to adjust. This will select only the object on that layer, so you can then apply an adjustment layer. Repeat for all of your items in the room.

FIGURE 3.44: By adjusting the levels, some pieces have brightened and some darkened, all becoming more realistic.

Next, let's give each piece its appropriate shading. Begin with a large piece of furniture, and apply a Drop Shadow effect (Layer > Layer Style > Drop Shadow) that is subtle and realistic in opacity, color, distance, and blurring (make sure Preview is checked in the Drop Shadow dialog so you can see your changes while you make them). Keep in mind when selecting the angle that the main light source is the left window, unless you've changed it.

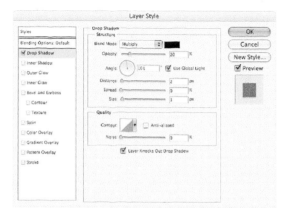

FIGURE 3.45: The Drop Shadow dialog box allows you to create subtle or dramatic shadows at any angle you choose.

You can now copy and paste this style onto your other layers using the Layer > Layer Style options. Not all of them will look perfect when you paste them, but we'll go back to them and tweak in the next step.

In my example, the distance and size settings I used for the couch shadow were too large for some of the smaller pieces in my room, such as the pillows and artwork. I double-clicked the f icon on my layers for the smaller pieces, and made the shading subtler.

On some pieces, the drop shadow that you'll apply might not make sense at all, particularly small pieces sitting on other surfaces such as tables, where the shadow should only be on the surface itself, not the other objects behind it.

But rather than remove the shadow altogether and start fresh, here's a handy tip: With your layer selected, go to Layer > Layer Style > Create Layer. This will turn your drop shadow effect into its own layer to which you can do anything you like. You can erase the parts that don't belong with your Eraser tool, or transform it to a more appropriate size or shape.

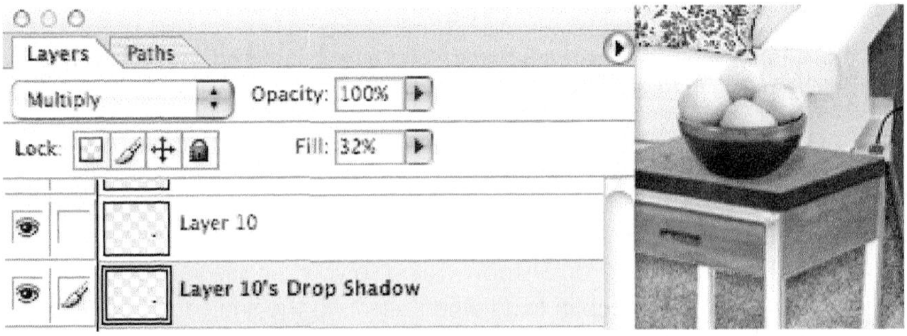

FIGURE 3.46: The bowl's shadow should be cast only on the table, so I made a new layer for the shadow and tweaked it.

If you need any additional highlights or shadows on your objects, you can finish up by using the Dodge tool and Burn tool in your toolbox. Dodging will lighten any part of the layer that you apply it to, while burning will darken. Both tools offer many variables in the Options bar, so you can experiment for just the right look. Lighting and shading is a difficult technique to master; just use your eye and do your best.

FIGURE 3.47: After a final bit of dodging and burning, my room is ready for guests.

When you're done, you should have a room filled with objects that look like they were there all along—an apartment people would love to visit.

Student Work

What have other designers done with this photo compositing project? Here are some projects created by Sessions.edu students:

FIGURE 3.48: Adam Benefield created an Asian-inspired meditation room, and he used some pretty complex selections (like those of the bonsai tree) to do it.

FIGURE 3.49: John Messinger's room is high-tech and masculine, with nice use of distortion to achieve realistic perspective and angles.

FIGURE 3.50: Melinda Langevin used lots of greenery (and very detailed selections) to create a tranquil, tropical room.

4 Illustrator Essentials

Designers starting out know Adobe Illustrator as "that program for designing logos," but it's capable of so much more: ads, illustrations, page layouts, and Web graphics, to name just a few applications. It's the industry-standard application for vector graphics.

You don't even have to be a virtuoso at drawing to create good Illustrator art. It helps, of course. But many designers who are not skilled illustrators are able to harness the program's drawing, selection, color, and effects tools to create powerful and detailed artwork.

If you're new to Illustrator (or just rusty), this chapter will get you well on your way toward understanding the fundamentals of using Illustrator to create vector graphics. Test your skills at the end of the chapter on an advertising design project.

FIGURE 4.1: Ready to let your imagination fly? Vector art created in Illustrator by designer John Schwegel.

In this chapter you will:

- Learn about the role of vector graphics in design.

- Learn to use Illustrator's drawing tools to create vector shapes.

- Learn to select and arrange objects on the Illustrator Artboard.

- Learn to apply colored fills and strokes to objects.

- Learn to modify vector objects using transformations and distortions.

- Learn how to use basic and specialized typography tools.

- Learn to apply transparency, filters, and effects to add complexity to objects.

- Design an outdoor advertisement using only vector art.

Illustrator and Graphic Design

Adobe Illustrator started as a simple drawing program intended to automate technical drawing tasks. Today? Illustrator has come a long way, baby. Its raison d'être is still illustration, the creation of line art. But along the way, its developers have added in a host of features that make it sophisticated and flexible enough for a range of applications.

Mastering Illustrator certainly isn't easy. The program's tough learning curve—compared with that of its ubiquitous pal Photoshop—is daunting to many who are most comfortable with the latter's painting metaphor. But for any serious graphic designer, Illustrator cannot be ignored.

Digital illustration is called for when a designer is looking for digital art with the special quality that only drawn art can impart. To produce an annual report, for example, an art director might commission an illustrator to create a set of icons and illustrations that run throughout the document, identifying chapters and reflecting its major themes.

FIGURE 4.2: Editorial illustrations such as these, by designer Heidi Schmidt, add grace to print layouts.

Professional-looking stock photography and clip-art graphics are so widespread these days that unique illustrations can really enhance the perceived quality of a project. Whether it's sketched in Illustrator or by hand, any piece of pictorial art is immediately grasped by the viewer as a symbolic representation—an imaginative rendering of a person, organization, or concept. People respond to such images differently than they do to photographs.

FIGURE 4.3: Ready to make your mark? Logo design is a core application for Illustrator.

From a design standpoint, one reason more people are learning Illustrator is that it offers tremendous flexibility in the creative process. With skill and good visualization, the basic building blocks of an illustration (such as lines, fills, colors, and gradients) can be easy to deploy and duplicate. Illustrations can be combined with the precise typography required for visual-identity design and print publication. And the results can be modified using a variety of popular effects such as distortion, transparency, and three-dimensional perspective.

Developing skill in Illustrator can open up many avenues in the design field. The program provides the crisp accuracy in the placement and proportion of lines and letters that's so essential in visual identity and packaging design. The ability to resize a vector-based graphic with no quality loss is invaluable; blow it up to billboard size and you'll still see a perfect result. Illustrator's precise typographical tools lend themselves to basic page layout projects such as promotions, magazine ads, and posters. Even Web graphics and pages can be initially designed in Illustrator before conversion to bitmapped format.

FIGURE 4.4: Futuristic, three-dimensional, and designed entirely in Illustrator.

At the professional level, the lines between photography and illustration in design are beginning to blur. Truly proficient Illustrator artists are creating art that looks just like photographic imagery by the skillful use of drawing tools, paths, shapes, and effects. Real or unreal? These images intrigue the eye, pulling us in. And they inspire people to learn Illustrator.

FIGURE 4.5: Designer Brooke Nuñez is renowned for her photo-realistic images. This rose uses complex gradient meshes in Illustrator.

Creating Vector Art

In this section, we'll work on the essentials of Illustrator—the ability to use the drawing tools; select and arrange your artwork; work with strokes, fills, color, and type; and utilize some basic effects. If you're new to Illustrator, that's a lot to cover, but it will provide a foundation for further study. As you'll discover in this chapter's project, a lot of creative work can be done using just these tools.

About Vector Art

To understand how Illustrator works, it's helpful to contrast it with Photoshop. If you've worked with photographs or artwork in Photoshop, you'll know that such images are composed of *pixels*—tiny dots, each with its own color. A group of pixels put together form what is called a bitmapped image.

Images created in Illustrator (and other vector-based software programs) don't have pixels. If you zoom in closely on them, you won't see any little dots. Illustrator artwork is referred to as *vector*-based; vector art uses mathematical equations to create lines and blocks of color.

Thankfully, you don't need to know a thing about those equations when you create your vector art. What you do need to know is that they contribute to the beauty of Illustrator. Vector art is infinitely resizable. Make your design much larger or smaller, and you'll experience no loss of quality—which is not the case with bitmapped images, which can get blurry and muddy when you resize.

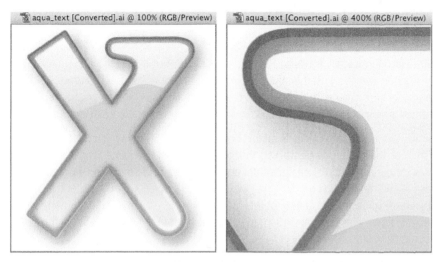

FIGURE 4.6: Size doesn't matter in the vector world. No matter how much I enlarge this vector graphic, it retains its crisp edges.

DRAWING TOOLS

If you're launching Illustrator for the first time, why not begin by exploring different ways to create lines and shapes? Illustrator provides a number of basic drawing tools that create different shapes but share common functionality and features.

SHAPE AND LINE TOOLS

Select the Star tool in the toolbox and click once on the Artboard. Doing so displays the options for this tool. You can access options for all the shape tools (Rectangle, Rounded Rectangle, Ellipse, Polygon, Star, and Flare) and line tools (Line Segment, Arc, Spiral, Rectangular Grid, and Polar Grid) in this manner.

In the Star options box, enter a value of *25* for Radius 1 (the star's inner radius) and a value of *50* for Radius 2 (the outer radius). Leave the Points value as is, and click OK. In doing so, you've drawn a shape numerically rather than with a mouse. Be sure to try this with the other tools.

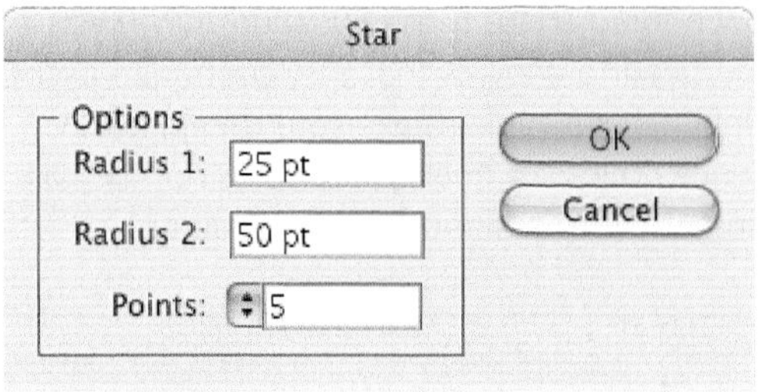

Star

Options
Radius 1: 25 pt
Radius 2: 50 pt
Points: 5

OK
Cancel

FIGURE 4.7: **Clicking with most tools on the Artboard gives you their numerical options.**

Drawing numerically is useful for precise drawing, but it may leave you feeling restrained creatively. Rather than clicking and entering numbers to draw, you can also click and drag with a mouse or drawing tablet—certainly a lot quicker than entering numbers. Illustrator accommodates whatever drawing style you choose.

If you draw with a mouse or tablet, hold down the Shift key to constrain shapes (such as the rectangle or star) so that all sides are of the same length (equilateral), creating squares, perfect stars and polygons, and so on. In the case of an ellipse, holding down the Shift key while you drag will create a perfect circle. To create a shape from a center point, hold down the Alt key (Option on a Mac) as you draw. Use both modifier keys together (Alt+Shift/Option+Shift) for additional control.

Those of you with sharp eyes might be wondering where, amid all the basic drawing tools, a Triangle tool is. Well, there is no such tool. To draw a triangle, select the Polygon tool and click and drag on the Artboard—but don't release your mouse button just yet. While dragging, press the down arrow key on your keyboard and note how the number of sides on the polygon decreases to three, the minimum. Instant triangle. And you can even draw a triangle numerically by clicking once on the Artboard with the Polygon tool and entering a value of 3 in the Sides input box.

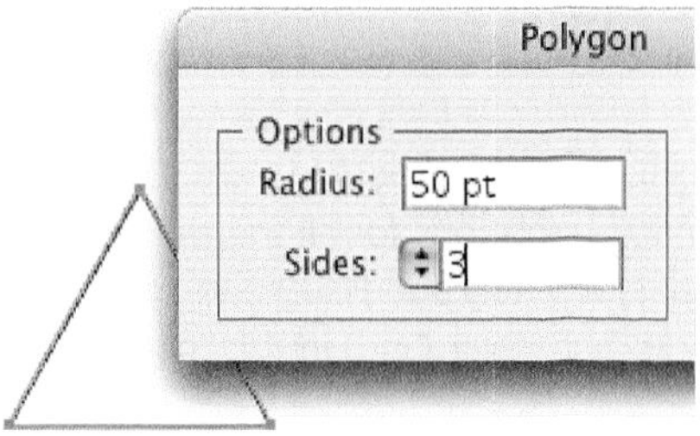

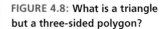

Polygon

Options
Radius: 50 pt
Sides: 3

FIGURE 4.8: **What is a triangle but a three-sided polygon?**

Want to try something really cool? As you draw with the mouse, hold down the tilde (~) for a dramatic wireframe effect. On a standard keyboard, look for the tilde on the accent key, just to the left of the 1 key. By pressing this key, you make a copy of the shape any time you move the mouse while drawing. Try it now with the Star tool—click and drag to create a star, but don't let go of the mouse button. Hold down the tilde key and give your mouse a spin.

Stop for a moment and look at the various drawing tools that all share this functionality. Just by using ellipses, line segments, rectangles, polygons, and other simple shapes and lines, you can construct a multitude of creations, from robots to landscapes.

FIGURE 4.9: **My handcrafted automaton. Basic shapes form the backbone of this robot illustration.**

FREE-FORM DRAWING TOOLS

Shape and line tools are certainly not your only drawing resources. Those who like to draw freehand will enjoy the Paintbrush and Pencil tools. The Paintbrush tool 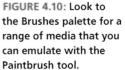 is a freehand drawing tool that's effective with a mouse and downright powerful with an electronic drawing tablet. The Paintbrush works in conjunction with the Brushes palette (Window > Brushes). With it, you can create artwork that emulates the look of watercolors, chalk, or even scribbles with a pen. Double-click with the Paintbrush tool to display its many options, such as Smoothness. Experiment with them to see a variety of painting possibilities.

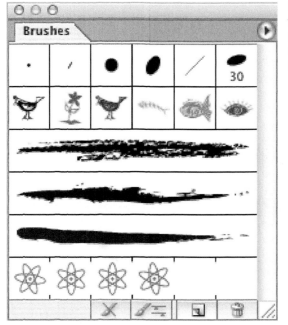

FIGURE 4.10: Look to the Brushes palette for a range of media that you can emulate with the Paintbrush tool.

The Pencil tool is practically an identical twin to the Paintbrush. They share similar tool settings (Fidelity, Smoothness) and functionality. While the Paintbrush automatically starts drawing with a brushstroke, the Pencil tool, by default, starts off with a 1-point stroke. The Pencil can draw with Brush palette brushes, but it does not do so by default. The Pencil and Paint Brush tools have been part of the Illustrator family for so long that if Adobe chose to combine the two into one, much chaos and mayhem would ensue.

FIGURE 4.11: **This cartoon piece of sushi was drawn with the Pencil tool. (The Chopstick tool is still being developed.)**

Finally, there is the Pen tool, which goes beyond the scope of this chapter— but you'll learn all about it later. The Pen provides the ability to construct ultra-precise paths, but has a learning curve almost as steep as that of the rest of Illustrator's features put together.

As you draw more and more shapes on the Artboard, they will invariably overlap. The newest shapes always appear on top of the older ones in what Illustrator calls a *stacking order*. Think of this as layers upon layers of shapes or objects. Up next, we'll look at how to alter the stacking order with the Selection tool.

Selecting and Arranging

If you've been trying out all of the drawing tools, your Artboard may be pretty crowded by now. Time to clean up. Select the solid arrow in the toolbox (in the top-left corner) .

THE SELECTION TOOL

This is the Selection tool, and with it you can select, move, rotate, and modify shapes on the Artboard. A shape or object in Illustrator must be selected before you can make any kind of changes to it.

When you select a shape, a bounding box consisting of an outline with eight points appears. If for some reason you don't see a bounding box as shown below, choose View > Show Bounding Box. To move a selection, click within the bounding box and then drag. To resize, move the cursor directly over a bounding box point until it turns into a double arrow. Click and drag to resize or reshape the selection. Press and hold the Shift key to resize proportionately. Hold the Alt (PC) or Option (Mac) key to constrain movement from the object's center.

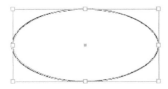

FIGURE 4.12: An object's bounding box and handles are visible when you select a shape.

To rotate an object, move the cursor just to the outside of one of the points until a curved double arrow appears. Click and drag in a clockwise or counterclockwise motion. Hold down the Shift key to constrain rotation to 45-degree angles. Reset the orientation of your bounding box after rotating by selecting Object > Transform > Reset Bounding Box from the menu bar.

To select more than one shape with the Selection tool, hold down the Shift key and click additional objects. If the object you're clicking does not respond, it may not be filled with a color. Try clicking on the outline of the object instead. Another way is to click the Artboard and drag a selection marquee around the objects you wish to select, just like making a marquee with the Zoom tool to zoom in on objects.

To make multiple copies, select an object, press the Alt (PC) or Option (Mac) key, and then click, drag away from the original object, and release. To deselect, click on the Artboard away from the selected object(s).

ARRANGING OBJECTS

Remember stacking order? It's time to shake things up and down. Draw two circles that overlap each other a little.

Select the bottom circle (with the Selection tool) and choose Object > Arrange > Bring To Front. The stacking order of the two circles changes. If you select the Send To Back command (from the same menu), the circle returns to the bottom of the stack.

If you try this and don't see any effect, make sure both of your objects have a fill. Select an object, and then click the miniature Fill and Stroke icon in the lower-left corner of the regular Fill and Stroke boxes in the toolbox.

FIGURE 4.13: Clicking this mini button gives an object a white fill and a black stroke.

Now, add another overlapping circle on top of the other two and make sure you can see all three. Select the bottom circle and choose Object > Arrange > Bring Forward. The circle moves between the other circles to the middle of the stacking order. Rather than jump to the top of the stack, this command can bring an object forward one position at a time in the stacking order. The Send Backward command has the opposite effect, sending an object back one step rather than all the way to the back.

FIGURE 4.14: You can control the overlapping of any objects, like these stars, by adjusting the stacking order.

If you have an object selected, you can also access the Arrange commands by right-clicking (Ctrl-clicking on the Mac) to display a pop-up menu.

Working with Multiple Objects

Why reinvent the wheel when you can so easily cut and paste it? That is the wonderful philosophy behind objects, which permit us to clone repeated design elements.

POWERFUL PASTE COMMANDS

Like most modern software applications, Illustrator features traditional copy and paste commands. They function as expected. You select an object, choose Copy or Cut from the Edit menu, and then click Paste. The new copy appears on the Artboard in the middle of the screen.

If you need to paste an object precisely in front (or back) of its original, however, these traditional commands are ineffective. To the rescue come the Paste In Front and Paste In Back commands. When you use either of these commands, found in the Edit menu, Illustrator will paste your copy either exactly behind the original or exactly in front.

The keyboard shortcuts for the special paste commands appear in the Edit menu.

For the skeptics in the audience, draw a circle, select it, and make a copy—Ctrl+C (PC) or Command+C (Mac). Select Paste In Front (Edit > Paste In Front). Nothing's changed, it would seem. Now select the circle and drag it across the Artboard. Notice the other circle now? That is the original; you are dragging the copy, which was pasted in front of the original. Voilà! The Paste In Back command works the same way but pastes the copy behind the original.

GROUPING

Next, let's take a look at the grouping (and ungrouping) of objects in Illustrator.

When you group objects, you effectively create a temporary bond. Group three stars together, and when you select one of them (with the Selection tool), you select them all. Fill one object with a color, and you fill them all. Rotate one object, and … you get the picture. Grouping is useful for organizing related objects in your document or for moving multiple objects about with little trouble. To group, select two or more objects and choose Object > Group or press Ctrl+G (Command+G on a Mac). To ungroup, choose Object > Ungroup or press Ctrl+Shift+G (PC) or Command+Shift+G (Mac).

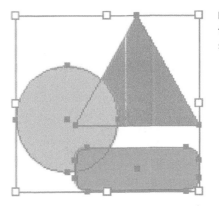

FIGURE 4.15: Just click any of the objects in the group to select them all at once.

You can group together object groups, and those groups can also be part of another group!

Working with Strokes and Color

Different strokes for different folks, they say. That is true in Illustrator too, once you gain control over your stroke palette.

THE STROKE PALETTE

Stroke may seem an odd name for something deserving of a palette, but you'll quickly come to appreciate it. A stroke refers to the outline of an object, whether it's a simple line or an elaborate polygon. The objects you're drawing so far are all (most likely) in black and white (until a few paragraphs from now!), and the stroke is the black part.

The controls on the Stroke palette affect both the style and width of the lines in your artwork. Since you can now select objects, grab a shape on the Artboard and enter a value of *5* in the Weight input box. As you do this, the line's thickness, or the stroke *weight*, changes on your object. Preset stroke weights are available from a drop-down menu; *spin controls* (the up and down arrows in the box) provide an alternate selection method.

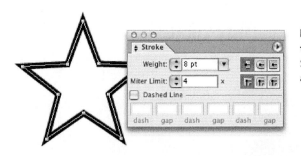

FIGURE 4.16: Thick, thin, or in between, the Stroke palette handles all your outlining needs.

The Cap and Join settings on the Stroke palette determine how a line terminates (the *cap*) and how one line meets the other (the *join*). A line or stroke can have one of three caps: a butt cap (a straight end), a round cap (a semicircular end), or a projecting cap (an end extending beyond the endpoint by half of the current line width). The three types of joins are Miter, Round, and Bevel. The Miter join has an input box below the Weight input, which allows you to select the Miter limit, or how long and pointy the join can be until one line turns into the other.

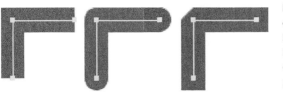

FIGURE 4.17: Cap and join options, from left to right: Miter join with a butt cap, Round join with a round cap, and Bevel join with a projecting cap.

As you might have guessed, the Dashed Line option will give you dotted or dashed lines. To activate it, click the check box and enter a value for the dash size (*1*, for example) and a value for the gap (such as *3*) between dashes. It's only necessary to enter a value within the first dash and gap box. The other boxes give you enhanced control over the dashed-line appearance by mixing dashes of different sizes and shapes with smaller or larger gaps. Experiment with different values in each box to see the result.

FIGURE 4.18: Strokes are found throughout this delightful Sonoma Joe illustration by Heidi Schmidt, particularly in its text.

By default, the stroke on any object is positioned above the color that fills it. As you increase the stroke weight, it begins to obscure the fill below it. This is most noticeable on text objects. To move the stroke below the fill, select the object you wish to edit and open the Appearance palette (Window > Appearance). This palette displays both the stroke information and fill information for the selected object. Click the Stroke appearance and drag it below the Fill appearance.

USING COLOR

Before we move deep into the territory of color, I want you to first look at the fundamental components of the shapes we're drawing. By doing so, you'll gain an understanding of what you can apply color to.

If you draw a circle in Illustrator, you'll see that the shape is made up of four points and four curved lines. The points are *anchor points*, and the lines are *path segments*. Together, the anchor points and path segments form either a closed or an open path. Squares and circles are examples of *closed paths*. A straight line, an arc, and a spiral are examples of *open paths*.

FIGURE 4.19: **A closed path comprises anchor points and path segments.**

With an object such as a square, the outline of the square is the stroke; the area within the outline is the fill.

In the toolbox are the Fill and Stroke color boxes. The Fill box is the solid square, and the Stroke box is the hollow square. The boxes represent the current colors used in newly drawn objects or the colors used in selected objects. Every object we have drawn so far has had a white fill and a black stroke, unless you have already changed these settings.

FIGURE 4.20: The Fill and Stroke color boxes are found at the bottom of the toolbox.

Some of the drawing tools, such as the Line Segment tool ⬲ and the Arc tool ◿, remove the fill color and use only the stroke color. If you drew objects earlier with these tools, the Fill box most likely has a red slash running across it, which indicates no fill color ◻.

Draw a circle on the Artboard and we'll change its colors. Be sure the object is selected once the circle is complete. With the Selection tool, double-click the Fill box to display the Color Picker. Click and drag in the color box or color spectrum bar (the thin vertical bar) to select a color. Click OK. The fill color of the circle changes to reflect your color choice.

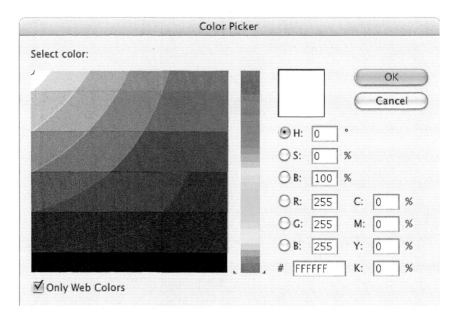

FIGURE 4.21: Checking the Only Web Colors box in the Color Picker shows only colors in the Web-safe palette. Leaving this unchecked will give you the full color range to choose from.

To change the circle's stroke color, double-click the hollow black square. The Stroke box is now the active color box since it is in front of the Fill box. Choose a color and click OK.

The double arrow in the upper right of the Fill and Stroke area lets you toggle colors back and forth between boxes. A single click on either box will make it active without displaying the Color Picker. To restore black and white default colors, click the mini Fill and Stroke box icon in the lower-left corner.

To see how the fill and stroke affect an open path, select the Spiral tool and click and drag on the Artboard to draw the shape. The fill color abruptly cuts off at the last endpoint on the outside of the shape. That cutoff connects the two endpoints of the path. Any open path can have only two endpoints; Illustrator will automatically connect them with the selected fill color.

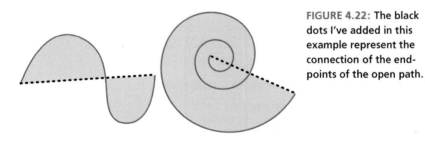

FIGURE 4.22: The black dots I've added in this example represent the connection of the end-points of the open path.

As another example, select the Pencil tool and draw a free-form line on the Artboard. Be sure to select a color for both the fill and the stroke. When you complete the line, Illustrator again connects the two endpoints.

In case you're wondering, a straight line can have both fill and stroke colors as well. However, because the path has no interior, the fill is not visible. To confirm its presence though, just look at the Fill and Stroke boxes in the toolbox.

REMOVING FILL COLORS AND STROKE COLORS

To set either the Fill or Stroke box to fill or stroke a shape with no color (making the area transparent), choose the None icon (shown as a red slash) just below the Fill and Stroke boxes.

A shape does not have to have a fill or stroke color. In fact, a shape doesn't have to have any color information whatsoever. Select an object you've drawn, and then click the Fill box to make it active. Click the None icon just below the Fill and Stroke boxes. Do the same for the Stroke box. Your object is now invisible, so to speak, but you can still select it to see its outline and bounding box.

The fill of an object can consist of a gradient rather than a solid color. A *gradient* is a smooth transition of one color to another. The stroke of an object cannot accept a gradient fill. Feel free to experiment with this on your own using the Gradient palette (Window > Gradient).

THE COLOR PALETTE

Slider controls beneath color bars on the Color palette (Window > Color) give you another way of changing and selecting colors. Depending on the color model active on the palette, you can also enter numeric and hexadecimal values in input boxes. Choose from among grayscale, RGB, CMYK, and other choices in the palette's option menu. The color spectrum bar or tint ramp that appears is also based on the color model.

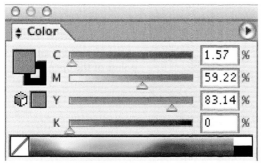

FIGURE 4.23: The Color palette —the entire spectrum at your service.

A miniature Fill and Stroke icon is displayed on the palette. As with the toolbox version, click either the Fill or Stroke box to make it active. The palette supports drag-and-drop features. Click the Fill box and drag its color onto an unselected object on the Artboard. The fill of the object changes to reflect the color on the Color palette. The toolbox version also supports this handy feature.

Swatch palettes give you a third choice in color selection. Choose Window > Swatch Libraries to display a menu of color swatches. Select Default CMYK to display its swatch palette. The palette features various CMYK color swatches (plus gradient and pattern fills as well) that you can drag onto selected or unselected objects, the Fill and Stroke boxes, or the Color palette.

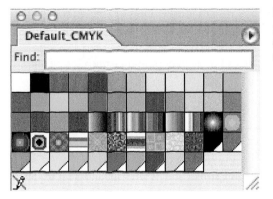

FIGURE 4.24: **The Swatch palette holds solid fills as well as gradients and patterns.**

To keep a swatch palette visible between Illustrator sessions, uncheck the Persistent option on the palette's menu.

Use the Eyedropper tool if you want to select or sample an object's color. To use the tool, select the Eyedropper and click an object on the Artboard. Both the Fill and Stroke boxes take on the sampled colors. Press the Shift key while using the Eyedropper to selectively sample colors for the active color box. This is particularly useful if you have a multicolored object and you only want to sample a particular color from it.

Another trick is to select an object, then click another object with the Eyedropper tool. This changes the color of the first object to match that of the second.

Using Type

Typography is essential to many design projects, so let's go over some of the text possibilities using the various type tools. Text in Illustrator behaves a lot differently than does text in a word processor, making it a little more challenging but a lot more powerful and flexible.

Let's start with the standard Type tool on a new, blank document.

THE STANDARD TYPE TOOL

Click anywhere on your document with the Type tool T. to set your cursor, and then type out a few words. The default is that the text is filled black, has no stroke, and is a small, standard font. But, like anything else in Illustrator, this can be changed by selecting (either with the Selection tool or by highlighting with the cursor) and applying a change using various palettes. The Color palette and Fill and Stroke boxes can be used on your text just like on any other object.

The most important typography features are found in the Character and Paragraph palettes (Window > Type > Character, Window > Type > Paragraph). The Character palette gives you all of your font face, font size, and spacing choices. The Paragraph palette handles the alignment and justification of lines.

FIGURE 4.25: This text has a **fill** as well as a stroke, and its letterspacing is set to –50 to pull it close together.

Lighten Up!

FIGURE 4.26: This line uses the default letterspacing, but the word *Up!* has a baseline value of 10.

Today's Specials

Pasta and Bean Soup
Mixed Greens with Chicken
Penne Bolognese
Tiramisu

FIGURE 4.27: These lines of text are centered in the Paragraph palette. For some breathing room, the line spacing was set to be much larger between the heading and the first item, and closer between the four menu items.

THE SPECIAL TYPE TOOLS

If you click and hold the Type Tool button in the toolbox, you'll see a series of useful (and a few not-so-useful) special type tools:

The Area Type tool ▣ is easy to use. First create a shape in Illustrator as you normally would, and select it. Then, with your Area Type tool, click in the upper left of the shape. (Try to click directly on the path; otherwise, you may get an error message.) Any text that you type will be formatted to fit inside the shape. Use the Justify All Lines button on your Paragraph palette so the text flows to both edges of the shape. The Vertical Area Type tool ▥ is just as simple, but the results usually aren't very readable—so this tool should generally be avoided.

This
block of text fills
an   ellipse   shape.
Type in an area usually
looks   best   when   the
shape and the font
are fairly simple.

FIGURE 4.28: Go ahead, type a few lines in any closed shape or path.

The Type on a Path tool ☑ can be a little trickier at first, but it's one of the most useful of the special type tools. First, create a path that you'd like your text to follow, like a curved line, using any drawing tool such as the Pen, Line, or Pencil. Make sure that this path is not an important part of your artwork— it will disappear after you enter your text. Click with your Type on a Path tool directly over the path or shape (if you get an error, keep trying to click right on the path)—when the cursor appears, you can begin typing. The Vertical Type on a Path tool works in the same way, but just like the Vertical Area Type tool, the effect isn't always very readable or attractive.

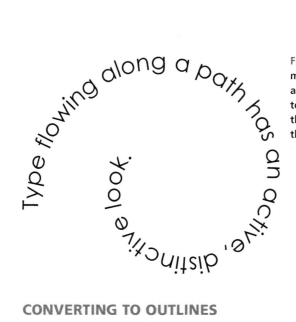

Type flowing along a path has an active, distinctive look.

FIGURE 4.29: If you need to move your type elsewhere along a path, use the Selection tool and drag the bottom of the I-beam that appears at the beginning of the text.

CONVERTING TO OUTLINES

If you'd like to give your text some other effects, like a gradient fill, for example, you'll need to convert your text to outlines. This means that the wording will no longer be editable (so check your spelling first!), but each letter will become a shape made of paths that can be edited just like any other Illustrator object. To convert to outlines, select your text with the Selection tool and go to Type > Create Outlines. Each letter will be its own shape, and the letters will be grouped together. If you need to work with the letters individually, you can ungroup them (Object > Ungroup).

Transformation

While we've been drawing, a heretofore hidden palette has been silently going about its business of tracking movements and displaying information about the tools we've been using and the objects we've been selecting.

THE INFO PALETTE

This surreptitious palette is none other than the Info palette (Window > Info). It provides *x, y* coordinates for the currently selected tool, color values of objects, width and height values of shapes and paths, font information for text tools, angles of rotation, and other useful feedback. I mention this palette now because it will come in handy when working with various transformation tools and commands that follow.

FIGURE 4.30: Now that's a lot of info!

X :	603 pt	W :	139 pt
Y :	598 pt	H :	152 pt
D :	205.973 pt	△ :	47.558°
C :	0%	C :	86.27%
M :	0%	M :	20%
Y :	0%	Y :	0.78%
K :	100%	K :	0%

ROTATE, REFLECT, AND TWIST

The Rotate tool may seem an odd thing to talk about since you already know how to rotate using the bounding box. The beauty of the Rotate tool is that it lets you rotate an object around any point you define. To see this, turn on the Smart Guides (View > Smart Guides), draw a circle on the Artboard, and then draw a couple of small stars close together nearby. Next, group the stars (Object > Group), keep them selected, and then click the Rotate tool. Position the crosshairs cursor over the center point of the circle and click. This defines the origin point for rotation. As you click, the crosshairs become a black arrow. If you click and drag with the black arrow, the stars now rotate around the center point of the circle. Notice that as you rotate the stars, the angle information in the Info palette updates. When you release the mouse, the crosshairs cursor appears again since the tool is still active.

FIGURE 4.31: You can move objects around any origin point you define using the Rotate tool.

Hold down the Alt/Option key and click again on the circle's center point. The options dialog for the Rotate tool appears. In it, you can enter values to set the rotation angle. Enter a value of *25* and, instead of clicking OK, click the Copy button.

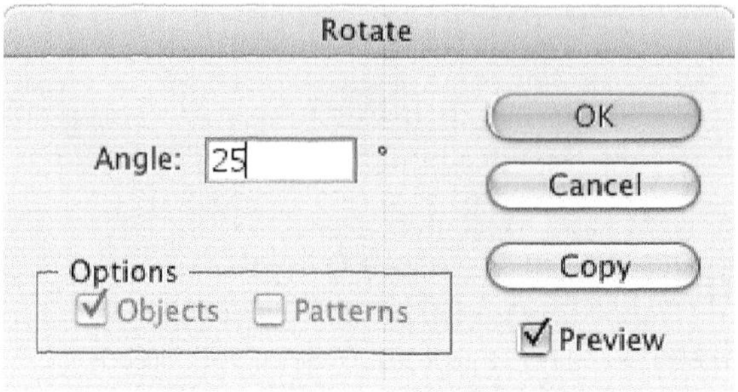

Rotate

Angle: 25 °

Options
☑ Objects   ☐ Patterns

OK

Cancel

Copy

☑ Preview

FIGURE 4.32: Defy your instinct and click Copy instead of OK to place a rotated copy of an object.

Press Ctrl+D/Command+D to repeat the last action. If you continue to press Ctrl+D/Command+D, copies of the stars eventually will appear at 25-degree angles all around the circle's center point. Rather nifty!

FIGURE 4.33: I needed to create an animation based on this graphic with a needle moving around a gauge. All I had to do was select the needle and then set its rotation origin with the Rotate tool to make it happen.

To demonstrate the Reflect tool, draw an arc (using the Arc tool) on the Artboard. When finished, double-click the Reflect tool 🔄 found within the Rotate tool fly-out menu. The Reflect options dialog appears with a choice of axes to reflect against (Horizontal, Vertical, or user-defined Angle). Select Horizontal and click Copy. A reversed copy of the arc is created across the horizontal axis of the original arc. The axis for an object originates from its center point.

Delete the copy of the arc, and select the original so that we can reflect an object with the mouse rather than via a dialog box. Click once on the Reflect tool (note the crosshairs cursor), and click just to the right of the arc. Press the

Shift key and click a little below where you just clicked. The arc reflects across the vertical axis we defined.

To make a copy of the arc across the axis, press both the Shift and Alt/Option keys before you click a second time. In this demonstration, the Shift key is used to constrain our axis to a straight line. Because an axis can be defined at any angle you choose, it is not always necessary to use Shift key.

FIGURE 4.34: If you want the object you draw to be symmetrical, you only need to draw one side, like I did with the shield shape here. Then use the Reflect tool to make a copy for the other side. Join the paths together to form a closed object to accept a fill.

SCALING AND SHEARING

The Scale tool ⬛ is useful for the precise resizing of shapes when used in conjunction with the tool's options. To use it, select the object you want to scale, and then double-click the Scale tool to display the options dialog. Here, you can enter a percentage value for uniform scaling, or an amount to scale the object horizontally or vertically. The Scale Strokes and Effects option, if checked, will increase the width of the stroke. For instance, if you scale a path segment with a 1-point stroke to 200 percent, not only will the object double in size, but the width of the stroke will also increase to 2 points. Effects applied from the Effect menu, such as glows and drop shadows, will also increase in size when this option is checked.

The behavior of this tool when using the mouse instead of numeric values is similar to that of resizing an object using the Selection tool and the bounding box. To scale with the mouse, select an object and click the Scale tool. For uniform scaling, click and drag out at a 45-degree angle while holding the Shift key. For horizontal scaling, drag the mouse horizontally while holding Shift . Drag vertically while holding Shift for vertical scaling. Other than constraining scaling movements, it's not necessary to hold down the Shift key when dragging.

To demonstrate the Shear tool , select the Spiral tool and draw a spiral on the Artboard. With the spiral selected, click the Shear tool, hold the Shift key to gain a modicum of control over this erratic tool, and then click and drag. If you drag along a horizontal axis, the spiral shape will slant or skew itself along this line. If you drag along a vertical axis or any other angle, the shape slants along that line. By default, the Shear tool sets the center of an object as its origin point. The origin point dictates where the slant will begin.

FIGURE 4.35: Put a new slant on your designs with the Shear tool.

For those who don't have the patience for such "toolish" nonsense, your best option is to use the Shear options dialog. By doing so, you can enter numeric values for precise control over your shear (or slant or skew—pick one!). As with most tools, you double-click this one to display its options. Set the value of the Shear Angle, choose an axis (Horizontal, Vertical, or user-defined Angle), and make a copy of the sheared shape from this dialog box. Clicking the Copy button instead of OK, and then repeating the command by pressing Ctrl+D/Command+D again and again, can quickly lead to chaos! Enjoy it.

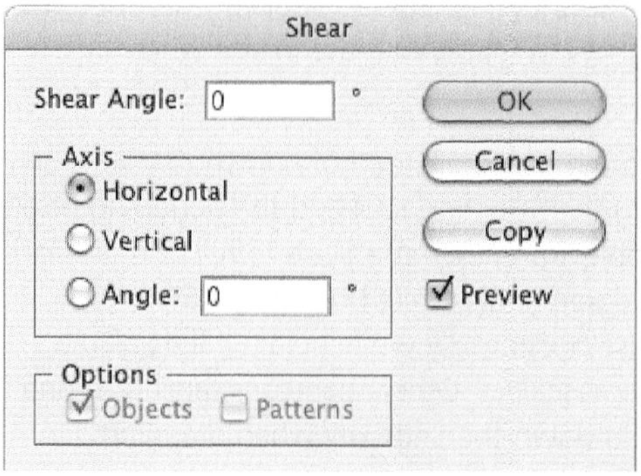

FIGURE 4.36: Gain more control with the Shear tool options dialog.

THE FREE TRANSFORM TOOL

The Free Transform tool  is the Swiss army knife of transformation tools. This one tool can resize, shear, rotate, and distort objects. Unleashing its full potential requires the use of modifier keys such as Shift, Alt/Option, and Ctrl/ Command.

FIGURE 4.37: **The billboard and the box images in this illustration by Leo Espinoza were distorted to great effect. When you need quick and dirty perspective angles, Free Transform is the tool to use.**

Since we've yet to use a rounded rectangle for demonstration purposes, draw one on the Artboard—the Rounded Rectangle tool is found in the Rectangle tool fly-out. To use the Free Transform tool, you must first select the rounded rectangle with the Selection tool, and then click the Free Transform tool. There are no visual clues that the Free Transform tool is active, other than the Info palette displaying some new information.

To resize or rotate the rounded rectangle, you use the tool in the same way you use the Selection tool and an object's bounding box. Click and drag a handle to resize, or click near a point to rotate. Let's move beyond these basic functions and distort the rounded rectangle with the tool.

Click and drag a bounding box corner. As you drag, hold the Ctrl/Command key. Notice that it affects only that corner of the object.

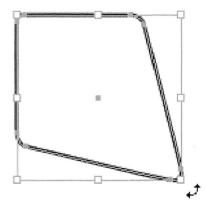

FIGURE 4.38: Object distortion using the Free Transform tool.

Now press the Shift key along with what you're doing. This constrains the distortion to the horizontal and vertical axis. Press a third key—Alt/Option—simultaneously to have an adjacent corner mimic the movements of your selected corner point. To shear the object, release the Shift key but continue to hold the Ctrl/Command and Alt/Option keys while you drag. You can achieve a variety of distortion effects by using practically any number of modifier keys while selecting any of the bounding box points. The key is to click and drag first, and then use the modifier keys.

FIGURE 4.39: Use the magic of Free Transform to create swanky boxes.

THE TRANSFORM PALETTE

Many of the functions found in the Free Transform tool can be found and modified numerically in the Transform palette (Window > Transform). As a reminder, an object must first be selected in order for this palette or any palette or tool to have an effect.

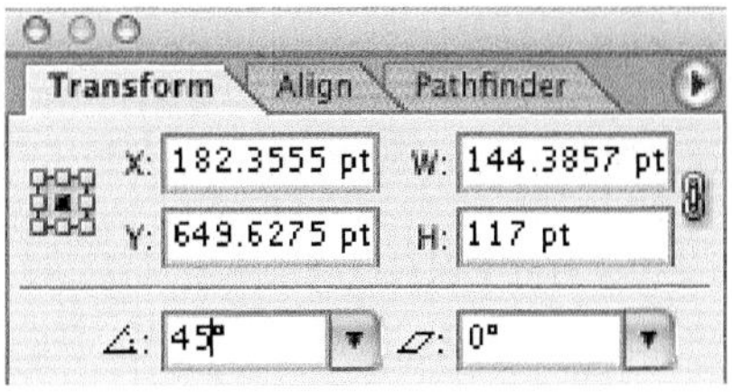

FIGURE 4.40: The
Transform palette.

By entering values in the input boxes, you can move an object along the *x*- or
y- axis, alter its width or height, rotate it to any angle, and shear it to any angle.
When a project calls for precision, this is the palette to have on hand.

The Transform palette features a miniature representation of a bounding box
that surrounds a selected object. Select a point on the bounding box icon from
which to originate changes. For instance, if you select the lower-left point of
the bounding box icon and then set a rotation angle, the object you're modifying will rotate around its lower-left bounding box point. The Transform palette's
option menu provides additional functionality. From this menu, you can choose
to reflect an object along a horizontal or vertical axis and check the Scale Strokes
and Effects option rather than accessing this function through the Scale tool's
options box.

Transparency

Transparency is simply the ability to see through an object. When designers talk
transparency, they often use the word *opacity*. Opacity is the level of transparency you give to an object.

FIGURE 4.41: The blue window's low opacity lets you
see through to the yellow
shape below.

To use opacity, select any object under the Illustrator sun—an object already sitting on your Artboard will do just fine. Open the Transparency palette (Window > Transparency) and enter a value from 1 to 100 in the Opacity box, or drag the slider that appears when you click the right-facing arrow on the Opacity box. The lower the value, the more you can see through the object. Objects are said to be opaque if the value is set to 100 percent. To be absolutely certain this is working, turn on the Transparency Grid (View > Show Transparency Grid). The grid should be visible through any object with an opacity level other than 100. To change the size or color of the grid squares, choose File > Document Setup and choose the Transparency option from the drop-down list.

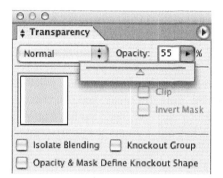

FIGURE 4.42: **The lower the opacity, the more you can see through an object.**

You can modify settings for the Transparency Grid by choosing File > Document Setup from the menu bar—select Transparency from the drop-down menu. These settings are document-specific, so don't expect to see your changes reflected elsewhere.

Other than the grid, you can use the Appearance palette (Window > Appearance) to determine whether your object uses transparency. If an object has an opacity level of 50 percent, an attribute in the palette will say Opacity: 50%. If opaque, it will read as Default Transparency. This palette will also display which blending mode an object uses.

FIGURE 4.43: This photo-realistic piece by designer Brooke Nuñez incorporates transparency settings in the sky and the face, in addition to exhibiting many other endearing qualities.

Since we're in learning mode, turn on all options for the Transparency palette by choosing Show Options from the palette's fly-out menu.

Note that if you stack multiple objects with transparency, they will gradually become more opaque where they overlap, because transparency is a cumulative effect.

KNOCKOUT GROUPS

Contrary to one's initial thoughts, knockout groups have absolutely nothing to do with a gaggle of rogue boxers roaming the streets wild and free. Rather, knockout groups serve a fundamental need in the world of transparency by preventing overlapping objects from applying their opacity levels to each other. Confused?

When you stack semiopaque objects, they become more opaque. Many times, this cumulative result is not desirable, such as when you've created semitransparent shadows that overlap. In real life, shadows wouldn't become more opaque—they'd just blend together.

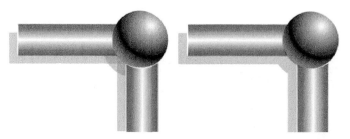

FIGURE 4.44: The shadows for the silver balls and the lines connecting them have the same opacity setting, 50 percent. Notice the clear distinction between shadows. This is caused by one 50 percent shadow being on top of another 50 percent shadow. From a design standpoint, it just won't do—knockout groups to the rescue.

When this problem crops up, just select the separate objects and group them (Object > Group). As you do this, the objects miraculously merge to eliminate the cumulative transparency. If you want to go back, uncheck the Knockout Group option in the Transparency palette.

Special Effects and Filters

Picture this scenario: You've got an outlandish vision for your next illustration, but you can't quite figure out how you're going to draw everything you want using Illustrator's basic tools and features.

Illustrator's special effects and distortion filters can lend a hand. These work-horse features alter your designs to give them an eye-catching complexity that your trusty drawing tools just cannot achieve (or not quickly enough, at any rate).

If you remember only one thing about this topic, remember this: Filters are final, effects are not. It isn't that filters are bad, they're just not as flexible as effects.

You can apply a whole range of effects to an object (as you'll see), and then save the file, lapse into a coma for years on end, open up the same file in Illustrator, and remove the effects—and the basic shape you began with will still be intact. If you were to apply filters to the same object, you would emerge from your coma to find that you're stuck with the pink drop shadow, the plastic wrap fill, and edges roughened by the Roughen filter.

What follows is a look at some of the filters and effects you can apply to objects. You are highly encouraged to experiment with them and others, keeping in mind that filters and effects require you to first select the object before you can apply them.

FILTERS

Got some bitmap art around, like a photo? Open it in Illustrator and go to Filter > Create > Object Mosaic. It converts the color values in a bitmap image to vector mosaic tiles, similar to a stained glass window. Control tile size, spacing, and number of tiles with the filter's options. Additional options constrain the width and height ratio, output the result in color or grayscale, and let you keep the bitmap image visible with the result or delete it.

FIGURE 4.45: **A photo of fish becomes an abstract design with the Object Mosaic filter.**

Filter > Create > Trim Marks places tiny marks around artwork to serve as guides for trimming or cutting after printing. It uses the dimensions of the bounding box around selected artwork. If you work in print design, you'll find this handy.

A wide range of Distort and Stylize filters are found in your Filter menu, and these do some pretty cool things to your art such as give it a shadow or pucker the shape inward. But hold your horses—the Effect menu has many of the same ones, so we'll look at them when we get to effects.

The remaining filters below the last divider line on the Filter menu (and the Effect menu) are borrowed from Adobe Photoshop. They are quite extensive, and because they are primarily raster-based filters, I will not discuss them here. If you use them in your work, I would advise using only the ones in the Effect menu so you can go back later to make changes. Feel free to experiment with them, though.

EFFECTS

Note that most of the effects described below will not work in CMYK mode. If you need CMYK mode, such as for a print project, start out your artwork in RGB when you create the document. Apply the effect you want, and then change the document's color mode to CMYK (File > Document Color Mode).

Effects are cumulative. For example, if you apply the Drop Shadow effect to an object over and over, the shadow gets progressively darker. To remove any of the effects from an object, choose Window > Appearance to display the Appearance palette. Select the guilty effect and click the trash can icon at the bottom of the palette.

Effect > Convert to Shape gives objects the effect of having the shape of a Rectangle, Rounded Rectangle, or Ellipse. In the Shape Options dialog (common to all three shapes), set Relative or Absolute width and height and adjust the corner radius (for Rounded Rectangle).

To give your shapes pointy spikes or rounded bulges, choose Effect > Distort and Transform > Pucker and Bloat. Pucker is great for creating interesting stars, while Bloat is useful for creating flowery shapes.

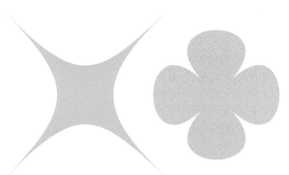

FIGURE 4.46: Boring squares become much more exciting with the Pucker (left) and Bloat (right) effects.

Effect > Distort and Transform > Roughen/Scribble loosens paths to give an almost hand-drawn feel to them. With some of the settings on Roughen, you can create both jagged and smooth paths.

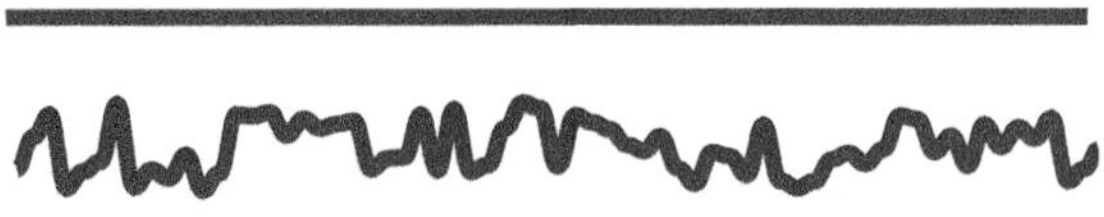

FIGURE 4.47: Try out the whole range of Roughen settings for a variety of results.

The Transform effect under Effect > Distort and Transform has many of the same features you'd find within the Transform palette, such as sliders and value boxes to control scale, rotation, size, and horizontal and vertical movement. Some of the controls are limited. What makes this effect special, though, is when you start playing around with the Copies and Random options. Select an object on the Artboard, choose this effect, check the Preview option, and start entering some values and moving sliders. You can get some really interesting effects by doing so.

FIGURE 4.48: Letting Illustrator create random transformations can yield some wild designs.

Enough with the twisting and twirling commands! There are no fewer than four commands in Illustrator to do such a thing, like Effect > Distort and Transform > Twist. If you've tried the Twist tool in the toolbox, you're 99.9 percent of the way there with this effect. However, because it's an effect, remember that you can always go back to the original shape.

For an instant wavy line, try Effect > Distort and Transform > Zig Zag. Draw a straight line, choose this filter, and uncheck the Preview box. Next, adjust the Ridges per segment slider, and then select Smooth from the Points section.

FIGURE 4.49: Instant wavy line!

The Effect > Rasterize command is similar to the Rasterize command found within the Object menu, and turns your vector art into a bitmap. But, as an effect, it will not do permanent damage. Remember that you're changing the appearance attributes of an object, not the object itself.

Add Arrowheads, found under Effect > Stylize, is useful for adding not just arrowheads, but also arrow tails to an open or closed path. Use Object > Expand Appearance (plus a few Ungroup commands) to work with the individual heads or tails.

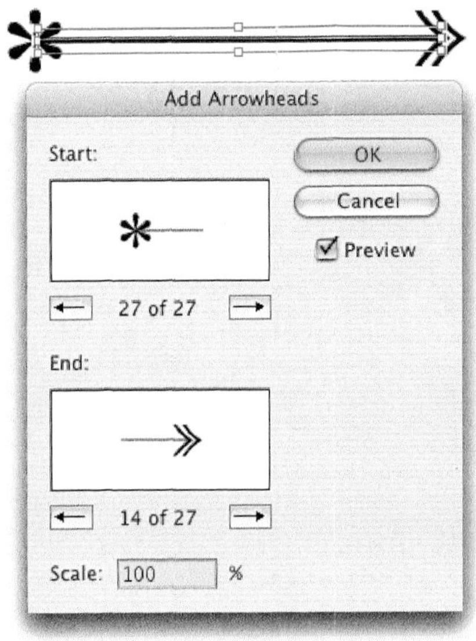

FIGURE 4.50: The Add Arrowheads effect has plenty of different heads and tails to choose from.

The series of Effect > Stylize > Drop Shadow/Feather/Inner Glow/Outer Glow adds soft (or hard) effects borrowed from the pixel world. The end result, however, is in fact a raster-based (bitmapped) effect added to an object, since the results still scale up and down without any loss in quality. These effects are good to have around the house, so to speak. The Feather effect is useful for creating a blurred look to hard-edged vector objects.

FIGURE 4.51: Drop shadow and other raster-based effects are shown here.

Need to emulate the rounded corners on a road sign or make a pointy star look friendly? Effect > Stylize > Round Corners will tackle those tasks with no effort. Setting the radius of the corners is the only option you get with this no-frills effect.

FIGURE 4.52: A simple effect with lots of uses.

So now you're armed with all sorts of methods for distorting simple and complex objects. Use these techniques in moderation, so as to enhance your creations rather than overpowering them. I know I can trust you!

Outdoor Advertising Project

Using type in a design can be just a simple way to communicate information, or an art form in itself. Illustrator provides the tools, type designers supply the typeface designs, but it's up to you to create dynamic and appropriate typography that communicates the message.

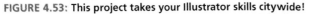

FIGURE 4.53: This project takes your Illustrator skills citywide!

In this project, you'll create an advertisement that wraps an entire city bus. In this moving medium, you'll need to think about how to make your text readable and stand out. You'll also need to use color and imagery to add life to the ad and make it eye-catching on the street.

Project Brief: Bean Mountain

A regional ad agency wants to make use of the area's extensive public transportation system to promote its newest client: a national coffee shop chain called Bean Mountain that's recently expanded into your city.

Your task is to create a colorful, stylized design to market the brand for placement on the city's buses. You will need to use the bus template provided below. To spur your ideas, think about the sample company name, slogan, and campaign copy below. You may include any of these copy elements in your design, or create your own.

- Name: Bean Mountain

- Slogan: Climb the cup to a higher taste

- Copy: Coffee drinker at the peak fitness

I place no stylistic demands on you for this project, except that you must design something appropriate for this type of client and product. I would, however, like to see you make use of the various typographic features you learned in this chapter. Don't cram them all into one design, but think about how a creative type treatment might call attention to the message.

As you're learning the basics of vector art, you are strongly encouraged to create your images entirely within Illustrator. If you use any bitmap imagery, please limit its use to no more than 25 percent of the overall design.

For ideas and inspiration, visit the Web sites of local and national coffee companies. Researching the company or product category is the first step in any design project.

Project Summary

Brainstorm and sketch advertising design ideas.

Use Illustrator's typography tools to set the copy for the ad.

Create a design that draws attention to the advertising copy.

1. Downloading and Using the Template

Access the bus template from your Images CD. The bus template file contains two layers: the Bus Frame layer (which contains a locked outline of the bus) and the Bus Clipping Mask layer. You can see them in your Layers palette (Window > Layers).

Read the steps below carefully so you understand how to use the clipping mask layer and avoid any unnecessary extra work.

The Bus Clipping Mask layer contains a light gray bus shape that represents the surface in which you will design. Hide this layer as you create your artwork by clicking the eye icon next to the layer name (clicking it again will show the artwork). Once you finalize your design, you will use the gray bus clipping mask.

A *clipping mask* is a shape that can hold other shapes within its boundaries or outline, like a picture frame. Don't worry about fitting everything within the design area—the excess will be hidden by the mask at the end of the project.

FIGURE 4.54: Any artwork that is outside the bus area will be hidden when the mask is applied at the end of this project.

2. Brainstorming Your Bus Design

Let's step aside from Illustrator for a moment to visualize the design. The coffee company is called Bean Mountain, so you might consider a literal approach, using drawings of coffee beans or mountains. Coffee beans are so irregularly shaped that you could draw them freehand pretty effectively with the Pencil tool, even if you're not a confident illustrator. Mountains are just triangles, right? Polygon tool!

For something less literal (and more abstract), think about what colors and shapes remind you of coffee. Peppy, bright colors and stars representing all that caffeine energy? Soothing colors and wavy lines to connote a delicious aroma wafting in the air? Consider the tools and effects you could use to make these ideas come alive, such as the Zig Zag effect.

Next, think about the typography you'll need to apply to the bus. What text should be the biggest? What font would be readable at a distance but indicative of the product? Consider whether you'd like to apply the text to a special shape or path, or leave it straight, and where you would like to place it in relation to your graphic ideas.

You may even want to do a few sketches on paper before you begin.

3. Creating the Bus Graphics

Click the Create New Layer icon at the bottom of the Layers palette, and drag the new layer so that it sits below the two other layers. Make sure your new layer and the Bus Frame layer are both visible and the Bus Clipping Mask layer is hidden.

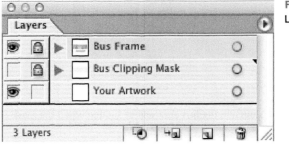

FIGURE 4.55:
Layers start here.

Now you can begin designing on your new, bottommost layer. The bus outline on the Bus Frame layer will help guide your placement of objects and text, but remember that you can let your art "bleed" beyond the bus since the excess will be cut off later.

Use your drawing tools to create the imagery you planned for your bus designs. You can be as detailed or abstract as you like, as long as it supports the goal of the advertisement. Keep these tips in mind as you work:

- Use Object > Arrange to modify the stacking order of your objects as needed.

- If you can't get the exact shape you want from a shape tool, try applying an effect from the Effect > Distort and Transform menu.

- Don't underestimate the power of freehand drawing with the Pencil tool —you may surprise yourself.

- Use the Stroke palette to apply thick strokes, dashed lines, and other special outline features.

- Try an interesting look by purposely making a large shape bleed off the edge of the bus shape.

- Group (Object > Group) selected objects in your design so that you're able to move them or scale them as a single entity. Just ungroup them if you want to edit them separately again.

4. Adding the Typography

Next up is the all-important task of setting type for the ad. Using the copy supplied above (or your own), set the typography on your design.

If you'd like to use type on a path or inside a shape you've drawn, you'll need to draw that first. When your path or shape is ready, choose the appropriate special type tool (Type on a Path tool or Area Type tool), click the path or shape, and enter your text.

You might be wondering how you can have type run along one of the graphics you've created already (like around the side of a coffee bean or along a mountain) without removing your graphic when you start typing. Here's what you'll want to do: Select the graphic and copy it, then use the Paste in Front command to put a copy right on top of your original. Then use the special type tool of your choice to input the type—the copy will disappear, but the original will stay underneath.

With your type in place, consider adding fill and stroke colors that will help the text stand out from your design as well as integrate with it for a cohesive look.

5. Applying the Clipping Mask

With your designs in place, it's time to put on the mask we talked about earlier and hide the excess space that surrounds the bus shape. Zorro, look out!

Make sure that your Bus Clipping Mask is above any layers that you have created artwork on (and below the Bus Frame layer). Make the Bus Clipping Mask layer visible, and unlock it by clicking the lock icon next to its name.

At first, this will obscure your artwork below. This is only temporary; it will return to normal once we create the clipping mask.

The next step is to select all the artwork and the clipping mask shape together. Do this by holding down the Shift key as you click the hollow circle on the artwork layer(s) and the Bus Clipping Mask layer. As you do this, the hollow circles become double circles, indicating that the artwork on those layers is selected.

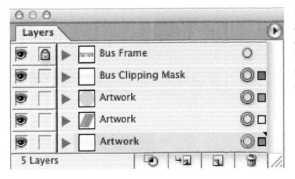

FIGURE 4.56: **Hold Shift and click the circle on your artwork layers and your Bus Clipping Mask layer to select all the objects on each layer.**

The final step is to choose Object > Clipping Mask > Make. This will cause your artwork to be masked inside the bus shape or bus mask.

You'll notice that any part of your design appearing over the windows shows up differently than on the rest of the bus. This is to simulate light showing through from the other side of the bus and gives the design a more real-world look.

Student Work

What have other designers done with this bus advertisement project? Here are some work samples from Sessions.edu students:

FIGURE 4.57: Jeff Weiner used gradients, type on a path, drawings of cups, and even a spill to cover his bus in the warm feeling of coffee.

FIGURE 4.58: Patricia Baumberger drew a coffee bean design that she copied, pasted, and transformed many times to cover the bus, and applied a variety of text effects.

FIGURE 4.59: Using thick black strokes, lots of repeated coffee beans, and type on a path, Stephanie Adams created a bus design as bold as the coffee it advertises.

5 Digital Imaging

Digital imaging is tough to nail down. One minute it's an abstract, futuristic-looking art piece on a company brochure, and the next it's a soft drink ad depicting a penguin in the Sahara. Real or surreal, literal or abstract, digital imaging is all about creativity and communication.

The fact is that with today's digital imaging tools—and some experience—you can produce any artistic concept that pops into your head. You have all the creative freedom in the world. But don't go Photoshop-crazy just yet. When you take on a professional graphic design project, your creative ideas and digital imaging expertise have a single goal: communicating the client's message.

As we explore a wide range of digital imaging techniques in this chapter, from photo touch-ups to realistic scenes created from scratch, consider the images you see every day on packages, in magazines, and on billboards. What do they communicate to the audience? How have retouching and other artistic techniques helped get those messages across?

FIGURE 5.1: Would you believe this image created by famous artist Bert Monroy is not a photo? This wow-inducer was painted from scratch in Photoshop.

In this chapter you will:

Learn to use the **Healing Brush tool** and **Patch tool** to retouch blemishes in photographs.

Learn to use the **Color Replacement tool** to change the hue of an area of a photo.

Apply a **Shadow/Highlight adjustment** to quickly repair lighting problems in a photo.

Learn to use **Levels** and **Curves** for precision lighting and color correction.

Learn to use a variety of **Filters** to create abstract artwork and modify its properties.

Explore the settings available in the advanced **Brushes palette**.

Learn to create and save **custom brushes**.

Create a photo-realistic image using custom brushes.

Communicating with Digital Imaging

If you're a digital artist creating art for art's sake, the world is your oyster—your work can communicate anything your heart desires, or nothing at all. For graphic design professionals, however, digital imaging has a very specific job to do. That job is to make images that look great and communicate. Sometimes you won't notice that any digital imaging work was done at all, which is quite a compliment to the designer. Other times, you'll be knocked out by the unmistakable application of digital imaging techniques.

The first category is the retouching and correction of original photographs, an important skill for designers in the publishing world. Such work can be as simple as making the sky more blue in a vacation ad or as extreme as lengthening the legs on a supermodel for a fashion cover. Designers go to town on model shots, performing such subtle tasks as slimming the waist, coloring the lips, enlarging the eyes, and correcting skin imperfections.

Even outside the world of glossy magazines, most photos that are published are first retouched and corrected, with the goal of removing features or blemishes that would distract the viewer or make a person or product seem less than ideal. These techniques also help designers and photographers out of some tough jams, such as when the lighting or weather on a photo shoot isn't ideal. Why reshoot when you can retouch?

Digital imaging also affords the designer the ability to make a surreal concept a reality that grabs viewers' attention and sticks in the memory. Let's say a pet food company asks you to design an upcoming campaign for a new cat chow that makes cats feel younger and more playful. You instantly picture dozens of kitties at the amusement park riding the coasters and bumper cars. It's not a situation that a photographer could ever hope to capture. With a handful of photographs and some digital imaging prowess, though, you could certainly make a scene that was convincing and memorable—and a moneymaker for the client.

FIGURE 5.2: Retouching is a common tactic in digital imaging. In this image, created by photographer Ken Milburn, the car and background were separate photos that were enhanced, then combined to make a finished scene.

Where Do You Draw the Line?

Every designer must ask himself this question when embarking on a digital imaging project. Since there are no limits to what you can do to an original photograph, some ethical concerns are raised. Digital imaging can be so realistic and convincing that it can be misleading. How perfect should you make that cover girl? Is it OK to put that guy's head on this other guy's body?

The answer to these questions depends on the medium. In the news media, for example, only minor corrections to color and lighting that help balance an image are permitted. *Newsweek* and *TV Guide* have both been in hot water over cover designs that included one person's head on another's body, leading readers to believe that the images were actual photos. In fashion magazines, where readers expect the ideal, heavier retouching is more acceptable.

In advertising and packaging, color and lighting corrections are used to make product images appealing but attainable. In a hamburger ad, for example, the lettuce and tomato might be touched up so that they appear more vibrant and appetizing, and reflections on the meat highlighted so that it seems extra juicy.

Creating a scene that is patently *not* real can also be acceptable. If floating that same hamburger in space or placing it on top of Mount Everest through digital imaging helps communicate a specific message, there's nothing stopping you. Viewers will understand that it is an unrealistic situation made to look convincing—just like the cats in the bumper cars—and will not feel misled.

What all the above scenarios have in common is the use of photography as source material. Most digital imaging assignments begin with photographs, obtained from photographers or stock photography sources. But it should be noted that photographs are by no means a requirement, as skilled Photoshop pros are able to create abstract and photo-realistic art from scratch. These pieces, formed with brushes, filters, and other tools, present an alternative when photos simply won't achieve the objective. The challenge of creating them helps keep digital imaging experts at the top of their game.

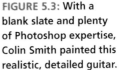

FIGURE 5.3: With a blank slate and plenty of Photoshop expertise, Colin Smith painted this realistic, detailed guitar.

Image Retouching

Because a photographic image is rarely perfect, Photoshop offers many tools for retouching and correcting images. Retouching deals with fixing or *touching up* the small details in an image. These tasks can range from something as simple as removing red-eye to something as complicated as smoothing wrinkles. Some may see this as cheating, but you're really just trying to enhance a photograph so that it looks its best.

I once heard Photoshop guru Scott Kelby speak about this issue at the Photoshop World convention. An audience member asked him how ethical it was to manipulate reality and change someone's appearance for the better. Scott's answer was interesting: He said that the purpose of retouching was to make a photograph look as good as real life.

When you're talking to a friend, so much is happening that you may not notice that he has a small blemish on his face or a feature that is just a bit off. But when you're looking at a photograph of him, you have nothing else to concentrate on but the photograph itself. Because a still image is a moment frozen in time, you're much more likely to pick up on any problems. That's a great way to think about image retouching.

So, with no further ado, let's jump right in and take a look at some of the image-retouching tools in Photoshop.

The Healing Brush

The Healing Brush tool ✎ allows you to cover up blemishes, wrinkles, scratches, or image damage. It works similarly to the Clone Stamp tool in that you sample from one area of an image by Alt-clicking/Option-clicking a source area and then paint on another area where you'd like to cover up blemishes. The way it works is by sampling the color, texture, transparency, and luminosity of the source area separately. Then, when painting, Photoshop merges the values of the sampled area with those of the target area.

If you choose the Healing Brush tool, you'll notice the Options bar changes to display a few settings specific to the selected tool. As with other brushes in Photoshop, you can change the Mode in which the brush paints.

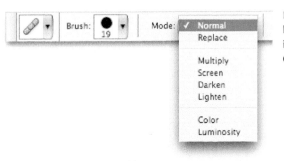

FIGURE 5.4: **Like other brushes, a Mode menu is available in the Options bar.**

The next group is the Source settings. Choose Sampled to use the pixels from the current image in which you're working. Choose Pattern to repair the sampled area with pixels from a pattern. The pattern can be selected from the drop-down list next to the check box. Another key setting is the Use All Layers check box on the right. It instructs Photoshop to use all layers when sampling or to use only the active layer.

FIGURE 5.5: **Choose whether you want to sample all layers or just the active one before you start using the Healing Brush.**

Note that it's best to work with small areas at a time. A general rule of thumb is to sample often. Even slight changes in texture and lighting values in the source image can wreak havoc on your healing abilities, so you'll want to make sure you're always sampling from an appropriate source.

FIGURE 5.6: **Various creases appear when a subject smiles, but we'll make them less severe with some retouching. The forehead creases will be smoothed with the Healing Brush tool, and then we'll use the Patch tool on the ones around the eyes.**

Political tip: When retouching photographs of your friends and family, never let them know that you've used the Healing Brush on them. As you can imagine, it's really not a compliment, and they'd be better off just thinking that they had a really good day at the time the photograph was taken.

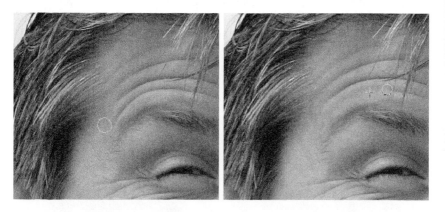

FIGURE 5.7: A small area of the skin is sampled (left), then painted over the wrinkle (right) to smooth it out.

The Patch Tool

The Patch tool is similar to the Healing Brush tool in both the applications for which it's useful and in the results that it produces. It works by repairing a selected area of an image with pixels from another area (or pattern).

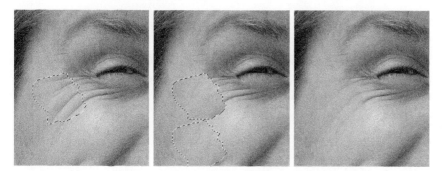

FIGURE 5.8: An area to patch is selected (left); the selection is placed over an area of smoother texture (middle); and the finished area takes on that texture.

▼ note

The Patch tool works only on the current layer. It doesn't offer the Use All Layers setting that the Healing Brush tool does, so be careful.

A handy feature of the Patch tool is that it gives you a preview of what effect will be applied to the target area. This happens after you first select the area to be repaired. You'll notice that as you search the image for a sample to repair from, the selected area will display the sample so you can see how they match.

To use the Patch tool, select an area to be repaired in the same way you select with the Lasso tool. Once you have selected a source area, position your cursor within the selection and begin to drag around the image to look for an area to sample from. Again, just like the Healing Brush, the Patch tool will try to match the color, texture, transparency, and luminosity of the sampled area with the source selection.

When you've found a suitable source to sample from, release the mouse button and Photoshop will do the rest.

FIGURE 5.9: The creases are now much softer (right), thanks to the Healing Brush and Patch tools, without being unrealistically smooth.

The Color Replacement Tool

The Color Replacement tool is similar to a regular Photoshop brush except that it does not overwrite all of the data on your image. Instead it manipulates the color on your image while retaining the image detail (texture, transparency, and luminosity).

Because the Color Replacement tool functions as a brush, it can be applied with more precision than some other color replacement functions in Photoshop. Also, because the Color Replacement tool performs image analysis on the fly, it saves you the step of extracting a particular area from your image before applying color changes.

FIGURE 5.10: The client wants a blush wine in the ad, and you've only got Bulgarian chardonnay? Not much you can do about the taste, but you can easily change the color.

That said, the Color Replacement tool is extremely easy to use. Once it's selected, you'll see various settings in the Options bar, like Tolerance, which you should be familiar with from other tools.

FIGURE 5.11: Familiar options for the Color Replacement tool.

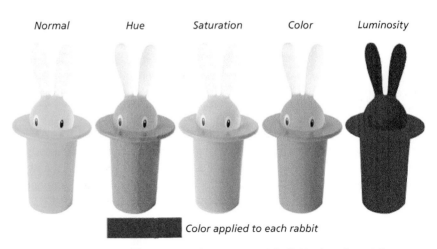

Normal   Hue   Saturation   Color   Luminosity

Color applied to each rabbit

FIGURE 5.12: Notice how the rabbit is affected by each individual Mode and the sample color.

The Mode settings determine the ways in which the Color Replacement tool can be applied:

- Color—Uses the currently selected foreground color to apply color to your image. It replaces the hue and saturation but preserves the luminosity of the source image.

- Hue—This option keeps the luminosity and saturation settings of the original image but replaces the original hue with the foreground color.

- Saturation—Adjusts the saturation of the image to match that of the foreground color.

- Luminosity—As you can probably guess, this option manipulates the luminosity (or brightness) of the source image to match that of the foreground color. However, the hue and saturation of the original will be preserved.

Image Correction

Image correction is different from retouching in that it concentrates on repairing portions of an image that should be different. Color casts, strong shadows, washed-out highlights, overexposure, and underexposure are all great examples of issues that might need corrected.

Shadow/Highlight Adjustment

Have you ever taken a photograph that's too dark or too light in certain areas? I'll bet you have. If so, the Shadow/Highlight adjustment, a recent addition to Photoshop, may be just what you're looking for. Used alone or in combination with other tools in Photoshop, the Shadow/Highlight adjustment has the ability to quickly transform your photographs into balanced, higher-quality images.

In my example photo, the little girl is hidden in the shadows. Due to the large amount of light in the background, the foreground was not exposed correctly.

FIGURE 5.13: Harsh backlighting hid the subject in shadow, but we can fix this with image correction techniques.

To fix this, I go to Image > Adjustments > Shadow/Highlight. The dialog box presents many options. (If yours doesn't, check the Show More Options check box at the bottom of the dialog box.) Often, the default settings work just fine. If not, note that the dialog box conveniently categorizes areas of adjustment such as Shadows. Experiment with these settings if you feel your photograph needs more work than the default. Remember to keep Preview checked so you can see the results as you adjust the sliders.

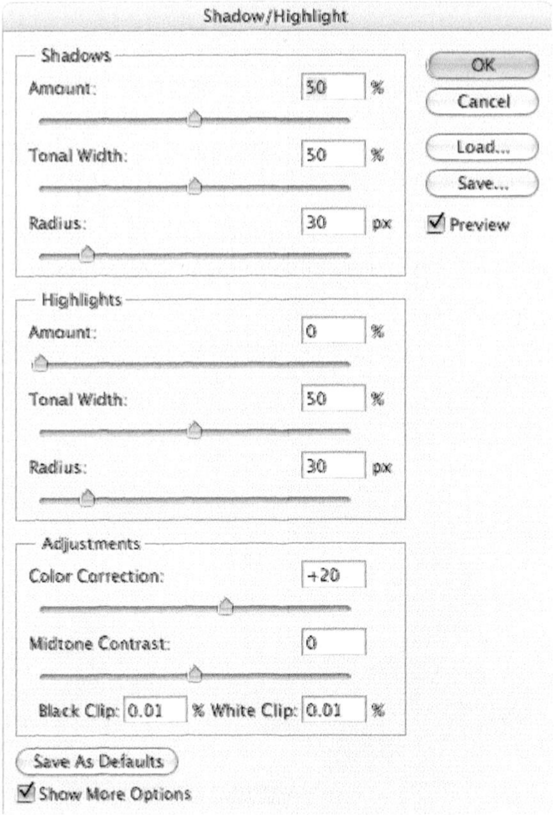

FIGURE 5.14: Check Show More Options in the Shadow/Highlight dialog box to see the full range.

The Shadow/Highlight adjustment works well in many cases. However, as you'll see in this lesson, other tools can work similar magic on your image and allow you more detailed control over the settings. You'll have to decide which is better by experimenting, as the various tools each work well in certain circumstances.

FIGURE 5.15: Looks much better, don't you think?

Adjusting with Levels

The Levels adjustment is the simpler of the two advanced color and lighting correction tools in Photoshop. It can be used for many things, but one of the most useful is extending the range of tones and colors already in an image. For example, photographs are often taken in situations where there is not enough light or too much of it. The Levels adjustment can redistribute the color information in the image to a more ideal range.

One of the nice features of the Levels adjustment is that opening the dialog box itself (Image > Adjustments > Levels) provides information about the image; you don't even have to do anything else. Go ahead and try it. Open a photograph that you're not happy with.

FIGURE 5.16: Dark photos are usually more salvageable than they look!

Choose Image > Adjustment > Levels. In this example, you can immediately see on each end of the graph that the grayscale values of the image don't extend to the full width of the possible range. You'll notice the graph is flat on both ends. You can immediately see that the left side (blacks) is heavily weighted with one large spike. However, the right side (whites) is not.

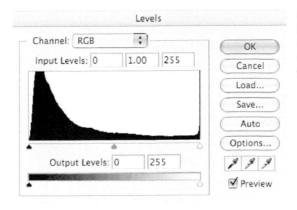

FIGURE 5.17: The Levels histogram shows you the distribution of grayscale values and lets you modify them precisely.

To reduce the tonal range of the photograph to a more ideal range, drag the middle slider toward the left where the histogram begins to climb. This will force those shades of black to lighter values while still retaining the lighter tones on the right side of the histogram.

FIGURE 5.18: Each slider—black, gray, and white—can be moved to even out the tonal range.

The Levels adjustment should be one of the first tools you choose when embarking on a color correction project. It can quickly help you fix overexposure or underexposure and many other related problems. However, keep reading, because you'll need to know where to turn when Levels doesn't work or doesn't do enough.

Curves Adjustment

The Curves adjustment allows us much more detailed control than Levels, as we can more precisely restrict our adjustments to certain ranges within the image. We also have more points available in which to adjust the tonal range of the image. Instead of just the three points that we have with Levels, we have 14 possible points with which to adjust.

In the Curves dialog box, we can strategically enhance an image. To see how, start with a fresh copy of the image you used to try out the Levels adjustments. When we applied a Levels adjustment on the photo, we ended up washing out the overall scene in our attempt to brighten the dark areas.

FIGURE 5.19: Levels helped brighten the dark areas, but they also brightened the entire scene more than we needed.

By moving the sliders from the left to the right in the Levels adjustment, we're brightening all colors in between, even if they were already fine. This is where we can turn to a Curves adjustment.

Press Ctrl+M/Command+M to open the Curves dialog box, or go to Image > Adjustment > Curves. Our first step is to figure out which part of the curve needs adjustment.

Use your pointer to hover over areas in the image and see where they fall along the curve. You may need to move your dialog box out of the way so you can see your image. As you drag your pointer over the image and click, you'll see a small circle appear along the curve in the dialog box. In our example we want to bring out the leaves, so drag over the dark ones (such as those in the upper right), click, and note where a small circle appears on the curve. That's the area we want to modify.

FIGURE 5.20: As you move your pointer along the problem parts of the image and click, you can see their corresponding areas on the curve in the Curves dialog box. In this example, I clicked a leaf in the upper right, and a circle appeared near the bottom of the curve in the dialog box.

At this juncture, you can either remember where that point is and add it manually (by clicking on the curve) or Ctrl-click/Command-click with the pointer on the image to actually place a point along the curve.

Now that we know what area to change, we also need to know what area to leave the same. Move the pointer and click around the waterfall, the bright parts of the rocks, and other areas you feel look fine as is. You'll notice that these points all tend to fall in about the top third of the curve. Add a point to the curve around the middle of this third to set a white point.

The default diagonal line represents no change to the image. So as we modify the curve in the problem areas, our goal will be to keep this acceptable area the same is it appears now.

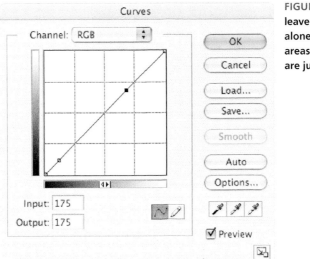

FIGURE 5.21: **We want to leave this part of the curve alone, since it represents areas of the image that are just fine.**

Now that we have the technical details behind us, you can go ahead and begin moving the point you created at the bottom left upward with the up arrow key. No need to go crazy here; just a small adjustment will make a big difference. As you do this, you'll notice that the dark areas all become lighter but the bright spots don't change.

FIGURE 5.22: **Our finished version is crisp and well-lit, without the washed-out feel that we got from Levels.**

Experiment with Curves as much as you can. This is the main tool used by color correction experts and is an invaluable part of Photoshop. Curves can do anything that other adjustment tools can, so if given an opportunity to pick only one adjustment tool to use in Photoshop, most experts would probably choose Curves adjustment.

Abstract Imaging

Given all of the great photo-retouching and correction tools in Photoshop, it's easy to forget that you can create amazing digital art from scratch for use in any graphic design project.

FIGURE 5.23: Renowned imaging specialist Colin Smith created this abstract design from scratch in Photoshop with filters and various other effects.

Follow along with me to create some high-tech, abstract art and learn a lot about Photoshop Blend Modes and Filters along the way.

First, you'll need some abstract elements to work with. Gradients, the Clouds filter (Filter > Render > Clouds), the Lighting Effects filter (Filter > Render > Lighting Effects), and the Gaussian Blur filter (Filter > Render > Gaussian Blur) will become your best friends here.

1. Start off by creating a new, 800-by-600-pixel canvas in Photoshop. Fill the background layer with black.

2. Use the Elliptical Marquee tool to draw a circle in the center of the canvas (on the background layer). Press D to set your foreground and background colors to the defaults, and then choose Filter > Render > Clouds. Deselect, and you should have something like my example. Alternatively, why not experiment with your own shapes?

FIGURE 5.24: In a few short steps, we'll turn this cloudy circle into a high-tech, abstract design.

3. Now choose Filter > Stylize > Extrude. Choose Pyramids as the Type, 30 pixels in Size and with a Depth setting of 255, Random. Or try your own settings in the Extrude dialog box. This filter, with my settings, will give you a three-dimensional, spiky-looking object.

FIGURE 5.25: The Extrude filter is one of the quickest ways to go 3D in Photoshop.

4. Color the object by choosing Image > Adjustments > Hue/Saturation. You can give it an orange color like mine, or experiment and choose your own. Be sure the Colorize box is checked.

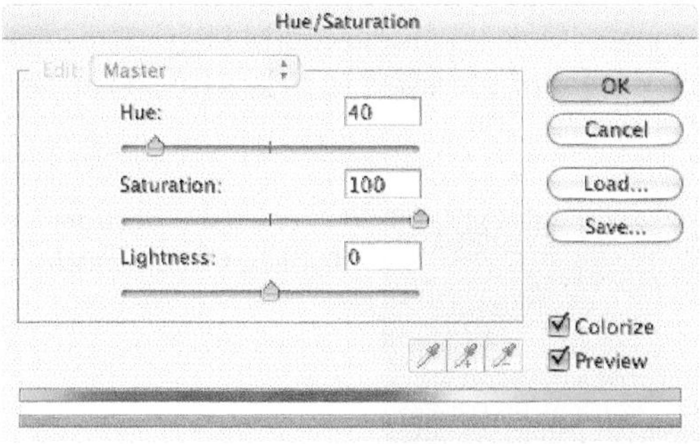

FIGURE 5.26: These settings will turn your spiky design bright orange, but you can use the sliders to choose any color you like.

5. Duplicate the Background layer (Ctrl+J/Command+J) so you have two layers. Select the top copy and change the Blend Mode to Color Dodge using the menu in the Layers palette.

FIGURE 5.27: The Color Dodge mode should be applied to the duplicated layer, above your background layer.

6. Duplicate the top layer and choose Filter > Blur > Gaussian Blur with a Radius setting of 6 pixels. Change the Blend Mode on this layer to Pin Light. You won't see the blur until you apply this new Blend Mode.

7. Duplicate the topmost layer again and change the Blend Mode to Overlay. Then link all the layers together and choose Merge Linked from the Layers palette options menu. Change the name of the Background layer to Layer 0 by Alt-double-clicking/Option-double-clicking the layer name. It will change to Layer 0 automatically.

8. Create a new layer below the orange spiky ball layer and fill it with black. Then change the Blend Mode of the layer above it to Screen. This shouldn't change anything yet; don't worry.

9. Duplicate the topmost layer five to ten times, positioning each copy randomly toward the left side of the canvas. Changing the Blend Mode to Screen in the last step allowed the black areas of the layers to be hidden so we can see through to each layer below it.

FIGURE 5.28: Abstract digital art from scratch!

In just a few simple steps, you turned a blank canvas into an abstract digital image perfect for a high-tech magazine article, a software box, or another graphic design project. You saw that filters don't just adjust existing imagery but, in the case of the Clouds filter, also create imagery to work with. Blend Modes added to the high-tech effect we were going for, and you can see how each affects a layer in a different way.

FIGURE 5.29: Add text, a grid, or other design elements to make an abstract piece work in a graphic design project.

Brushes

Painting with brushes is another way to create digital imagery from scratch, and Photoshop gives you amazing flexibility in its Brush tool.

Basic Brush Settings

You've got a few ways to view brushes in Photoshop. Let's start with the simplest view containing the fewest options. When you click the Brush tool ✎ in the toolbox, you'll notice that the Options bar changes to reflect the current tool's available settings.

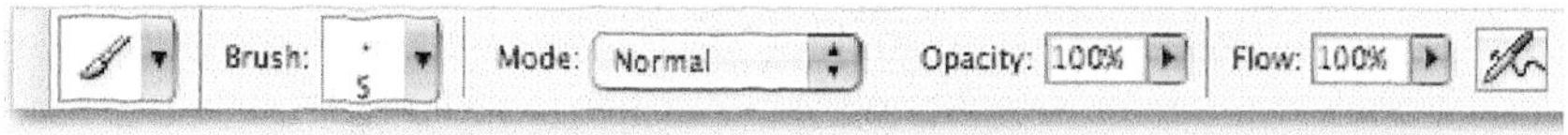

FIGURE 5.30: **The Brush tool options.**

By exploring these options, you'll find the most basic settings that can be applied to a brush:

- Master Diameter—This setting controls the size of the brush. Enter a value in pixels or drag the slider to change the setting.

- Hardness—This setting controls the size of the brush's hard center, or crispness. It is expressed as a percentage of the total brush size. Setting the hardness to 100 percent means that the brush's hard center extends out to the full width of the brush—the edge will be crisp. At 50 percent, the center (50 percent) of the brush is hard and the remaining portion (50 percent) becomes softer toward the edge of the brush.

- Mode—This setting controls how the current brush affects the pixels in your image, like the Blend Modes you've used in the Layers palette.

- Opacity—This setting controls the opacity of the brush. At 100 percent, the brush will be applied at full opacity. Anything less, and you'll begin to see through the brushstrokes.

- Flow—Flow determines how quickly the brush applies paint. A lower setting produces a lighter stroke.

- Airbrush—The Airbrush button ✍ allows you to apply gradual tones to an image, simulating traditional airbrush techniques.

tip

To change brush sizes quickly as you paint, press the left and right bracket keys. Press the [key to reduce the brush size and the] key to increase it. The increment of change depends on the brush size. A brush size between 0 and 100 pixels will change by 10-pixel increments each time you use this shortcut. A brush between 100 and 200 pixels will change by 25 pixels; a brush between 200 and 300 pixels will change by 50 pixels; and a brush between 300 and 2500 pixels will change by 100 pixels.

Advanced Brushes Palette

Here's where we get into the meat of Photoshop's powerful brush engine. The advanced Brushes palette contains the options for re-creating traditional media brushes as well as options that allow you to generate random textures and designs quickly. This is the palette in which you'll be spending most of your time when doing advanced painting in Photoshop.

Starting from the top, let's work our way down the palette and see what each option can do for us.

- Brush Tip Shape—You've already seen what the Diameter and Hardness settings can do. This view offers even more options regarding the tip of the brush.

- Angle and Roundness—Angle specifies the angle at which the brush is applied to the canvas. Roundness specifies the elliptical shape of the brush—from a perfect circle to a thin oval. Use these settings together to produce calligraphy-like effects with a round brush.

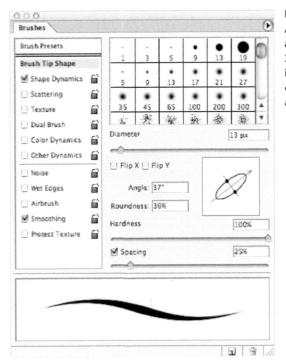

FIGURE 5.31: **With an Angle of 37 degrees and a Roundness of 36 percent, the brush is a narrow, slanted oval and will produce a calligraphic stroke.**

- Spacing—Spacing determines how closely the Brush tool spaces each brush mark. A small value produces very tight spaces between brush marks. A high setting makes the brush appear to skip as you paint.

- Shape Dynamics—The Shape Dynamics section controls three aspects of the brush stroke appearance: size, rotation, and perspective. The variations for each parameter are specified with sliders.

  You'll see the word jitter used throughout the Brushes palette. Essentially, Adobe uses this term within certain brush settings to determine variation in the individual instances of the brush's tip. Think of it as the maximum range of allowable values. Jitter-based settings allow you to achieve random effects with brushes, as they produce different results each time.

- Scattering—Scattering spreads copies of the brush tip's shape along the path of a stroke.

- Texture—The Texture setting in the Brushes palette uses a pattern to make strokes appear as if they were painted on a textured canvas.

- Dual Brush—The Dual Brush option adds another brush tip to the one selected as the Brush Tip Shape. The second tip is overlaid using the Blend Mode at the top of the Dual Brush section of the Brushes palette. This section is a cross between the Brush Tip Shape and Scattering sections. In addition to selecting the second brush tip and Blend Mode, you adjust the second tip for diameter, spacing, scattering, and count. Count refers to the number of times the second brush tip appears in each stroke of the initial brush tip.

- Color Dynamics—The Color Dynamics section hosts more settings that really let you save time and randomize your brushes. Color Dynamics looks at the current foreground and background colors (set in the toolbox) and interprets colors between them based on the settings in this section. It then applies those colors randomly to each instance of the brush tip that is applied to the canvas.

- Other Dynamics—Other Dynamics contains settings only for opacity jitter and flow jitter. These two settings operate just like the opacity and flow settings discussed earlier, but the added jitter lets you vary the application of them.

The various Control drop-down menus let you specify how you'd like to control the variation of certain elements of brushes. You can choose not to control, fade, or vary a brush based on Pen Pressure, Pen Tilt, and so on.

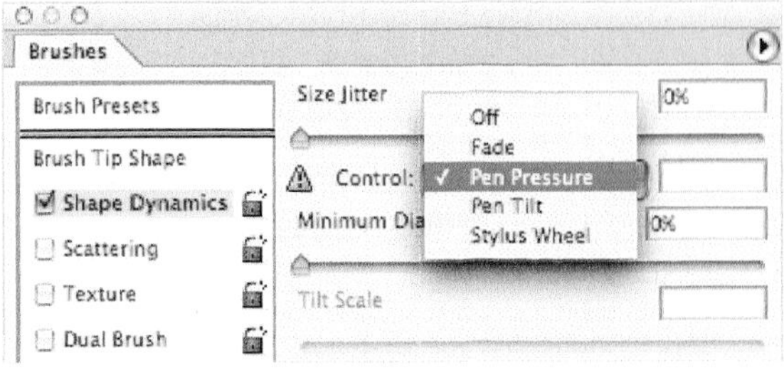

FIGURE 5.32: These controls are available if you're using a pressure-sensitive drawing tablet.

Pen controls are available only when you're using a pressure-sensitive digital drawing tablet rather than your mouse. A warning icon appears if you select a pen control but have not installed a tablet.

Custom Brushes

Custom brushes are a great way to enhance your creative painting options in Photoshop. They let you go beyond what Photoshop has provided and create a brush tip shape out of nearly any object you can imagine.

FIGURE 5.33: Another stunner by Bert Monroy. In this Photoshop painting, the leaves were created using a customized brush tip and settings.

To create a new brush tip, use any selection tool to select the area of an image you'd like to use as a brush. Once it's selected, choose Edit > Define Brush Preset. Your new brush will now appear in the brush tip presets seen in the Brushes palette discussed previously.

Saving your brushes to your computer is similar to saving the contents of any other preset in Photoshop. Once you have the custom brushes you've created in the Brushes palette, just expand the options menu at the right of the palette and select Save Brushes. Name the file accordingly, and your brushes can now be backed up and reloaded should you ever clear your current brushes or if Photoshop crashes and deletes the current settings.

Saving your Brush tool presets is slightly different from saving the actual brush tips. Suppose you've created a complex brush preset using the advanced Brushes palette. You've got it just the way you want, but you realize it's time to create another brush preset. What do you do? You don't want to lose those settings and have to re-create them. Writing them down hardly seems like a good alternative.

Never fear; Tool Presets to the rescue! To begin, create the brush you'd like to save, then open the Tool Presets palette (Window > Tool Presets). Choose New Tool Preset from the fly-out options menu. Give it a meaningful name, and you're set. Just as with brushes, you can save these Tool Presets.

Photo-Realistic Imaging Project

Custom brushes and the advanced features inside the Brushes palette can be useful for any type of illustration or design work for Web or print. However, I find them particularly important when working to create photo-realistic art. In this project, you'll design a photo-realistic golf ball scene using custom brush features to give your image a lifelike appearance.

Project Brief: Photo-Realism from Scratch

Here's your chance to impress (and fool) your friends. Your goal when working with photo-realistic graphics in your design projects will be to make the viewer ask, "Is it a photograph or is it Photoshop?"

FIGURE 5.34: Fore! Tee up your Brush tool as you embark on a photo-realistic journey to re-create a golf ball in the rough.

Your client, a leading golf ball manufacturer, wants to showcase his product up-close-and-personal in a realistic situation.

The Photoshop file for the golf ball is available on the Images CD.

FIGURE 5.35: The golf ball from the Images CD should be the only part of the image you don't create from scratch.

Project Summary

- **Brainstorm a scene for the golf ball, and create a sky relevant to the scene.**

- **Consider how the lighting would affect the coloring of the grass, and set Color Dynamics accordingly.**

- **Use a default and/or custom brush to create realistic grass in the foreground and background, blurring as necessary for a depth-of-field effect.**

- **Expand the scene using a custom brush to create trees, birds, or other realistic features.**

Project Steps

I created the example version using one of Photoshop's default brushes and a golf ball I extracted from another image. The effects used most prominently in creating this illustration were the Shape Dynamics, Scattering, and Color Dynamics sections of the advanced Brushes palette. Let's look at my steps.

Use the RGB color mode to create your image. The final dimensions of the file should be 500 by 375 pixels.

1. Background and Lighting

When you design your golf ball scene, think about the depth and lighting on the landscape. I included a blue gradient background behind my scene to establish that it is a bright, sunny day.

Try various gradients and shades of color to get the sky the way you like it for your version. It can be bright blue like mine, gray and overcast, or even a vivid sunrise or sunset. Don't worry about clouds just yet—you'll add those later.

When you consider your sky and how bright the lighting is, consider that the grass will need to display various green hues that represent this type of lighting. You'll want to use brighter, highly saturated greens for sunny daytime colors and slightly less saturated colors if it's overcast outside. Plus, not all golf courses are plush green all year round. (Mine are, of course, because I live in Florida.) This would be a great place to expand and come up with some autumn colors. And yes, nighttime golf does exist, glow-in-the-dark golf balls and all. In that case, the grass would need to be dark shades of blue, with a moonlit sky in the background, perhaps.

All of this translates to choosing an appropriate foreground and background color when working with the Color Dynamics section of the advanced Brushes palette.

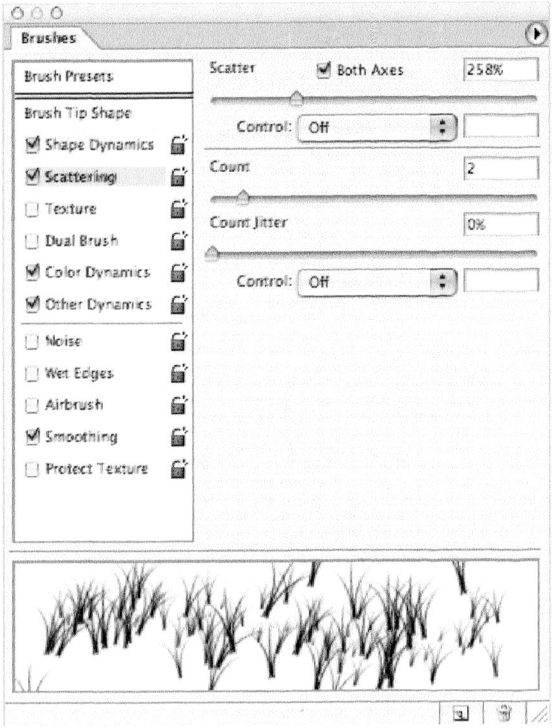

FIGURE 5.36: I applied these custom Color Dynamics settings to Photoshop's default grass brush. Notice that I used the Jitter sliders to make my grass vary widely in brightness, somewhat in saturation, and just a bit in hue. Too much Hue jitter and my grass would have been multicolored!

Recall that the Color Dynamics settings apply variations of color between the current foreground and background shades, which in my case are a light green and dark green.

With the foreground and background colors chosen, you can begin creating your grass.

2. Foreground and Grass

I created my grass using a default brush, included with Photoshop, which you'll find in your menu of brushes. However, feel free to create your own grass brush for a more advanced application. Also, you may want to place some rough, longer grass in one part of the image using the default brush, and short, well-groomed grass in another with a custom brush—as on a real golf course.

To create a custom brush for the grass, make a handful of grass in a new document using any drawing or painting method you choose. Select the area of the image you'd like to use as a brush, and choose Edit > Define Brush Preset. Your new brush will now appear in the brush tip presets seen in the Brushes palette.

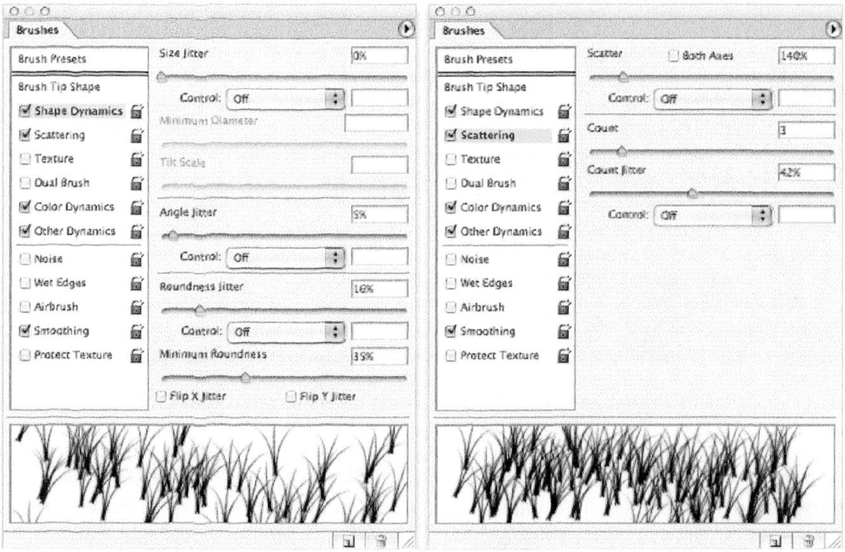

FIGURE 5.37: These are my Shape Dynamics and Scattering settings, but yours may differ depending on the effect you want.

Several grass layers were created to portray the illusion of depth, with some in front of the ball and some behind. The golf ball is not right up against our fictitious camera, so you can blur any grass in front of it to create a depth-of-field effect. The same goes for grass behind the golf ball. You can achieve these effects after you create the grass by applying a Gaussian Blur filter (Filter > Blur > Gaussian Blur) to those layers. Your blurred areas may vary depending on where your ball is in the scene.

FIGURE 5.38: Notice that the closest and farthest layers have a slight blur.

Also, as objects recede into the distance, something known as *atmospheric perspective* takes place. This causes the colors to appear less saturated with color and more gray. Next time you're around a mountain range, see if you can notice it. This effect can be applied to the golf scene by adding a Hue/Saturation adjustment layer to the background layer(s) of grass (Image > Adjustments > Hue/Saturation) and reducing the saturation setting.

The image still needs a little something, don't you think? We'll add to it next.

3. Ideas for Expansion

With your pretty sky, lush grass, and ball sitting in the scene, your next task is to expand your image to include at least one other element that uses brushes. You can include nonbrushed elements too, but something created with the Brush tool should be your first priority.

In my example, I used clouds. I'll admit I extracted my clouds from a separate photograph. But you can create your own clouds with the Brush tool and some experimenting. You don't need to include clouds per se—I'd really like to see some creativity here.

FIGURE 5.39: Here's my final version with some clouds. What will you put in yours?

Here are some other ideas for expanding this project with brushes:

- Create a custom brush of a tiny, faraway, flying bird, and populate the sky with some of them.
- Design a forest in the far background of the scene. Use Color Dynamics and lots of jitters to achieve a random look.

Student Work

What have other designers done with their golf ball scene? Here are some work samples from Sessions.edu students:

FIGURE 5.40: Mareile Paley created a paradise of a golf course with brushes to create grass, waves, and distant bushes.

FIGURE 5.41: In addition to using brushes for the grass and clouds, Don Noray gave this scene a creative perspective and added a tee.

FIGURE 5.42: Sabine Welte used the single-blade tip and other brushes to create a truly stunning piece presenting the golf ball at dusk.

6 Color

Color is the visual appearance of an object created by the specific quality of light it reflects or emits. *Primary colors* are the theoretically pure colors from which all other colors can be mixed. The colors, or *hues*, of a printed project, such as a poster, are created by the *reflection* of light from the paper the design is printed on, each printed image reflecting a particular range of the color spectrum. The hues visible on a *monitor* screen are created by mixing the color components of *transmitted* light in varying intensities, also forming a full spectrum of color. Color has three visual qualities: *hue* (its apparent, named color, such as red), *value* (its degree of lightness or darkness), and *intensity* (its degree of saturation or purity) **(Figure 6.1).**

The color model for print projects is called the *subtractive model.* In this model, *cyan, magenta, and yellow (CMY)* are the primary colors of reflected light, and are the ink colors intermixed to create the full spectrum of color. White light (as would be reflected from a white sheet of paper) is comprised of *red, green, and blue (RGB)* (added together, they create white light). In the subtractive color model, if an object (or image) absorbs (subtracts) red light but reflects green and blue light, the color you see will appear as cyan. If blue light is absorbed, the reflected color appears as yellow, and so on. In theory, when CMY are combined in print, they produce black. However, creating black by overprinting CMY requires too much ink, resulting in drying problems and extra expense. In practice, black is used to add density to the CMY image, thus the four colors are called *CMYK.* The letter *K* is used to signify black, so as not to confuse it with *B* for blue, and also because it is the key image plate, usually carrying the most image detail. Projects printed in CMYK are also called *process color, full-color,* or *four-color.*

CMYK also called: process color
Full color
Foour color.

color palettes and variations

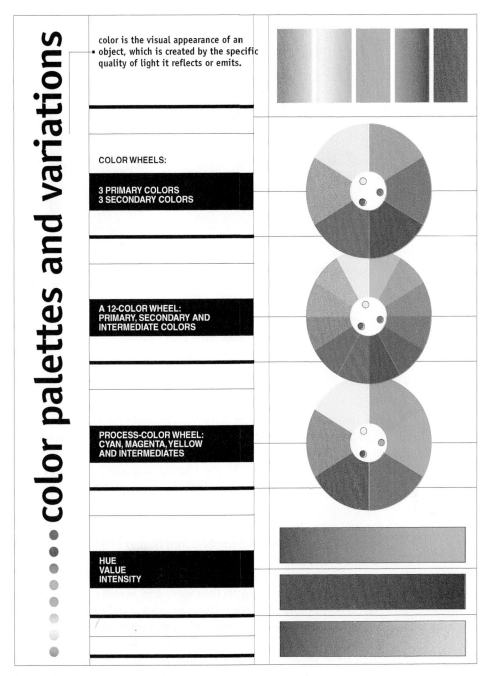

color is the visual appearance of an object, which is created by the specific quality of light it reflects or emits.

COLOR WHEELS:

3 PRIMARY COLORS
3 SECONDARY COLORS

A 12-COLOR WHEEL:
PRIMARY, SECONDARY AND
INTERMEDIATE COLORS

PROCESS-COLOR WHEEL:
CYAN, MAGENTA, YELLOW
AND INTERMEDIATES

HUE
VALUE
INTENSITY

FIGURE 6.1: Color palettes and variations.

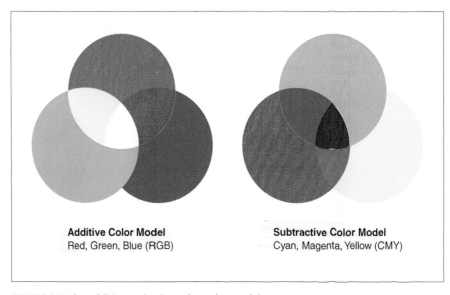

Additive Color Model
Red, Green, Blue (RGB)

Subtractive Color Model
Cyan, Magenta, Yellow (CMY)

FIGURE 6.2: **The additive and subtractive color models.**

The color model for *electronic* projects (those using transmitted light, such as a display monitor) is called the *additive model.* Transmitted light is comprised of red, green, and blue, or RGB. When full intensities of RGB are added together, the light appears as white. When no light is being transmitted, we see that area as black. Therefore, varying intensities of RGB are used to create the full color spectrum. When designing for the Internet, a reduced *(Web-safe)* color palette may be desirable to ensure consistent display **(Figure 6.2).**

The designer uses the color wheel, comprised of primary, *secondary,* and *intermediate* colors to create hue combinations appropriate to the content and character of a project. Different combinations of colors create varying degrees of visual contrast and affect the emotional ambiance of the design. Colors opposite one another on the color wheel, such as red and green, are called *complementary colors.* Depending on their value and intensity, *complementary pairs* can be high or low in contrast. Using an orange and green of the same value and intensity, for example, produces a high degree of visual vibration—hard on the eye, but appropriate for a "psychedelic" effect. Yellow and violet, on the other hand, are quite different in value, the violet significantly darker than the yellow, and can be used together without creating such a dramatic visual effect. *Triadic complements* are sets of three colors equidistant from one another on the color wheel, such as blue, green, and orange. With the addition of one more color, a wider range of color possibilities becomes available. *Near comple-*

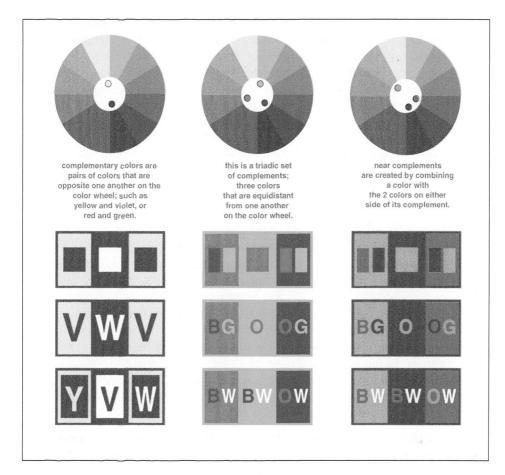

FIGURE 6.3: Complementary colors.

ments are created by combining a color with the two colors on either side of its complement. A palette of near complements usually utilizes secondary and intermediate colors, such as orange with a secondary violet and blue, resulting in a more subtle visual statement. Complements can be superimposed in various combinations, for example dark on light, light on dark, blue on orange, orange on blue, blue on orange on green, orange on blue on green, and so on. Two or more pairs of complements can be used together, as well as pairs of triadic sets. The possibilities are almost unlimited **(Figure 6.3).**

As mentioned above, color has three visual characteristics, hue, value, and intensity, and the designer exploits all three of these qualities. Even the most limited use of color offers these three possibilities. A one-color job using *a spot color* of red, for example, provides the designer with the solid, 100 percent red hue, which has a particular degree of intensity as well as a step-scale of tint percentages or values of the basic red, such as 80 percent, 70 percent, 60 percent, and so on. In a job using two or three spot colors, each individual color has this full range of value, or tints, and each color and its tints can be combined with each additional color, resulting in an extraordinarily comprehensive color palette. Depending on the colors initially chosen, intermixing or overlaying colors and tints (*offset printing inks* are transparent) produces a value range from dark to light in the most subtle of neutral tints **(Figure 6.4).**

Color is universally employed to symbolize cultural ideals, social, political, and spiritual attitudes, and a broad spectrum of emotional and physical conditions. Colors gain their symbolic meaning through association, such as blood red to symbolize energy and life, the luminous yellow of the sun to express warmth, or leaf green to convey health and growth. Color is also used to express more esoteric states, such as violet to represent spirituality, or blue to communicate melancholy. Some colors are more visible than others, making them useful as signifiers, such as the familiar yellow used for school buses, the red of a stop sign, or the red, yellow, and green of a traffic signal. Social and political positions can be suggested using color, such as green for an ecological subject, or red to symbolize revolution. Color is used to improve the visual appearance as well as the communication level of a design.

The usefulness of color to the designer is, of course, in the effectiveness of its application. Using the color models discussed above, the designer has an enormously broad range of groupings from which to choose. The expressive range of color is vast; it can be passive or aggressive, and it can express quality or cheapness, strength or weakness, joy or grief. Each particular color combination influences the overall appearance and effectiveness of a design, while at the same time expressing a distinct attitude **(Figures 6.5, 6.6).**

Leo Lionni, a pioneering art director, graphic designer, and illustrator, emigrated from Italy to the United States in 1939. He used color as a key element in *Epictetus on Philosophy,* from the Container Corporation of America's public service series Great Ideas of Western Man **(Figure 6.7).** Lionni's design is based on an excerpt from Epictetus's *Discourses,* of the first century, "Here is the beginning of philosophy: a recognition of the conflicts between men, a search for their cause . . . ." The significant concept of the ad is "conflict resolution." Lionni's powerfully iconic design of three standing figures portrays a central, mediating figure, flanked by two armed combatants. The starkly black stylized

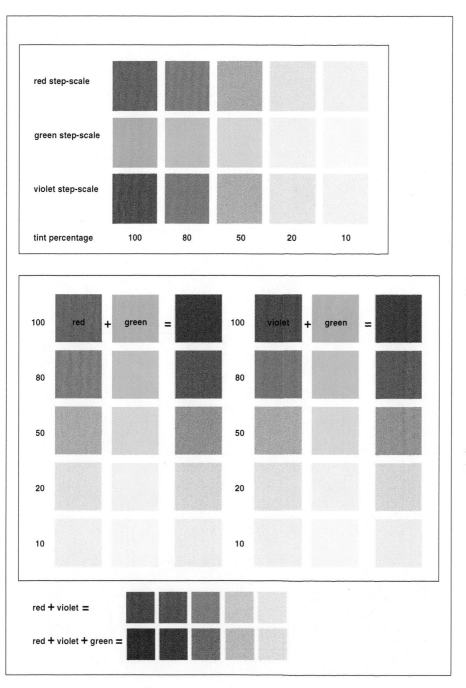

red step-scale

green step-scale

violet step-scale

tint percentage 100 80 50 20 10

100 red + green = 100 violet + green =

80 80

50 50

20 20

10 10

red + violet =

red + violet + green =

FIGURE 6.4: Tint scales and color combinations; hue, value, and intensity.

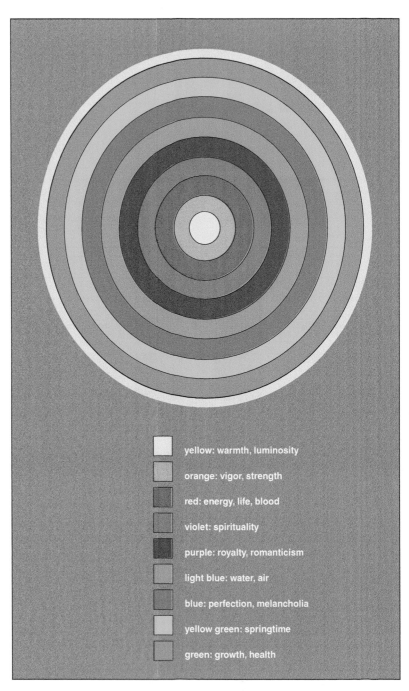

FIGURE 6.5: The expressiveness of color.

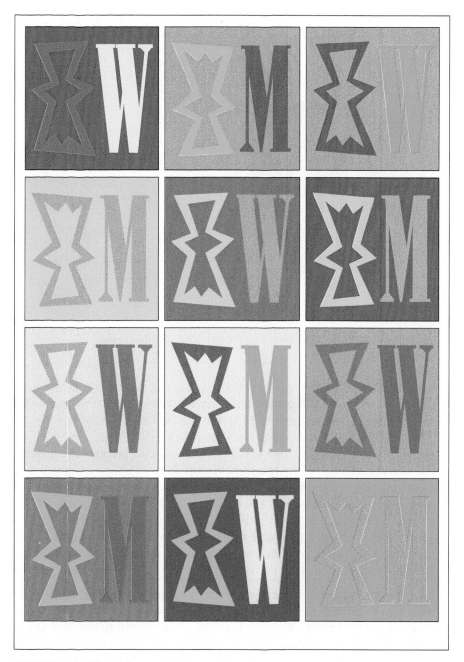

FIGURE 6.6: **Applying color.**

FIGURE 6.7: Leo Lionni, institutional advertisement, *Epictetus on Philosophy.* Great Ideas of Western Man series, Container Corporation of America, 1951–1952 series.

figures, appearing to be roughly cut from black paper, like paper dolls, are a perfect foil for the intense primary and secondary colors that fill the negative spaces between the protagonists. The colors are used to express both difference and unity. Bright red-orange is linked to the left-hand figure, while bright green (the complementary color to red-orange) signifies the figure on the right. The dramatic vibration of the two complements, both aggressive in nature, serves to further isolate the adversaries. Concurrently, placing colors in the sharply defined negative spaces also helps to draw the three figures together, uniting them with a common backdrop. Enriching the concept further, two additional colors border the middle figure: bright yellow imparts a hopeful, positive attitude, while purple lends dignity and gravity to a difficult state of affairs. The appearance and the effectiveness of the design are improved with color.

Full-color printing, and, of course, electronic full color, is ubiquitous in our visual environment. Limited color, or less than full color, however, doesn't have to limit creativity. In fact, limited color actually stands out in contrast to the more familiar full color, and can be deliberately exploited for its uniqueness. Each year, Jeff Neumann, the designer of the *Seattle Times* entertainment tabloid, *Ticket,* has to create a cover for the summer concert issue. Each time, the challenge is to find another way to visually symbolize both music and summer.

FIGURE 6.8: Jeff Neumann, cover, *Shake and Bake. Ticket, The Seattle Times,* 1999.

For the 1999 cover, Neumann used color to smartly integrate word, image, and symbol in an unexpected way **(Figure 6.8).** The key to the cover design is Neumann's witty spin on the headline, "Shake and Bake" (the popular batter mix in a bag) and the subhead "The summer simmers with hot concerts." The predominant image, a sculptural black and white photograph of a woman, taken from the back, has been given a terribly painful sunburn, with a single music note skillfully reversed out of the red. The analogy is immediately clear: when you sit in the sun all day, shakin' to the music, you're likely to be baked to a crisp! Text, photograph, and music symbol are intimately united. The second color, cleverly added to the monochromatic photograph in a dramatic, yet understated manner, effectively reinforces the elegant simplicity of the concept.

For the summer 2000 cover of *Ticket,* Neumann used color in both a descriptive and a symbolic fashion **(Figure 6.9).** Titled *Cultivating the Classics,* the issue reviews summer classical music festivals around the state. The principal image, a beautifully decorative silhouette of a violin-playing idyll, establishes a classical aura while flowers emanating from the violin symbolize music. The silhouette, completely lacking interior anatomical detail, is filled instead with a flat pattern of green grass, simultaneously expressing both summer and the outdoors. The flowers, in contrast to the almost monochromatic grass, are full color, their form as rich, lyrical, and dimensional as the music they symbolize.

FIGURE 6.9: **Jeff Neumann,** cover, *Cultivating the Classics. Ticket, The Seattle Times,* 2000.

Just as color can be employed to express a mood or emotion, it can also be used to make evident certain social or cultural associations. René Galindo's cover design for *Diseño Grafico en Mexico,* a juried annual published by Quorum, a professional graphic design organization, unites form and color to exemplify Mexican design **(Figure 6.10).** The most immediate impression projected by the cover design is that of color; the entire wheel of primary, secondary, and intermediate colors is represented, each color intensely saturated for maximum effect. Complementary pairs contribute to a sumptuously rich palette, while soft tints are used to create a subtle third dimension. The color statement suggests Mexican folk art, wedded to the geometry of Aztec or Mayan architecture. The central image, heavily outlined in black, serves quadruple duty: a stepped pyramid, a technical pen or pencil, a modern skyscraper, a pixilated electronic design. Looking closer, one also sees the hot magenta sun, surrounded by a high purple sky, and, just beneath the horizon line, the bright green of the fertile earth. With each element firmly locked into place, the symmetrical design epitomizes the essence of classical graphic design.

The versatility of full-color printing is thoroughly exploited by designer Joe Erceg in his poster for a celebratory fireworks display **(Figure 6.11).** Touted as "A Theatre of Fire, Color and Sound," the project provided the perfect opportunity

FIGURE 6.10: **René Galindo, Signi,** book cover, *Diseño Grafico en Mexico, Volumen I.* Quorum, Consejo de Diseñadores de México, 1997.

FIGURE 6.11: **Joe Erceg,** poster, *Fireplay.* Twentieth Anniversary of Lloyd Center, Portland, Oregon, 1980.

FIGURE 6.12: Rick Valicenti, Mark Rattin, Thirst, poster, *Mother.* Society of Graphic Designers of Canada, Alberta Chapter, 1994.

to link color exploration with subject matter. Erceg's insistently symmetrical poster is bright, playful, and energetic, somewhat reminiscent of a nineteenth-century *broadside*. The showpiece of the poster, a dazzling pinwheel of fire, explodes out from its center point, leaving waning trails of tiny colored stars in its wake. Four fireworks towers flank the central design, each carrying pin-wheels on their armatures, the artwork saturated with various combinations of the process ink colors (CMYK). Erceg cleverly reversed the tone of the night sky, making it white rather than black *(achromatic),* simultaneously emulating the explosive white light cast by the fireworks, accentuating the radiant colors of the pinwheel, and silhouetting the awestruck children watching the show.

The full-color technology of print and electronic media makes possible the emulation of "natural," or photographic color, as well as infinite tints and color combinations. Computer technology enables designers to profoundly alter real color to either enhance communication or create artistic effect. Rick Valicenti and Mark Rattin of Thirst Studio, uncompromising, passionate explorers of new directions in design, manipulate media in a celebratory spirit of graphic self-expression. In their collaborative poster, *Mother,* advertising an extended lecture and design workshop by Valicenti, conventional, full-color imagery is united with digitally manipulated form to create an enticingly abstruse visionary icon **(Figure 6.12).** A physically manipulated vernacular typeface is used for the background text, its rough-hewn texture in deliberate contrast to the smooth, full-color perfection of the heavily art directed fashion photo of "mother." Subjected to further processing in a *3-D modeling* program, the typeface reappears as an essentially monochromatic word sculpture, uncomfortably floating at, or on, the model's neck, tagging her as "mother." The forward-looking, emotionally detached figure drifts up and into the layout from off-camera, her torso rendered in smeary shades of full color, disturbingly biomorphic. Ingeniously, the designers melded conventional and experimental technology to create a stunningly memorable graphic entity.

Key Words—Vocabulary for Study, Discussion, and Critique

1. Achromatic
2. Additive color model
3. Broadside
4. CMY (cyan, magenta, yellow)
5. CMYK (cyan, magenta, yellow, black)
6. Complementary colors
7. Complementary pairs
8. Electronic media
9. Four color
10. Full color
11. Hue
12. Intensity
13. Intermediate colors
14. Monitor
15. Monochromatic
16. Near complements
17. Offset inks
18. Primary colors
19. Process color
20. Reflected light
21. RGB (red, green, blue)
22. Secondary colors
23. Spot color
24. Subtractive color model
25. 3-D modeling
26. Transmitted light
27. Triadic complements
28. Value
29. Web-safe palette

7
Digital Illustration

Digital illustration is an exciting medium for creating art on the computer. With just a few strokes and clicks (OK, more than a few), you can create wonderful line art in Illustrator, using your screen as a canvas. No pencil sharpeners required, just a mouse—or a drawing tablet if you get really obsessed.

Digital illustrators use the traditional principles of drawing and painting, using line and shape to represent form, space, and light. But once the work is created, the medium has no limitations. A digital illustration can be easily edited, resized, duplicated, and applied to a whole host of graphic design projects in print or on the Web.

In this chapter, you'll learn some ways to "see" objects as an illustrator, and then you'll explore how to create them using Adobe Illustrator. Don't worry if you don't have much traditional drawing experience. Digital illustrations can be created in many different ways; you may find that you can draw something amazing onscreen that you could never do on paper.

FIGURE 7.1: Designer Joshua Hood created this simple but effective logo illustration with a stylized approach to color and curves.

In this chapter you will:

- Learn to use Illustrator guides to position objects on the Artboard.

- Create a stylized alarm clock using basic shapes, colors, highlights, and eye-catching details.

- Learn time-saving ways to duplicate objects and create complex shapes from very simple ones.

- Use the Pen tool to create closed paths and join existing paths.

- Learn to create smooth curves and hinged curves with the Pen tool.

- Create a stylized TV and tennis ball using Pen tool paths, colors, highlights, and other details.

- Learn to use the Pathfinder to create complex objects from the intersections of simple ones.

- Create an illustration of an everyday object of your choice using shapes, the Pen tool, the Pathfinder, and other features.

Illustration Fundamentals

Illustration, by hand or on the computer, is the translation of form, space, and light into a picture. Do you remember your first black-and-white pencil sketches as a child? Childhood doodles are the essence of drawing, which is the attempt to capture exactly how things look in a simple, recognizable form.

In our first drawings, we often sketch the outline of an object: a house or flower, for example. But look closely at most objects in the world, and you'll see that there are no outlines that go all the way around an object. Instead, you'll see *contours*: lines and shapes formed by contrasts in texture or color on an object and by the light that falls on it.

FIGURE 7.2: Illustrations like "California" by Chris Varricchione can combine surrealism and creativity with great attention to realistic contours. The result is a piece of art that makes a viewer stop and stare.

If you could see the world in black-and-white (imagine your television was broken), you would see contours everywhere: on some edges of an object, around areas of empty space, or as lines on the surface of an object, such as craters or wrinkles.

Some illustrators attempt to capture every detail in a shape. Others stylize and simplify their drawings, capturing the boldest contours and hinting at tones, shapes, and lighting without trying to capture every little nuance. This approach can be really effective in digital illustration, where illustrations can be created by either using a digital pen on a Wacom drawing tablet or using your trusty mouse to create simple shapes and colors in Illustrator.

Before we dive into the hands-on part of the chapter, I want to mention some techniques that I find helpful for digital illustration. First, perspective is important—some type of depth is required to keep things from looking flat. Simply varying the thickness of my contours can give the drawing much more volume and life. Second, to make sure you're thinking about contour, you may want to limit your colors initially to two tones, dark and light.

But don't stop there—once your basic composition is coming together, the use of color can also contribute to the dimension of your work. Flat color can be quite beautiful in drawings—just simple fills of outlined shapes—or you can use gradients to mimic the lighting and depth of real life. Darker shapes can form shadows, lighter shapes can become highlights, and less saturated (less intense) shapes can represent areas that are farther away. Keeping it simple, you'll want to tweak your design so that the finished work has naturalism and charm.

Creating Visual Concepts

One important item to mention is the the need to brainstorm before you draw. When you're hired to create an illustration for a graphic design project, the primary goal is to communicate the client's message. Because illustrators are often called upon to communicate abstract concepts (technological change, say, or job satisfaction, or the rising stock market), the brief from the client can be a little vague—sometimes nothing more than an idea.

This leaves the illustrator to brainstorm the concept—to come up with a visual idea *and* carry it out. A conceptual illustration can be handled very literally—for example, if the client wants to convey the flavor of a product, you may want to draw a juicy strawberry. But often the illustration goes in a less literal direction. Editorial graphics for an advertisement or a magazine article, for example, must give the viewer something to think about and draw conclusions from.

Try to sketch or write down as many different ideas as you can before you start drawing. One of my magazine clients needed an illustration on the topic of email security and how easily hackers can snatch email messages. I started by brainstorming, writing down everything I could think of related to email and theft. I thought awhile about using an image of Sherlock Holmes, but realized that would be too complicated and some people might not recognize him. Then I thought, "Why not draw the computer as an email thief, and represent the email message as a letter?" The client loved it because it was very clear without being too literal. I was certainly glad I had taken the time to brainstorm various options before beginning to draw.

FIGURE 7.3: Lots of brainstorming and sketching leads to creative concepts that clients love.

Watching the Clock

We're going to start this exploration of digital illustration with a fun (and easy!) clock drawing using just the basic drawing tools. Follow along, and you'll end up with a clock like mine.

FIGURE 7.4:
My finished clock.

Using Guides

Let's begin by opening a new document in Illustrator. Go to File > New and click RGB. Leave the Artboard size at the default, which is U.S. letter size (8.5" by 11"). Save the file as Clock.ai.

Go to View > Show Rulers. You will see ruler units on the left and top of the document window. Depending on your current preferences, you'll see the ruler unit in either points or inches. Throughout the chapter, we will use inches.

To change the ruler units, go to Edit (or the Illustrator menu in Mac OS X) > Preferences > Units & Display Performance). Change General to Inches. Leave the rest as is, because type is better adjusted in points.

Click and drag guides from the left and top ruler, and release the mouse in the center area.

Drawing the Clock with Circles

Now you are ready to draw! We'll play with the Ellipse tool, drawing circles where the two guides meet. Let's call this point of intersection the "crossing guides" from now on.

FIGURE 7.5: Drag guides from the horizontal and vertical rulers to form the crossing guides, circled here.

We will start by creating an outline of a clock. Go to the toolbox and select the Ellipse tool ⬚. Position the pointer at the crossing guides. Press the Alt/Option key, and the pointer will change to a round icon ⬚. Click once and a dialog box will appear. Type 3 in for both the width and height.

A color may already be filled inside the circle you just drew. It depends on how your color fill is set up. If the circle doesn't have a color, go ahead and give it one. Go to Window > Color to bring up your Color palette, and choose RGB mode from the option menu on the palette.

With the circle selected, type 255 in the Color palette's R (red) field, 191 in G (green), and 0 in B (blue) to put a cool orange color in the circle.

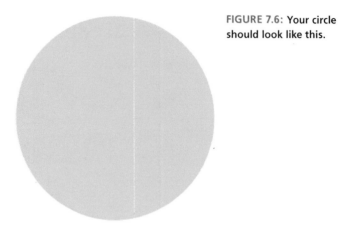

FIGURE 7.6: Your circle should look like this.

Now, we will draw shades. We will make two. One is a half circle, the other a full circle. We will call the half circle shade A and the full circle shade B.

FIGURE 7.7: Our two simple shades (left, middle) will add up to a more interesting shape (right).

Shade A will be a half circle, but we will use a full circle to make it. Draw a new circle using the same process as before, but this time type 2.7 in for both width and height. You've created a circle slightly smaller than the first.

You will turn this into a half circle by deleting an anchor point. With the Direct Selection tool 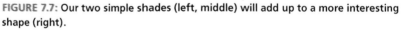 selected, click the right anchor point of the circle. Now you'll see that the only anchor point is selected. Press Delete. You will see an open path. Choose the Pen tool and click one of the end points, and then click the other end point to close the path.

FIGURE 7.8: When you have an open path, it's a good idea to close it.

We will pick an orange color for this, different from the first. Go to the Color palette and type 255 in R, 140 in G, and 0 in B.

Now we will rotate the half circle. Select the shape (with the regular Selection tool ▶), and choose the Rotate tool ◌. With the Alt/Option key pressed, click the intersection point of the crossing guides. A dialog box will appear—type 45 for the angle.

Make another circle, again using the same process as for the first, but now type 2.3 in for both the height and width in the dialog box. You just drew shade B, which you should make the same color as shade A. Cool!

Let's make one more circle from the crossing guides, the same way as before but with 2.1 in for the height and width. This will be the glass cover on the clock. In the Color palette, type 0 in R, 160 in G, and 198 in B to make a cool blue.

Drawing the Clock Hands

This is the beginning of a Pen tool study. In this section, we will create simple clock hands using the Pen tool. The Pen tool is a very useful part of creating vector graphics. I would even say, "No Pen tool, no Illustrator." Sound harsh? That's how important it is. But don't panic. After we create a couple of illustrations, you will master the tool, and you'll even start to enjoy the precision and control it gives you.

Select the Pen tool in the toolbox. Make sure the fill color is set to None and the stroke is black. We will draw the long hand of the clock first.

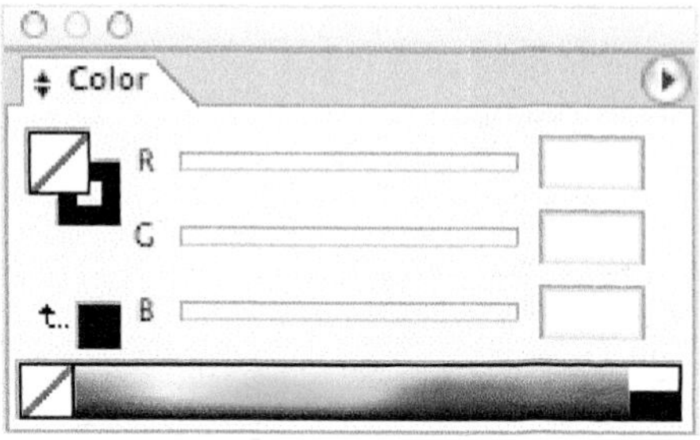

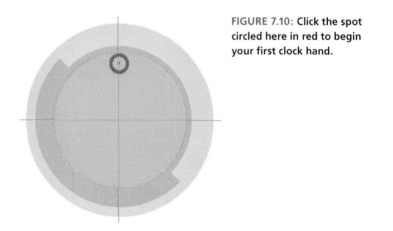

FIGURE 7.9: **Check the Color palette to make sure your fill is None and your stroke is black.**

First click along the vertical guide. This is the starting anchor point. With the Shift key pressed (holding Shift while you drag vertically or horizontally will make a straight line), click the intersection point of the crossing guides. Good! We just created the clock's long hand.

FIGURE 7.10: **Click the spot circled here in red to begin your first clock hand.**

Move your Pen tool toward 7 o'clock and click. This will be the short hand. Play with the hand—it could point to any hour. You are the master of time!

Now let's look at what we've drawn. Aren't the lines too thin to be clock hands? They sure are, so let's change the line weight. Go to the Stroke palette (Window > Stroke). Type 8 in the Weight field and select the Round Cap button. Choosing a round cap creates nice rounded ends for the clock's hands. They should be much more realistic now.

Adding Legs and a Shadow

Now we have to give legs to the clock, right? Otherwise, it may fall over.

Before we begin, I'd like to recommend that you be creative with these details. As you'll see, the legs don't have to look like those in my original drawing. They could be longer, skinnier, or fatter. After we create the left leg, we will use the Reflect tool 🔄 to copy it to create the other leg. That will save you time.

Let's start with the left leg. Select the Pen tool. We will draw a triangle with three anchor points. Once again, yours doesn't have to look the same as the original drawing.

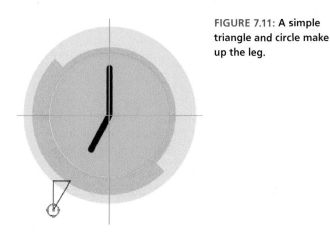

FIGURE 7.11: A simple triangle and circle make up the leg.

Next, position the Ellipse tool pointer on the bottom anchor point of the triangle, and draw a circle. All right! You've created a leg. Once the object is grouped, you can move it around at will, so let's do that now.

First, select the triangle and the circle that make up your leg together (hold down Shift while clicking with the Selection tool to select multiple objects). Then, go to Object > Group to group those two images. Now you can move them together with the Selection tool. Find a perfect spot for the leg.

Let's add a color. You may see the leg outlined in black. If so, go to the Color palette, and click Stroke (the open square) to activate the stroke color. It will come forward. Click None ⊿, and the stroke color will be gone.

While the leg group is selected, click Fill (the solid square in the Color palette) to activate it. Type 255 in R, 140 in G, and 0 in B.

Uh-oh—is the left leg sitting on top of the clock? Don't worry. In Illustrator, the most recently created object always sits on top of the other objects. In this case, you should send the leg backward, behind the clock. Select the leg, and go to Object > Arrange > Send to Back. You will see that the top part of the leg gets hidden. It was sent to the back. And I mean all the way back.

FIGURE 7.12: **Send to Back places objects at the very bottom of the stack.**

Now let's reflect the leg group to make another set. While the leg is selected, go to the toolbox and double-click the Reflect tool. Choose Vertical and type 90 as the angle. Click Copy (not OK!). You will see another leg appear, reflected.

With the Selection tool, drag the leg horizontally until you find a proper location, and release the mouse.

Next comes the shadow below the clock. This is easy. Just draw an ellipse with the Ellipse tool. While it is selected, go to the Color palette and type 3 in R, 74 in G, and 94 in B (for the fill, not the stroke).

Drawing Bells Using a Gradient

We're getting there. We will draw two alarm bells on the top of the clock. Once again, if you want to try something on your own, that's fine. I'd like some variety.

Draw any size circle that you think is a proper size for an alarm clock bell. I used 0.4" for the width and height. Place your bell toward the upper left of the clock.

FIGURE 7.13: It doesn't matter what color your bell is filled with, since we will change it to a gradient next.

Now, we will try out the Gradient tool ▣. Let's open the Gradient palette (Window > Gradient). We will use a Radial gradient here. In a Radial gradient, the beginning color is the inside color, and the outside color is the ending color.

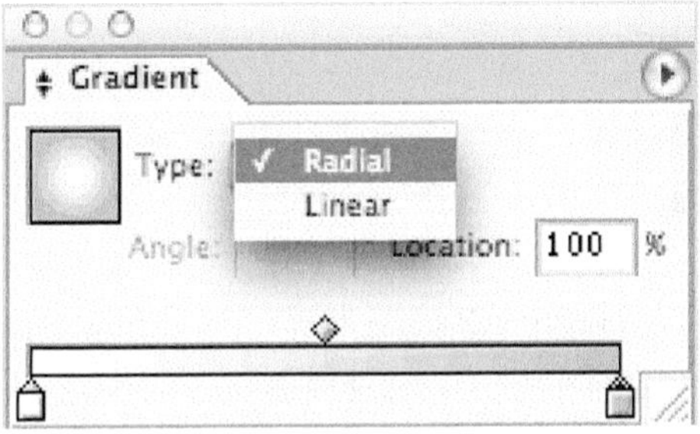

FIGURE 7.14: The gradient default is black and white, but you can click the sliders to change the colors.

To set up colors in the gradient, you must choose the colors from the Color palette. Drag the Color palette right next to the Gradient palette for your convenience.

Click the left slider 🛆, and go to the Color palette. Pick a color, whatever you like. I chose white. Now you'll see the left slider filled with the color you just picked. Next, select the right slider. Choose any color for the ending color. For this example, I chose gray (163 in R, 163 in G, and 163 in B). Now you're finished with the color settings for your gradient.

With the Selection tool, select the circle you've just created. Go to the toolbox and choose the Gradient tool. Click where you think the beginning of the gradient should be, drag, and then release where you think the ending should be. Also make sure you get rid of the stroke outline for the bell. Cool!

Let's connect the bell to the clock using a stroke. With the Pen tool, click the center of the bell, and then make another click anywhere that looks good. Make the stroke weight 3 points.

FIGURE 7.15: **Two clicks of the Pen tool, and your bell is connected.**

It is on top of the bell. Let's send it to the back, like we did earlier with the leg. With the Selection tool, click the stroke you just created, and go to Object > Arrange > Send to Back.

The next step will be to make the echo of the bells. We will use four circles to draw this. The center of the bell will be the center point of the four circles.

Draw four circles with no fills (their sizes do not matter as long as they're all different) and stroke color settings of 255 in R, 191 in G, and 0 in B. Give them all a weight of 2 points.

With the Direct Selection tool, select two anchor points of each circle, and delete. Quite easy, huh? Let's group the remaining pieces. Select the whole bell unit, including echoes and connection lines, and go to Object > Group.

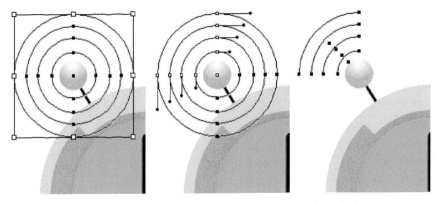

FIGURE 7.16: The center of the bell should be the center of the four circles.

Click the bell group with the Selection tool. Double-click the Reflect tool to make another set. The setting will be Vertical and the angle should be 90 degrees. Enter these in the dialog box and click Copy. Move it to the appropriate location, then send to the back: Object > Arrange > Send to Back.

Highlights of the Clock

Wow! Look at what you've done so far. The clock we created looks pretty good and is nearly complete. Let's keep it up. We're almost there. Even though the clock looks good, something's missing. What could it be? The highlights.

FIGURE 7.17: Let's add some highlights so our clock won't feel so flat.

Highlights are the brightest spots in an illustration. Adding highlights adds a sense of depth to an image. You should always have highlights in your illustrations.

Let's think about what color we should go with. We will put a highlight on the glass cover. It should be brighter than the color of the glass, right? I simply added more white on the highlight. The color setting I will use is 191 in R, 231 in G, and 241 in B.

First we'll make a circle. With the Alt/Option key pressed, position the Ellipse tool at the intersection of the crossing guides and click. Type 1.8 in for both width and height.

For the highlight, we will use only a quarter of a circle. We will get rid of two anchor points to make it. Choose the Direct Selection tool, click two anchor points, and delete.

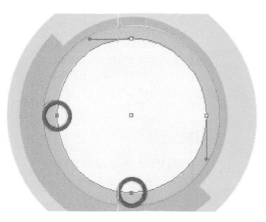

FIGURE 7.18: Select and delete the two anchor points circled in red to get a quarter circle.

Now the path is open. Let's close it using the Pen tool. Click any open end, and then click the intersection of the crossing guides. Lastly, click the other end. Good. Let's rotate it. Select the highlight using the Selection tool. Then select the Rotate tool and position it on the intersection of the crossing guides. With Alt/Option pressed, click once. In the Rotate dialog box, type –45. Click OK.

FIGURE 7.19: Rotate the highlight to give it a more interesting position.

Adding Eye-Catching Details

We added a highlight. So far, so good. But a block of color looks kind of dull, doesn't it? And the other parts of the clock look too symmetrical for my taste. I'd like to add some action—something live. We can add a few line touches so that the highlight pops out. This could be the eye-catching element of the composition.

Eye-catching elements are little exaggerated light effects, colors, or delicate shapes. They're not realistic (usually), but they are crafted to be intriguing to the eye. "What's that?" asks your eye. Let's try it.

We will start by using a couple of circles. Select the Ellipse tool. With Alt/Option pressed, click the intersection of the crossing guides and type 1.5 in for the width and height value. Let's draw another circle, this time with 1.1 inches as the width and height value.

Select those two circles and give them no fill but a stroke color setting of 0 in R, 0 in G, and 0 in B, which is solid black. (This color setting will be changed soon.) Make the stroke weight 4 points. Let's place these circles on the clock as depicted in the beginning of the chapter. As you see, we will use just a quarter of the circle. We'll do this the same way we did the bell echoes.

Choose the Direct Selection tool, then click two anchor points of each circle and delete.

FIGURE 7.20: **Delete the anchor points circled here, and you'll have two arcs.**

With the Selection tool, click to select the strokes. We will rotate these strokes from an axis of the crossing guides. Select the Rotate tool and position it on the crossing guides. With the Alt/Option key pressed, click once. In the Rotate dialog box, type –30 and click OK.

Let's change the stroke color settings to 0 in R, 160 in G, and 198 in B.

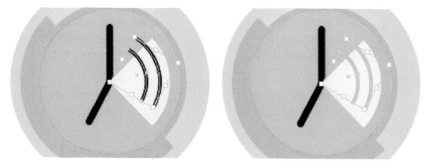

FIGURE 7.21: **A color change makes all the difference.**

Done! Let's look at the whole image. To have a clearer look, hide the guides (View > Guides > Hide Guides).

Adding a couple of lines in the highlight gives a very different look. Remember that big changes don't always make an illustration better. Sometimes just a minor touch can give you a better look.

FIGURE 7.22: **All done!**

Once again, you can add whatever you want on top of this illustration. Just try!

The Pen Tool

You might say, "What, the Pen tool again?" I know what you mean; all of this emphasis on the same tool can be trying. But in this section, you will not only practice what you've learned so far with the Pen tool, but also take it even further by using it with just about every type of path you can think of. Remember: No Pen tool, no Illustrator!

I consider the Pen tool the most powerful tool in the whole Illustrator kingdom. In time and with practice, you can use it to draw anything you imagine!

FIGURE 7.23: Designer Todd Macadangdang uses the Pen tool in this illustration to create the contours of this woman's face, later filling them with gradient meshes for realistic shading.

As we explore the Pen tool, I recommend you turn on the drawing grid (View > Show Grid) and its snap-to feature (View > Snap To Grid). This will constrain the tool to the grid lines and help you learn how the tool behaves. When you are more confident, you can get rid of the drawing grid and draw freely.

CREATING A CLOSED-PATH OBJECT

We will start our study with a closed-path object, so select your Pen tool now. You'll see an X next to the Pen tool pointer ✎. That means the Pen tool is ready to begin a new path segment. Click somewhere on the Artboard and then click again somewhere else to create a straight line. Now the X is gone ✎, which means you're drawing! If you hover over the second anchor point now, a pointer showing a small arrow appears ✎. The arrow means the Pen tool can create a cusp anchor point (we'll talk about that later) or remain a corner/ straight anchor point. We'll keep this as a straight anchor point by clicking another part of the Artboard to draw a second straight line.

Place the pointer above the first anchor point we drew. Now there is a circle next to the pointer ✎. That means that once you click, you will close the path.

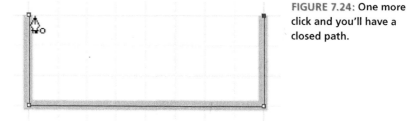

FIGURE 7.24: One more click and you'll have a closed path.

ADDING AND SUBTRACTING ANCHOR POINTS

Let's try another quick study. Draw two separate path segments beside each other but not touching. To end a path and start a new one, press Enter before you draw the second path.

Select the first path segment with the Selection tool and position the Pen tool near the center of it. The Pen tool now has a plus sign pointer ✎, which means you'll add a new anchor point if you click. Try it. Now move the Pen tool to the new point you made. See the minus sign on the pointer ✎? When you click the point, it will be deleted. Try this too.

FIGURE 7.25: Try it out—add a point to a segment, then subtract it, watching your Pen tool pointers.

You can also add and delete points using the Add Anchor Point tool and Delete Anchor Point tool in the toolbox. So many options!

CONTINUING AND JOINING EXISTING PATHS

Next, move the Pen tool over one of the anchor points on the end of either path segment. The pointer has a forward slash, which means you can continue a previously drawn path ✎. Click the anchor point, and then move the Pen tool over an anchor point on the other path segment. Now the pointer is a box with a line on both sides ✎. That means if you click, you'll join the paths. Give it a try.

FIGURE 7.26: **Clicking now will join the two paths.**

Creating Curves

You can also use the Pen tool to create curved lines (also called *Bézier curves*) similar to the way you create straight lines.

CURVED LINES

How is it done? Instead of clicking, you click and drag. When you drag, direction lines and handles appear. The direction lines show the path a curve will follow when you click to create another anchor point.

Let's make a curve. Click and drag with the Pen tool to create an anchor point with direction handles. Click and drag somewhere else to complete the curve. As you drag, you can change the rotation and length of the direction lines. Longer direction lines create steep curves, shorter lines create soft curves.

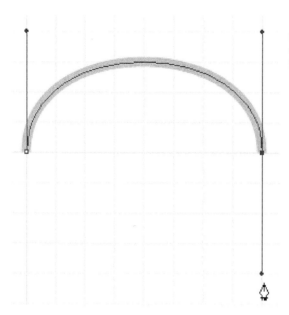

FIGURE 7.27: I made a symmetrical curve using vertical direction lines of the same length on both sides.

If you click a previously drawn curve with the Direct Selection tool, you'll see its direction lines. You can move the direction lines with the Direct Selection tool too. Practice drawing lots of curves. Select the segments, and study the angles and lengths of the direction lines to see how they change the path as you see in Figure 7.29. A tip to keep in mind is that the fewer the anchor points, the smoother the curve.

HINGED CURVES

In a *hinged curve*, two curved lines meet to form a *cusp point*. It may sound weird, but it's actually very handy.

There are three types of anchor points in Illustrator: corner points, smooth points, and cusp points. Straight lines use corner points (which we drew earlier with our straight, closed path); curved lines use smooth points; and hinged curves use cusp points.

Follow along, and we'll make a hinged curve.

Click and drag upward to drag out direction lines. For the next point, click and drag downward to pull out direction lines—but do not release the mouse, OK? Hold the Alt/Option key to drag the bottom direction line and align it with the top direction handle, and then release. Create a third point by clicking and dragging down to pull out the direction handles. Does your path look like the letter M? Great! The two points on the outside are smooth points, and in the middle is a cusp point.

FIGURE 7.28: **Just practice!**

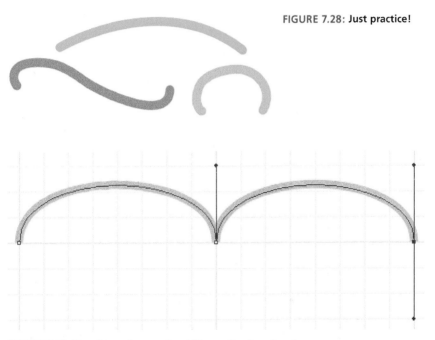

FIGURE 7.29: **Your hinged curve should be pretty close to mine.**

IDENTIFYING AND CHANGING ANCHOR POINTS

Select any anchor point with the Direct Selection tool to see what kind of point it is. Corner points do not contain direction lines; smooth points always have two direction lines (in a straight line above and below the anchor point); and cusp points have either one or two direction lines at different angles.

Are you wondering whether you can change one type of anchor point to another? I hope so—you can do it with the Convert Anchor Point tool ⌐⌐⌐ under the Pen tool in the toolbox.

To convert a smooth point or cusp point to a corner point, just click the anchor point with the Convert Anchor Point tool. Try it out on a curved path segment or on a circle. The smooth and cusp points lose their direction lines, and the path segments lose any curve information.

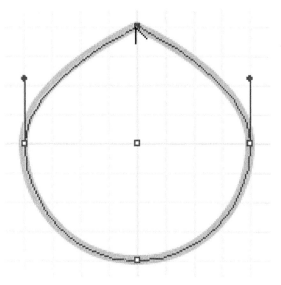

FIGURE 7.30: **This was a circle until I converted an anchor point.**

To convert a corner point or cusp point to a smooth point, click and drag the anchor point with the Convert Anchor Point tool. As you drag, direction lines appear and the path segments leading into the point begin to curve on either side of the anchor point.

What about converting a smooth point to a cusp point? That's a little trickier. First, draw a circle to practice on. Select the bottom anchor point on the circle with the Direct Selection tool to see the direction lines. Hold the Alt/Option key, and click and drag a direction point. Notice that the other direction line stays put. Wow, this a lot of information to digest! But lots of practice with the Pen tool will make you a master of it soon.

Two Objects Interacting

Before we start this next piece, I'd like to share some thoughts on illustration.

When I was in college, I was frustrated about not being as good as van Gogh (he is my favorite painter). But once I entered the workplace, I realized that pure talent is not everything, because I work for clients! They are the ones who judge my artwork. Sometimes they make me feel like van Gogh, sometimes like nobody.

To keep my clients happy, I put a lot of effort into conceptualizing the design, sketching out various options before I get started. I tend to avoid abstract concepts, because almost every design has to make sense to a lot of people. I aim for realistic concepts and add my point of view. And I try to pull it all together through composition.

When I move forward with the design, I pay a lot of attention to the little details. Simplicity is the goal, so I try to avoid boring and unnecessary details. I concentrate instead on elements that hold people's attention. Sometimes it's the smallest thing. For example, if I have to draw ten straight lines horizontally, I would never draw ten lines with the same length and angles. I would make sure that I produce my lines with slightly different angles and lengths. Try it! I know it will make people more interested in your artwork.

Making Guides from an Object

We're going to make an eye-catching illustration that involves composing two different objects and making them interact. Along with our trusty Pen tool, we're going to play with the Pathfinder and some other cool Illustrator features.

FIGURE 7.31: **This finished illustration involves planning, composition, and … the Pen tool.**

Start a new Illustrator document that is in RGB color mode and U.S. letter size (8.5" by 11"). Save the file. Let's call the document TV.ai.

There are many different ways of creating guides. The one you learned earlier, dragging from the rulers, is a basic method. This time we will use a rectangle to create guides. Huh? That's right. In Illustrator, any object can be used to create guides. You will see how.

First of all, let's draw a rectangle. Go to the toolbox, select the Rectangle tool, and click in the center of the document. Type 1.55 in for width and 1.17 in for height.

With the rectangle selected, go to View > Guides > Make Guides. It's that easy.

FIGURE 7.32: The initial fill on your rectangle (left) doesn't matter since it will become a blue guide (right).

We will illustrate a TV on top of this, so let's lock this guide so that it doesn't get moved by accident. Go to View > Guides > Lock Guides. Most of the time, guides start out as locked.

Drawing a TV Using Guides

On top of the guides we just made, let's draw a TV set. Select the Pen tool and move the pointer inside the guides. Just make two angled shapes similar to my example. It is not that hard, right? To create these angled brackets, you'll just use straight lines. They don't have to be proportional or perfect; in fact, it's better that they're not.

FIGURE 7.33: Our TV will be very stylized, starting with these angled shapes.

You've just created an outline of a TV, so now add a fill color. It will be 51 in R, 51 in G, and 153 in B.

Now with the Pen tool, draw a leg, the left one. It is just a triangle. We will use the same color we used for the TV outline.

FIGURE 7.34: The second leg will be a simple duplicate of the first.

Because the two legs I'm using are the same, we will make a copy to use as the right one. With the Selection tool, click the left leg and drag it to the right with the Alt/Option key pressed. That will make a duplicate. Find an appropriate place, and release the mouse.

We may need more guides for other parts of the TV later, but we don't need the rectangle guide anymore. To avoid confusion, let's delete it. Go to View > Guides > Clear Guides.

The TV's body and screen are next. Using the Pen tool, draw a (slightly off-kilter) rectangle with fill color settings of 102 in R, 102 in G, and 255 in B. It will be a TV body. It's currently on top of the frame we made, so let's send it to the back. Cool.

Notice that the upper-left corner in my example is not fully covered by the rectangle. I meant to create this highlight by using negative space. Sometimes you can create highlights out of light effects without adding anything to the illustration. In this case, omitting the corner of the TV creates a light effect with negative space.

FIGURE 7.35: Sometimes you don't need to draw anything extra to make an interesting effect.

For the screen, select the Rounded Rectangle tool and click with it on the Artboard. Use 1.12 in for the width and 0.85 in for the height, and give it a Corner Radius of 0.2. Place it in the middle of the TV and give it a fill. I used 51 in R, 204 in G, and 255 in B to get the bright aqua color.

Now just add a circle of 0.13 in for width and height. This will be a channel dial.

FIGURE 7.36: Now we have the basic TV shape finished.

Modifying Shapes with the Pathfinder

In this section, we will use Pathfinder commands to modify shapes. The Pathfinder uses special commands to create new shapes using the intersections between simpler objects. We will try it out by creating some objects here. Let's begin.

First, we'll draw an antenna base using a half circle. We will start with a full circle that's 0.33 inches in width and height. Now draw a rectangle a little bit bigger than a half of the circle.

Select both objects with your Selection tool, holding down Shift. Go to the Pathfinder palette—if you don't see it, go to Window > Pathfinder. Click the Subtract from Shape Area button in the Pathfinder (the second button in the Shape Modes row.

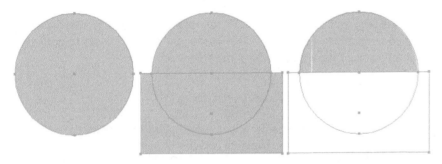

FIGURE 7.37: **When we use the Pathfinder, the intersection of the two shapes will be removed (right).**

You will notice that the front rectangle and the intersection of the circle are gone. Now you have a perfect half circle. Fill it with the same color as that of the TV frame.

Now we will add two antennae to the base in the same color. Just draw two triangles in any shape, and add two circles to their peaks.

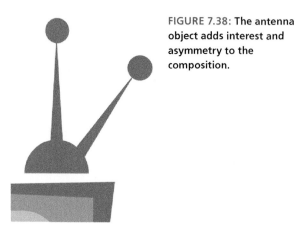

FIGURE 7.38: **The antenna object adds interest and asymmetry to the composition.**

We are almost finished drawing the TV set. How are you doing? Your TV looks great so far, but look again at the final illustration. We have a way to go! Let's keep up our hard work and do some more Pen tool studies.

The Curved Segments

We'll put what you learned earlier about curved paths to work here. You just need a little practice to create beautiful curved segments.

With the Pen tool selected, click in two places on the page, outside of your main drawing. You will see a line connecting two points. Grab the Convert Anchor Point tool. Click and drag slightly the two points you just created, one at a time. You'll see direction lines and direction points appear.

Just play around with the direction points for now. You can click and hold them with the Direct Selection tool and move them around. Why don't you spin one 360 degrees slowly and see how the curved segment changes?

You can also play with curves using a circle drawn with the Ellipse tool. Make one now, and use the Direct Selection tool to pull one of the direction points down. Wow. See how it changed? The longer the direction line, the longer the curved segment with the strange angles. It's a rule!

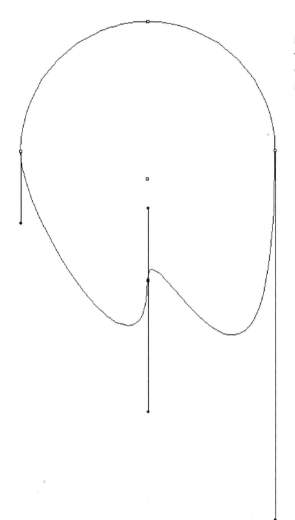

FIGURE 7.39: You can move the direction points on any object—a circle, a Pen tool path, a star, you name it.

Don't forget to delete the practice shapes once you are done with them.

Accents on the TV

The TV looks good, but it still needs some accents to pull the eye. I'd like to put some around the corner of the TV set. Let's do it. This requires the Pen tool skills you just practiced.

First, we need a swoosh shape in the top-left corner. I just put a guide in blue to show you what kind of a shape we will draw. With the Pen tool, click and (somewhere toward the top of the screen) slightly drag the line toward 11 o'clock. Don't worry about the precise direction too much—you can change it later.

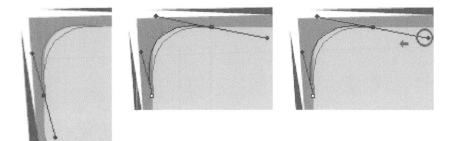

FIGURE 7.40: The blue guide shown here is the shape you will make with these direction line tweaks.

Move the Pen tool to the right. Click and slightly drag toward somewhere between a 3 o'clock and 4 o'clock direction. Notice that the bottom direction line of the first anchor point disappeared. Why? Because you are not using it in that direction. But it will appear when you close the path.

Now here comes the tricky part. We must go back to the first anchor point, keeping the sharp edge. You can't do it without changing the direction of the direction point. If you just go back to the first anchor point without changing it, you will lose the sharp edge. Just try it (and use Edit > Undo when you're done). It's good to experiment.

OK. We will change the direction point toward a 9 o'clock direction. Press Alt/Option and click the direction point. Drag the point toward 9 o'clock. You kept the sharp edge and just changed the direction.

With Alt/Option pressed, click the first anchor point (to close it) and drag it toward 6 o'clock. If you get confused here, it's OK. Even though you drag it down, you may see a direction line pointing upward, instead of downward. That's all right. You're dealing with the hidden direction line of the first anchor point.

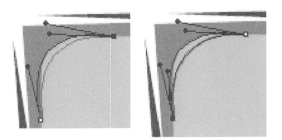

FIGURE 7.41: **Close the path, and make your direction lines like mine.**

If you find this hard to believe, just go back to the previous stage by going to Edit > Undo or pressing Ctrl+Z/Cmd+Z. Then, close the path without pressing Alt/Option. You will now see both direction lines.

The reason to press Alt/Option when you close the path is to keep the direction point and line 1 of the first anchor as is and change the other direction point and line 2 of the first anchor point to keep the sharp edge and smooth curve. If you don't press Alt/Option, you will lose both the direction point and line of the first anchor point and control of the shape.

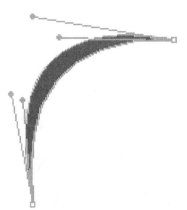

FIGURE 7.42: **A close-up look at the shape you created and its direction lines**

Play around with it until you get it right. Then just add a fill color: 51 in R, 51 in G, and 153 in B.

Now, just add a couple more swooshes next to it and at the bottom right. This will give you some more practice.

FIGURE 7.43: Practice your curves by adding some new swooshes.

Next, we will add a visual effect in the middle of the tube, where the tennis ball we draw later will come out. I used the Star tool 🟊 and modified its shape with the Twirl tool 🌀. Here's how:

First, select the Star tool and click in the center of the TV screen. A dialog box will appear—type 0.2 in for Radius 1, 0.4 in for Radius 2, and 12 for the number of points. Now you have a star with 12 points.

Select the Twirl tool, and click and drag it around. The star will start twirling from the center.

FIGURE 7.44: Little touches like the twirled star make your illustrations feel alive and active.

Now let's add a background image. We will start by using a circle, as in my example. We will use only a section in yellow for the background. In order to do that, we will have to add a rectangle with edges that are similar to the TV outline, then cut out the intersection and the rest of the images using Pathfinder.

FIGURE 7.45: We'll create this yellow background in the Pathfinder.

Draw a circle that's 1.45 inches in width and height, and then use the Pen tool to draw a rectangular shape that has a similar edge to the TV outline. Overlap them like in my example. Then use the Pathfinder's Subtract from Shape Area button to cut out unnecessary images. Color it with 255 in R, 255 in G, and 0 in B.

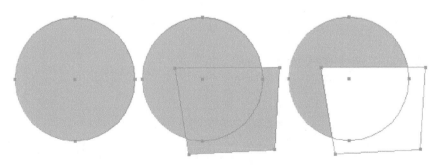

FIGURE 7.46: The TV-shaped intersection area is removed in the Pathfinder (right).

Masking the Ball

In this section, we will illustrate a simple ball and its tail. The tail is a swoosh that creates motion. This part of the illustration requires masking skills and very delicate lines. Sounds tricky, but I'll help you along.

As you work, you'll need to use layers to keep everything organized. This illustration is getting complex! If you don't see the Layers palette on your desktop, go to Window > Layers. Name the current TV layer TV layer.

Let's create a new layer and name it tennis ball. We will illustrate the ball objects on this layer because the TV layer is too busy. To avoid a traffic jam, we will temporarily hide the TV layer by clicking the eye icon. Done? Now you won't see anything on the Artboard.

Click the tennis ball to make it active. Let's draw a ball using a 1.1-inch circle in yellow (255 in R, 255 in G, 0 in B). This will be the outline of the ball. Add a green circle (0 in R, 255 in G, 0 in B) of 0.89 inch on top of the yellow circle.

Create two more circles with yellow strokes (255 in R, 255 in G, 0 in B) and no fills. The stroke weight should be 3 points. Put them in the appropriate place, referring to my example. We just drew a tennis ball.

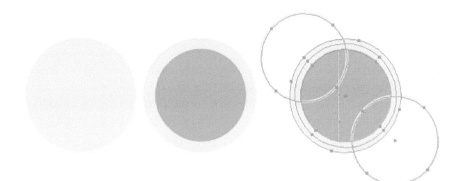

FIGURE 7.47: Wimbledon, here we come!

We are about to put a mask on top of the circles to hide the outer rings. First draw a 1-inch circle. Select all the circles around, including the mask, and go to Object > Clipping Mask > Make. You will see only the properties inside the last circle. Cool! The ball is finished.

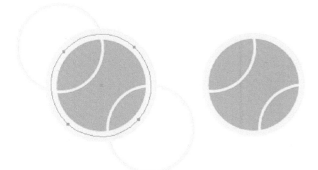

FIGURE 7.48: **Only what's inside the last circle is visible.**

Let's hide the tennis ball layer for now. Click the eye icon to hide it. We will show it again later.

Drawing the Ball's Tail

You'll find drawing the tail-like path of the ball to be highly challenging. Let's think about how could it be done in the easiest way.

First of all, go to the top of the page and look at the outline of the tail. How could it be done? That's right; I created it with two circles: a big one for the outer shape and a small one for the inner one. Then I used the Subtract from Shape Area to crop out the intersection of the two circles. Bingo.

First, create a new layer for the tail and name it tail. Now draw two circles. The big one is 2.65 inches and the small one is 1.6 inches. Move the smaller circle on top of the big one and arrange them like in my example. With both circles selected, click Subtract from Shape Area from the Pathfinder palette. The intersection is gone. To make sure, just add any color to it as a fill. Cool.

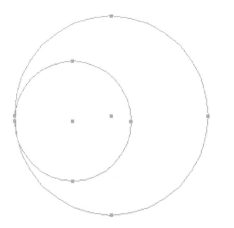

FIGURE 7.49: **Arrange your two circles like these.**

If you look at the completed illustration, you'll notice that only the bottom half of the image is used. So we will crop out the top portion.

At this point, working with colors makes it hard, so let's switch to Outline view (View > Outline). We won't worry too much about colors now, since we can change them later. When you're done with Outline view, you can return to regular view by selecting View > Preview.

Go to the toolbox and select the Rectangle tool. Draw a rectangle. It's got to be bigger than the top half of the tail image.

Place the rectangle on the top half of the tail image. Click the Subtract from Shape Area button from the Pathfinder palette. The top half of the tail should be gone.

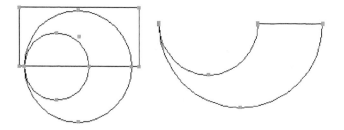

FIGURE 7.50: **Draw a rectangle over the top, then subtract this area with the Pathfinder.**

Now we need to draw a circle, which goes on top of the tail. It will become the outline of the ball. As you can see from the finished artwork, these objects are filled with a gradient. Notice that the ball will sit on top of the circle. Hmm. Then it will be complicated, right? Just to make it easier, let's combine these images into one.

Select both images, then go to the Pathfinder window and click Add to Shape Area. Now they are one object.

FIGURE 7.51: A simple circle is united with the tail and given a snazzy gradient.

Fill it with a gradient: Select the Gradient tool and go to the Gradient palette. Choose 153 in R, 255 in G, and 255 in B for the beginning color; 102 in R, 102 in G, and 255 in B for the ending.

Now we must locate this object on the TV set. Let's make the hidden layers visible (a tennis ball and TV layer). The end of the tail should be in the center of the TV screen, so it looks like it is coming out of the TV. Let's move the ball onto the head of the tail. Drag the tail layer below the ball layer in the Layers palette. The illustration will look like my example.

FIGURE 7.52: **Make all layers visible, and bring the ball and tail to the same location as mine.**

Finally, we will draw three little tails inside the big one. Make sure you're in the tail layer. Go to the toolbox and select the Pen tool.

Ready? Try to produce an angle similar to that of the outer tail by modifying direction lines to produce the curves. It doesn't have to be perfectly accurate, but it should look like it is coming from the same place. Color it white and add another small tail right next to it, then one more.

FIGURE 7.53: **These are the last elements of our illustration.**

What do you think? It looks great! It's a fun interaction between two different illustrations, and it really shows off your Pen tool and Pathfinder skills. Great job.

FIGURE 7.54: That was hard work! Time for a TV break.

Illustrating with Dimension

The clock and TV illustrations in this chapter should have warmed you up to the idea of drawing with Illustrator and working with the Pen tool. With simple shapes, curves, and colors, we were able to capture the essence of the objects they represent without making them too realistic. All it took was a little creativity and some observation of the actual objects to figure out what was worth drawing and what we could leave out.

You'll continue with this idea of drawing stylized objects in the next project, but we're going to take it a step further. An image doesn't need to be flat to be stylized—you can work with color and perspective techniques to give realistic dimension to your drawings.

Project Brief: Accessories with Style

A new clothing and accessories shop is working on the in-store signs that will mark each product department (for example, hats, shoes, neckties, jeans). They'd like you to pick a single department and create one illustration for it before commissioning you to do the rest.

The illustration should contain a pair of items (such as matching gloves or two different shirts) that should have some depth but still be stylized. The illustration should be only of the two items and not include other elements or text—and it must be drawn completely in Illustrator; no bitmapped art allowed.

FIGURE 7.55: For this project, an illustration of a pair of shoes, I combined stylized contours and an illusion of depth using color and detail.

Project Summary

- Brainstorm and sketch illustration ideas for a pair of clothing or accessory items.

- Use the Pen tool and other drawing or shape tools to create the outer and surface contours of your items.

- Apply color fills that represent the highlights, midtones, and shadows to give the items realistic depth.

- Introduce details to the items that maintain a stylized appearance and contribute to the illusion of depth.

Project Steps

Before you begin, choose the items that you would like to draw. Select a pair of items that suits your skill level in Illustrator so far. It's best to use items that you have on hand so you can set them up however you like to sketch. But you could use a photograph of items from a magazine, the Web, or elsewhere.

It's also recommended that you choose solid-colored items so you can focus on their shapes and lighting rather than on intricate patterns or color changes.

1. Sketch the Pair of Items

Arrange your items so that one is in front of the other, and angle them however you like for an attractive setup. With just pencil and paper (yes, really!), create a rough sketch of what you see.

As you sketch, first look at just the contours—the lines and curves around the objects and on their surfaces. Which ones are most important in helping a viewer understand the shape? Which ones could be exaggerated for effect or removed because they are unimportant?

After contours are drawn, look carefully at the lighting on and around your items. Try to pinpoint the middle tones—the ones that are neither very bright nor very dark. Shade these midtone areas lightly in your drawing. Avoid shading areas that are bright—the highlights of the scene. Shade more heavily the areas that are shadows on the items or cast by the items. As you look at the high-lights, shadows, and midtones, also think about their colors and how you might represent them in Illustrator—because that's what you're about to do.

2. Draw the Front Item

In a new Illustrator document in RGB mode, use your Pen tool (or shape tools, depending on the item) to draw the outer contour of the front item of your pair. Make sure the finished path is closed and has no stroke. Take your time to get it pretty accurate, but remember that you can adjust what you've drawn with your Direct Selection tool.

Fill the shape with a color that you feel closely matches the main midtone shade of the object. What you have now should look like a silhouette of your item, since it's just a flat, filled shape that has no details, highlights, or shadows yet.

FIGURE 7.56: Depending on your item, the silhouette might not look like much now. Adding highlights and shadows will make the shape much clearer.

Notice the highlights and lighter midtones on your objects and on your paper sketch. Your next step is to draw those areas and fill them with the appropriate lighter colors.

This can be a little tricky, so let's think back to the highlighted areas we placed on our clock and TV drawings. To make those, we reshaped simple objects like circles or drew little shapes using the Pen tool. The shapes themselves were pretty abstract, but they followed the main object contours nicely and were in realistic locations.

You may use several shapes to build up to bright white highlights, using colors closer to the midtone for the larger shapes and colors closer to white for the smaller ones.

Now it's on to the shadows, so check out your actual items once again, as well as your sketch. As with the highlights, draw shapes that follow the item neatly and fill them with the appropriate darker tones.

And don't forget about the shadows your objects may cast on the surface. Remember that for our clock all we needed was a simple gray oval. Maybe that's all you'll need for your object, or you might need to draw something with the Pen tool if your item is complex.

FIGURE 7.57: You can see my highlights and shadows here. My use of abstract shapes and flat colors keep the stylized look that I like but give it instant dimension.

Here's a handy trick that works for those shadows that items tend to cast. Copy your midtone silhouette shape and paste it on your Artboard as a duplicate. Fill it with the appropriate shadow color (such as a light gray) and put it at the bottom of the stacking order. Then just move it, rotate it, or transform it as necessary.

3. Draw the Back Item

You might think that drawing the back item would be just like doing the front one, but I've got even more tricks up my sleeve that will help you achieve realistic-looking depth in your piece.

Start on a new layer above your front item. When you're done, you can simply drag this layer below the front item layer to change the stacking order. You may also want to hide your front item's layer so it doesn't get in the way.

Draw the shape of your back item and fill it with a color, just as you did for the front item. But instead of the same midtone color you used in your front item, use a slightly lighter and less saturated version of the hue. This instantly makes it look farther away.

Your back item should also be smaller than the front one—the smaller you make it, the greater the perceived distance between the two objects.

Next, as before, add in your highlight and shadow shapes. These should be a bit subtler in color than the ones you made on your first item, and you can make them a little less detailed—all contributing to the illusion of depth.

FIGURE 7.58: My back shoe is lighter, smaller, and less detailed than the one in front—what a difference that makes to the illusion of depth. Cool!

Imagine where else you can use this handy technique. How about in an illustration of a group of people? The detailed people with more color contrast will appear closer than less detailed, softer, smaller people in the group, even though it's still just a drawing made of colored shapes.

4. Add the Finishing Touches

Spend some time comparing your Illustrator image with your actual items. Most likely you have left out many of the details—which is good, since we want the illustration to be simple and stylized.

But, like with our clock and TV, there may be some accents or details that you feel are key to these items and give them some punch. Maybe it's a touch of color around the brim of a hat, or a small starburst shape indicating a sparkle on a belt buckle or eyeglasses lens.

Go ahead and add these now, and recall that these would be best placed on the front item (and only very subtly on the back item) to maintain the depth of the image.

Student Work

What icons have other designers created? Here are some work samples from Sessions.edu students:

FIGURE 7.59: Brent Brooks made his sunglasses more realistic by including gradients and transparency. Finishing touches add sparkle to the final project.

FIGURE 7.60: Jane Boss used the Pen tool very carefully to work with the challenging folds in these shirts.

FIGURE 7.61: Strong reflections can make the highlights tricky, but Jonathan Swihart was up to the challenge and created realistic shine and depth on these boots.

Poster Design

Poster design is a fundamental challenge for any graphic designer. A simple composition in two-dimensional space, a poster is put to a thousand uses, ranging from advertising and event promotion, to public service announcements.

The designer's challenge is to use the medium to engage, inform, and finally motivate passersby. Walk down a city street, hop on the subway, or visit a museum, and you'll see posters everywhere. The best pull us in, present their message with alacrity, and leave us thinking about them afterward.

In this chapter, we'll explore some principles of composition that can be helpful in developing effective poster designs. You'll learn approaches to achieving unity, balance, and rhythm in your posters to make them stand out on the street.

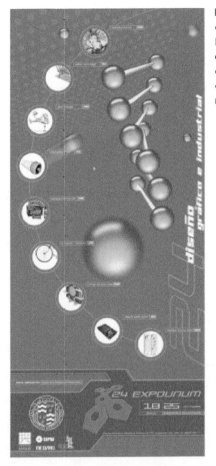

FIGURE 8.1: Posters like this one by designer Gabriela Monroy use balance, repetition, and other intriguing compositional techniques to communicate effectively and make a lasting impression.

In this chapter you will:

Learn about different methods used in poster design to deliver effective messages.

Explore methods of creating unity in the design of a poster: proximity, repetition, continuation, and underlying color.

Learn how and why to create symmetrical and asymmetrical compositions.

Learn how different methods of balancing a composition influence its effect.

Learn about three types of rhythmic approaches to composition.

Learn about proportions found in art, nature, and design.

Explore some applications of typographical rules in poster design.

Design a poster for a music festival considering compositional techniques, imagery, typography, and the display environment.

Poster Design Fundamentals

The poster has been around for about as long as people have had something to announce, and it shows no sign of going away. Why is this, when one might have expected video ads and billboards to take over our public signage? One answer is that a well-executed two-dimensional design still has the power to entrance us.

FIGURE 8.2: Urban construction projects generally prohibit posters. Soon after the hoardings go up, posters appear anyway..

Posters are all about economy of expression—using a minimum of information to get a lot across. Sometimes poster designers are asked to whittle down information and translate it into a visual form; at other times, to create a compelling message with typography alone. Finally, designers are sometimes asked to find a way to organize a daunting mass of details and make it accessible.

A designer's choice of image can clearly make or break a poster. The function of an image is to simplify the message—to avoid having to present part of the message in a more complicated way, through lines of text. Images most often represent what a product is, who's providing it, or whom it's for. They are a shorthand explanation for something that's hard to describe, like "providing working-class people with loans to buy a house they couldn't otherwise afford."

FIGURE 8.3: How do you communicate the names of dozens of performers and composers without information overload? Make them into an attractive piece of art! In this poster for Lincoln Center, the clever use of type works with the photo as a single image to draw viewers in and get them to read more.

A poster designer must also have a strong grasp of typography. It may come as a surprise that typography is so important when text on a poster is used so sparingly (compared with, say, a product package or a magazine spread). But it's an unwritten rule of design that the fewer elements you use, the more carefully you need to use them. Oftentimes the goal of a poster is to communicate a specific text message: "U2 concert on Friday the 12th," or, "Entrance closed for repairs." The designer's choice of typeface, text layout, and balance between text and images will all determine whether this message is actually read and remembered.

Finally, keep in mind that the poster composition itself must intrigue us to attract our attention. Even the simplest images and wording can get lost in an ineffective composition. How do you create a strong design, direct the viewer to the most important elements first, and make the whole thing memorable? It all comes down to composition, so we'll look at a variety of classic approaches in this chapter.

▼ note

A poster's "stickiness" is just as important as its initial impact. Viewers may see a poster for mere seconds, but some aspect of the poster must leave a lasting impression.

Achieving Unity

Let's face it: Designing a poster series, like any graphic design job, can be chaos. Photographers? Missing in action. Writers? They're wrestling with deadlines and inner demons. Marketers? They're changing their minds every two minutes.

At this point in the process, the designer must bring order through composition. Literally. Poster designers must somehow create a sense of unity from a confusion of headlines, blocks of copy, photographs, and logos. Without unity, a poster becomes chaotic and unreadable. All the parts of a design must fit together to make a coherent whole.

How do we create a "unified" composition? Let's explore some of the classic principles of art and design to find out.

Proximity

The first principle of unity is *proximity*, also called grouping. Proximity is based on a natural principle: Things that belong together, go together. When we see objects that are grouped together on a page, we tend to associate them. We think of them as groups—regardless of whether those objects are actually similar or related. It's like guilt by association.

This law of proximity can assist the poster designer in a number of ways. First, the grouping of people, objects, and text can enhance the message. Think of a billboard in which a customer photo, product shot, and ad slogan are all interwoven. The type of person depicted (kid? grandpa? overworked parent?) will be inevitably associated with the product. If the typography is handled well, it will look like the customer is saying "I always use Bleacho," not the advertiser.

Second, grouping elements together can give them greater impact than if they were standing alone or apart from one another. When several items are placed in close proximity (for example, an interlinked group of watches in different styles), the eye moves smoothly from one to the next. The items become one visual unit, providing a single message for the viewer to look at instead of a set of discrete items.

If a group of items is the most prominent part of the poster, the structure will hold together the overall composition and draw attention to it. Any remaining elements will be viewed as secondary.

FIGURE 8.4: In this diagram, notice how your gaze flows from one circle to the next. The individual items are recognized as parts of the whole, which is the focal point of the design.

Repetition

Another way to create unity in your designs is to repeat shapes, colors, or values. When we see a design element repeated on different parts of a page, our eye naturally follows them, linking them visually even if they are not grouped together. We can't help playing connect the dots.

The simplest way to use repetition is to create a pattern of repeated shapes in the background of the poster. A tiling effect in the background can create a visual interest and structure that ties the foreground elements together. In this type of composition, repetition is a secondary element.

Another way of using repetition is to use a line of repeated elements to lead the eye to an important message, logo, or image. Repeated elements can form a path that draws the eye, creating a sense of suspense—where is this going? It's a way of telling a story and compelling a viewer to look at an item you want him to focus on.

FIGURE 8.5: The series of caterpillars leads the eye directly to the INNU logo. The repetition continues past the logo with the butterflies, which represent how you'll feel after a visit to the salon.

Repetition can work extremely effectively even when objects themselves are not repeated. The mere repetition of a shape or color in a few places can really pull a composition together. It can be very subtle. For example, a poster for a new nail polish might show a large drop of the polish. Elsewhere in composition, the same shape and color may be echoed in the bottle of polish and the model's nails. Without our realizing it, our eyes are drawn to this repetition.

FIGURE 8.6: Here, the dots that are an essential part of the logo are repeated in the illustration—creating unity, getting attention, and reaffirming the brand.

In posters for consumer products, repetition is also an effective strategy for persuading viewers to compare related items. An ad poster might be covered in a dozen pairs of shoes, all different. The initial message (shoes!) is easy to understand because related items are repeated, but a secondary effect is that the poster invites the viewer to look at each pair individually.

Another popular design technique is to present a row or set of items that are all exactly the same except for one that breaks the mold. You might design a grid of 15 squares, 14 of which are blue and 1 that is bright pink and contains a company logo. I know which square people will look at. This stand-out-from-the-pack approach is useful for helping viewers focus on the uniqueness of a product, company, or event. Repeated elements feel mundane, less important, and less exciting than the single, unique one.

It's also worth noting that repetition creates the consistency that is essential when constructing a poster series, whether the posters are to be viewed simultaneously or on separate occasions. A set of outdoor ads designed for a summer concert series must work as a team; seeing one should remind you of other posters in the series. The repetition of positioning, color, scale, or imagery can make a series a cohesive group and promote the recognition and absorption of an overall message.

Continuation

What other techniques for creating unity are there? Continuation is another method for attracting and leading the eye. It's often used in conjunction with repetition, and you've seen it in the prior examples. When a designer uses continuation, the edges of shapes in a composition are aligned to lead the viewer's eye from one item to the next.

This principle uses the properties of lines to help a composition hang together. When we see a line, our eye instinctively wants to follow it, to find out where it leads. The edges of objects can be used in the same way. Any objects in a set can appear disjointed when they are placed on a page. If items just float in space, the viewer has to do too much work to find and ultimately understand the message. By aligning the edges, however—horizontally, vertically, or diagonally—the composition can be unified.

FIGURE 8.7: Continuation is used in this poster to lead the eye vertically, from the text to the U or vice versa. The left and right sides of the U and text line up perfectly, and if "U" look more closely, you'll see the E and C of "PEACE" align with the inner lines of the U.

This technique works with images on a poster, leading the eye to information and branding, but it is also a great choice for text-based designs. Continuation makes it clear which elements (such as headlines and subheads, or photos and captions) are meant to be read together.

Underlying Color

How do you unify a composition where there are a variety of objects with no shapes, colors, or edges in common? A simple solution is to place them on a solid color field.

Now this might beg the question, Why would you place unrelated objects in your poster in the first place? Ordinarily, you wouldn't. For most commercial posters where you need to get a message across quickly, you will generally have access to some related shapes or colors.

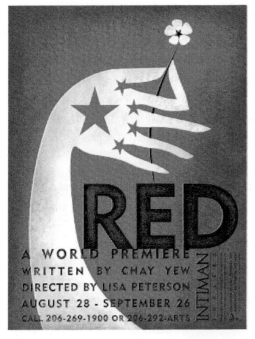

FIGURE 8.8: In this poster, "Red" is not only the name of the performance and an allusion to its political theme, but it's also the color that holds the elements of this design together. Proximity is used along with a strong sense of balance to make this an incredibly strong piece.

For art events or posters where the viewer will have some time to interpret the piece, however, discordant elements can provide an interesting, experimental look. Occasionally an advertiser will ask for a surreal combination of items. Using an underlying color as a background for disjointed elements can ground them so the viewer understands they relate.

Achieving Balance

Balance, or a lack thereof, is a powerful tool for any poster layout. And that's because a lack of balance is disturbing. From a young age, we learn to avoid leaning trees, rocks, furniture, and ladders as potential dangers. Seeing imbalance in a design causes a similar visceral reaction: Are we going to fall over? Is something going to fall on us?

In composition, we assume a center vertical axis and expect to see equal weight on both sides. Balance is especially important in a poster design, because a poster will often need to stand alone, with nothing outside of the design to stabilize it. (Some designs, like magazine ads, can be balanced by the adjacent page or another nearby element.)

> **tip**
>
> A word of warning: Don't use the underlying color method as a quick way to avoid a properly aligned or otherwise unified composition.

Symmetrical Balance

Nature is full of examples of symmetrical balance. Butterflies, maple leaves, and snowflakes can be evenly divided down the center. Humans are attracted to symmetrical designs partially because our own bodies are symmetrical (well, mostly).

Designers play with these visual expectations. In creating a poster, a designer will often place a main image or block of text along a vertical axis, distributing equal portions of the object on both sides. This makes the viewer feel comfortable—everything has been neatly ordered for him. When the "object" placed symmetrically is a face or body, it can help viewers make an emotional connection to the composition.

Symmetrical balance also occurs when multiple objects are placed in the same position on each side of a central vertical axis. This combines the benefits of repetition and symmetry to create a completely balanced, rock-solid design.

FIGURE 8.9: This striking design for Champion Athletic is almost entirely symmetrical along the vertical axis, making the design (and thus the product and brand) feel solid and comfortable. Bold color, lines, and use of negative space give it even more strength.

However, symmetry can have drawbacks. We don't always want a design to feel so solid, so comfortable, or so passive. By their nature, posters are often used to introduce new products, events, or ideas with the purpose of persuading viewers to take action. A more energetic composition may be required for such posters. Note that this doesn't mean developing a composition that is unbalanced—it means using balance in a different way.

▼ note

Symmetry on a horizontal axis can also make for a balanced design, though it doesn't generate the comfort level of vertical symmetry.

Asymmetrical Balance

Asymmetrical balance is a common strategy for adding oomph to a poster design. Designers use color, value, shape, and position to balance dissimilar forms without letting chaos rule. Truly asymmetrical balance can be difficult to achieve—if the sizes, colors, or other elements are just a little off, the equilibrium will be as well.

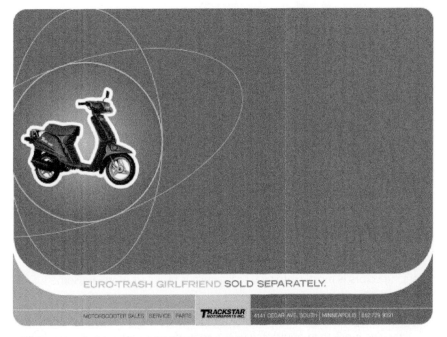

EURO-TRASH GIRLFRIEND **SOLD SEPARATELY.**

MOTORSCOOTER SALES | SERVICE | PARTS   **T**RACKSTAR   4141 CEDAR AVE. SOUTH | MINNEAPOLIS | 612 729 9021

FIGURE 8.10: The asymmetry in this Trackstar Motorsports poster makes the image arresting, and you can almost feel the scooter moving to the right.

Let's look at several types of asymmetrical balance and examine ways to achieve them.

BALANCE BY COLOR

Have you ever wondered what made the painting of Dutch artist Piet Mondrian tick? Mondrian devoted a great deal of his work to the balance of weight in colors. For example, one of his paintings features mostly white blocks with a large yellow block in the upper left and a small blue one in the lower right. The small area of blue perfectly balances the large area of yellow. To form such a balance, Mondrian moved colors around the grid until they were just right.

FIGURE 8.11: In this design exhibition poster, the large yellow field is beautifully balanced by the small black bar and color photos along the bottom.

Balancing colors is mostly intuitive, so practice is required. Here are some guidelines:

- A small area of color can balance a much larger neutral area. Color attracts the eye more than neutrals, giving a spot of color equal weight to a large neutral area.

- Warm colors carry more weight visually than cool colors. Oranges and reds jump out at us, while blues and greens tend to recede. Therefore, a large area of a cool color is needed to balance a small area of a warm color.

- The more vivid the color intensity, the greater its weight. A richly saturated blue will seem heavier than a dull blue. How do you work with this? Balance small bits of vivid color with larger areas of muted color.

BALANCE BY VALUE

Asymmetrical balance is based on equal eye attraction, which occurs when dissimilar objects are balanced so that they are equally interesting to the eye. One element that invariably attracts our attention is *value difference*, the contrast of light and dark. Black against white creates a strong contrast. Gray against white creates less contrast and less visual weight.

How do you balance values to enhance a poster design? You can do it by balancing light and dark values intuitively, the same way you balance shapes—across the surface as a whole. Test your intuition by blocking out any questionable area and looking at the remaining picture. Then unblock it and see whether you feel better about the balance of values and shapes in the design.

> **tip**
>
> If you're not sure about the values of the color choices in your design, convert your image to grayscale momentarily. Seeing just white, gray, and black will give you a better sense of how your lights and darks balance.

FIGURE 8.12: Balance by value is used in this Cub Scouts poster. The blue dots on white create an illusion of very light blue—much lighter than the rich red in the lower section. The elements in each section also balance by value—notice the dark truck and the white lettering.

A contrast of values on each side of a poster creates so much eye interest that a tension is created between the sides. The eye skips from one to the other, wanting to pull the two components together. A visual energy and a subconscious excitement are created simply by the interaction of different elements in the composition.

BALANCE BY SHAPE AND POSITION

Balancing shapes will also help bring unity to your poster design. A large, simple shape (or image or text area) can be balanced by smaller, more complex elements. The larger shape will generally attract attention to the overall composition. The smaller elements will be viewed as secondary, but they can be just as important to the visual equilibrium of the poster.

FIGURE 8.13: In this diagram, the detailed field of varying stars is balanced by the simple, solid wave.

FIGURE 8.14: This type of balance works great in photography-based posters. The large, simple focal point of the man and sneaker balances against the distant and detailed street scene below him.

The positioning or placement of the elements plays an important role in balance. The farther an object is from the center of the page, the more visual weight it will suggest. This visual association is based on our experiences with balance in the real world: On a seesaw, for instance, a child on the end of a beam can lift an adult sitting near the center.

FIGURE 8.15: This outdoor ad for a technology firm dramatizes the concept of customization by showing different sizes. The balance between the XL and XS tees draws the eye to the poster.

A single, very small element can counterbalance a large one (or group) if placed all the way to one side of a poster. For example, a tiny logo might sit flush against the right edge of a horizontal ad while a large photo of a model takes up much of the left side. Although the logo is no match for the large image on its own, its position in the outermost edge of the composition levels the design.

This method of balance applies to angled compositions as well. A large object angled in one direction will usually require a counterbalance in the opposite direction, or the whole poster will appear crooked.

Creating Rhythm

Music creates a structure through rhythm, the repetition and variation of groups of notes. When we hear a musical phrase, we hear the timing of each note and mentally record the spacing from one note to the next. If the rhythm is memorable, we will recognize it every time it is repeated or varied throughout the musical composition.

Rhythm in design works the same way. When you put together a sequence of items for your viewer, you can arrange them rhythmically to make them memorable and moving. This goes beyond the concept of repetition we explored earlier, as you can create visual rhythm in a number of ways.

Repetitive Rhythm

Repetitive rhythm is the successive appearance of groups of elements. A flow of elements with variation is required to make it rhythmic. Think of all the ways that rhythm is achieved in music: Over an underlying pulse, the composer can create long, flowing phrases or short, abrupt ones. Space is necessary, too; the listener must have time to absorb one group of elements before hearing the next.

As a designer, you might repeat a circular shape 20 times in a single poster composition. Repeat the color, position, and contents of the circles to establish a "beat" and provide variety to keep the eye entertained.

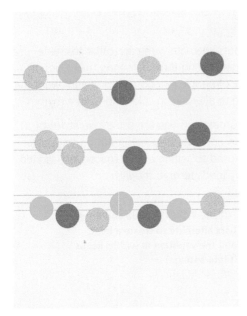

FIGURE 8.16: The circles in this diagram are repeated elements that entertain the viewer as they vary throughout the composition.

FIGURE 8.17: The repeated circle is both a structural and a thematic element in these public service posters – an intriguing visual element and a statement about protecting children.

Alternating Rhythm

In alternating rhythm, two or more motifs alternate with each other to create a sequence or pattern. It's like two singers taking turns delivering their lyrics. If you're working with an image of a row of people in a poster, you might want the models' pants (or even their skin tones) to alternate in color and form a rhythm.

The same goes for the typography in a poster. If you are using two styles of a typeface or two colors of type, you can alternate between them on the poster to create a rhythmic order. We are so used to seeing evenly spaced left-aligned type that any such unusual typography tends to grab the eye.

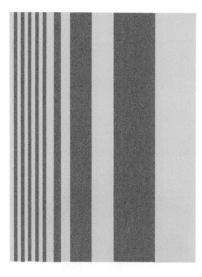

FIGURE 8.18: **The aqua and brown bars alternate to create a beat, and the variation in widths keeps it interesting.**

Note that alternating elements do not need to be boldly different from one another—even subtle variations (such as alternating heights of people in a row) can give a poster added interest. Viewers might not even consciously notice what you are alternating in this case, but the effect will still draw them in and help make the experience memorable.

Progressive Rhythm

In progressive rhythm, the idea of change or at least gradual variation in forms is explored. As the rhythm continues, the forms become more or less intense. The color may become more (or less) vivid, for example. Progressive rhythm is the visual equivalent of a song's crescendo or diminuendo—its increase or decrease in volume.

FIGURE 8.19: A cascade of dancers adorn this dance school poster, creating a visual crescendo that leads to eye from top left to bottom right.

The elements that make up a progressive rhythm—whether they're images or words—must have some qualities in common and some that vary. You might create a diagonal row of butterflies that are all the same shape but gradually change their color, size, and rotation, or a series of identical words that progressively fade, receding into the background.

Progressive rhythm can add depth to otherwise flat posters such as those containing two-dimensional illustrations or only typography. The feeling that something is morphing or coming toward you can make the poster feel more active and lively.

Using Proportion

Most designers rely on their intuitive sense of proportion in approaching a poster. When our intuition hits a roadblock, however, the principles of proportion can be very helpful in determining the correct division of space within a layout. Let's look at some basic ones now.

The Golden Section

The golden section, discovered by the Greeks in the fifth century B.C., was once referred to as a "key" to proportion. The *golden section* is a ratio that divides a whole into two segments so that the smaller segment has the same proportion to the larger that the larger has to the whole. This can be expressed algebraically as *a:b = b:(a+b)*. The sides of a golden rectangle have a proportion of 1:1.618.

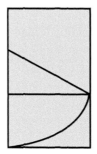

FIGURE 8.20: To construct a golden rectangle, begin with a square. Draw a diagonal from a midpoint of one side to an opposite corner, and then draw an arc from that diagonal.

Whether they realize it or not, most people prefer a rectangle with proportions close to the golden section. A composition using a golden rectangle feels more balanced, comfortable, and natural to the viewer.

Golden section proportions are used in works of sculpture, painting, and architecture. In addition to man-made works, golden section proportions can even be found in humans, plants, and animals.

note

Like vertical symmetry, the golden section is found in nature, which is why it feels familiar and comfortable in a design. Nautilus shells, sunflowers, and pinecones all have features that are closely tied to the golden section ratio.

If you look at a variety of posters, magazine ads, and other rectangular compositions carefully, you'll find that they are often divided into two parts using the golden section, or that the point of interest tends to lie along the line that forms the golden section.

FIGURE 8.21: Loosely based on the golden rectangle, like many posters are, the action in this Theatre Project poster by Spur Design is broken up into a square section (containing the illustration) and a smaller section (containing the type and branding).

The Root 2 Rectangle

Root 2 rectangles are also used in poster layouts, though their proportion is approximately 1:1.414, slightly different from that of the golden rectangle. (If you're wondering how this rectangle got its name, 1.414 is the approximate square root of 2.) The root 2 rectangle is said to be sacred or a symbol of birth, and can be found in some ancient artworks.

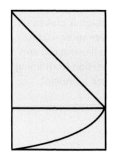

FIGURE 8.22: To construct a root 2 rectangle, draw a diagonal across a square, and then draw an arc from that diagonal.

In poster design, root 2 rectangles are used in the same way that golden rectangles are, forming two balanced sections or providing compelling placement for a point of interest.

FIGURE 8.23: Like posters based on golden rectangles, root 2 posters have a square area as the focal point, as with the bull image in this Professional Bull Riders design. The other section, in this case containing the type, is slightly smaller than that of a golden rectangle design.

Using Typography

The general public usually thinks of graphic design as a nontextual medium—and yet the printed word is considered by many designers to be the most important component of visual communication.

Think of the most compelling, seductive poster you've found on your commute to work. Sure, that grainy image of young lovers running through crashing waves is evocative. But without the skilful use of typography—the company logo, the clever tagline, those small letters declaring *London, Paris, New York, Tokyo*—what does it communicate?

Typography is an essential tool for poster designers, partly because type is so powerful, and partly because it must be used economically to get a message across quickly. Typography today includes everything related to the publication of text and the placement of words and images on the page—so much more than just picking a typeface.

Nevertheless, when designing a poster, choosing a typeface is where typography begins. With thousands of different typefaces available, where do you start?

The desktop publishing revolution encouraged everyone to go mad with fonts. To provide visual consistency, however, an individual poster should use no more than three typefaces. When two or three different typefaces are used, they should be fairly distinct from one another—they should contrast. Alternately, if using multiple variations of a single typeface, each should still be distinct in some way. The items' contrast should indicate which ones are most important. If they are too similar looking, it's confusing for the reader. Especially on a poster, where the message must be delivered quickly, the hierarchy of information should be extremely clear. Care should be taken not to overuse bold and italics. In certain fonts, bold and italics look very different from their parent typefaces.

The Virtues of Typography

Of the many tenets or virtues in typography, perhaps the most important in poster design are simplicity and restraint.

It can be very tempting to use highly decorative fonts. There's no doubt that this can draw attention to your poster design—but not all attention is good attention. The wrong choices, particularly overly decorative ones, can undermine your message. In many cases, a decorative font is not necessary. If there

tip

Just like overly decorative fonts, banal fonts (both simple and decorative) can undermine the message. Try not to rely on the default options that came with your computer—find typefaces that are fresh and work best with the design.

are busy elements in the design, such as photographs or many repeating elements, a simple font and perhaps a variation of it may be all you need to get your message across. It will balance out the other busy elements and call attention that way.

In a simpler overall design, a more complex font can be introduced for your main text. This can serve two purposes. First, it helps to decorate the design and add interest to the entire look. Second, it draws attention to the main text. A simple font can get lost in an ultrasimple design.

When using a decorative font, though, it's important to use it as sparingly as possible, such as for just a word or two of the main text rather than all of the copy in a design. Using a cleaner font for secondary type will balance with the decorative font and will more strongly convey the hierarchy of text.

This leads to the other important virtues in font usage: balance and contrast. The tension between these two elements can help a design capture attention or stand out from the crowd. Balance and contrast can be created between typefaces or between text and other elements, like images.

FIGURE 8.24: An ad campaign to raise public support for hosting the 2012 Olympics in New York City began with an image – a logo that combined an image of an athlete with and image of the Statue of Liberty. The logo appeared all around the city, even on subway trains.

FIGURE 8.25: The outdoor ad campaign for the NYC 2012 bid was pure typography: aspirational messages in the many colors of the Olympic rings, depicting the feeling of the witnessing the event, some horizontal and others hanging banners of text.

Think back to the compositional tools we talked about earlier, like asymmetrical balance and repetitive rhythm. These aren't limited to images and geometric shapes. Juxtaposing text against text or image against text works just as effectively with these techniques.

Finally, there's the virtue of placement—not the placement of text on the page, but the placement of your poster in public. Will it be in a subway car, where you have time to read several lines of text? Or on a street poster that you're zipping past in your car? Your poster's surroundings should determine your use of text—including your choice of typeface, the size and spacing around the text, and the level of contrast against the background.

Poster Design Project

Throughout this chapter, you learned how to direct the viewer's attention using a variety of compositional techniques. Now you'll use this knowledge to design an event poster that interests and informs.

Your client is giving you a lot of creative freedom for the poster, so use it wisely. Consider methods for getting the message across economically with a killer composition and use of typography.

Project Brief: Mozart Festival

You have been commissioned to design a poster for a touring Mozart festival that's visiting your city. The festival, which originated at New York's Lincoln Center for the Performing Arts, celebrates the compositions of Mozart plus a few other classical music icons such as Beethoven, Schubert, and Haydn.

Your client would like an effective poster design that captures the sophisticated but fun spirit of the festival. The poster will be displayed outside your town theater, so it must be designed to be viewed from a distance. Pedestrian passersby will see it, as will commuters on bikes and in cars.

FIGURE 8.26: **Arts organizations like New York's Lincoln Center for the Performing Arts rely on posters to advertise a multitude of events and performances to passersby.**

The festival is aimed at classical music fans, who are typically older and more affluent, but organizers are also hoping to get a younger crowd interested in classical music.

The dimensions of the poster are 20 inches wide by 30 inches tall, to fit in a vertical marquee, but for the purposes of this project you may scale it down to 10 inches wide by 15 inches tall, or 4 by 6.

The copy should read:

The New York Traveling Orchestra presents:

Mozart Festival

Discover Mozart, Beethoven, and more

[insert your local venue name]

[insert a date of your choice]

Project Summary

- Research the subject and location for the poster, and find appropriate images to use in the design.

- Conceptualize the poster design, considering the target audience and your research.

- Choose the compositional techniques you feel are appropriate to delivering your message.

- Produce the poster, considering the focal point, the hierarchy of information, and the presentation of typography.

Project Steps

Like every good design project, this one will start with some research and conceptualization—then it's onto your creative composition.

1. Research the Subject and Location

Unless you're quite the classical music aficionado, you'll need to spend some time understanding the graphic style typically used in this genre. CD covers, Web sites, other classical music event posters—all of these should be part of your research. Ask yourself some questions as you work:

- What colors are common in this genre? What feelings do they evoke?

- What styles of type are used? What do they tell me about how the music might sound?

- Are photographs or illustrations used? How are they used, and what effect do they have?

As you view the artwork, try to put yourself in the shoes of a typical member of the target audience, and consider the location of the poster outside the theater. If you can, visit a theater in your area to see what environmental features may enhance or get in the way of your poster. For example, if the theater's exterior is red brick, you may want to stay away from a dark red main color so as to keep the poster from blending in too much.

FIGURE 8.27: This poster for the Cascade Festival of Music has a goal similar to that of your poster project, and achieves it with balanced composition, text with a rhythmic beat, and an image that suggests both the location and the music.

2. Conceptualize and Find Images

With research in hand, plan a concept that integrates your city and the Mozart/ classical music theme. And don't forget the audience! How will you design your poster to reach true classical music fans as well as energize young newcomers?

As you conceptualize, don't worry too much about specifics. For now, just get a sense of the direction and tone you think your poster should take, what types of colors and images are appropriate, and how you can get the message across quickly within its environment.

From here, you can begin finding the images you plan to use, if any. (A text-based design is perfectly valid, too, as long as it is effective.) If possible, take your own photos or make your own illustrations—but you may use other sources for your images as you see fit.

3. Sketch Out Your Composition

If your concept is developed and you know which text and images you will use, you can plan your composition. Decide which part of the design is the focal point, how you will move the viewer through the design, and how you will create a hierarchy of information.

Before you begin, review the techniques for unity, balance, rhythm, and proportion. Start sketching while you consider the following:

- How will you unify the various elements of your poster? Should any elements be repeated, aligned, or grouped? How will your choice influence the recognition of the poster and the delivery of its message?

- How will you balance this vertical poster—symmetrically or asymmetrically? How will this choice help draw attention to the poster? If asymmetrically, how can you use your design elements to form the balance? Consider color, size, position, value, and so on.

- Is a rhythm or "beat" appropriate to this poster? If so, how will you create it using your design elements?

- Do you plan to work with a golden rectangle or root 2 rectangle? If so, how? Remember, you can break up the poster according to the golden section or root 2 proportion, or you can place your point of interest along its dividing segment.

4. Produce Your Artwork

Don't confine yourself here. Begin on a fresh Photoshop canvas in the size you'd like to work with (4" by 6", 10" by 15", or the actual size of 20" by 30", which is great for your portfolio), and produce your background elements. To help you along, you may want to overlay a grid on your canvas (View > Show > Grid), or show the document rulers (View > Rulers).

With background elements in place (colors, patterns, geometric areas, and so on), you can bring in your photographs or illustrations. If you need to edit them or clean them up, do that first, and then position them according to the composition decisions you made.

Nothing is set in stone—take a step back and see if this composition truly gets your point across in the best way possible. Simple tweaks to the placement, value, or size of your images can often turn an off-kilter layout into a more balanced one.

5. Incorporate Typography

Now you can add your typography. As you set all of the wording supplied by the client, consider the virtues we discussed—simplicity, balance, and placement. How will you make the text easy to read (but still interesting!), balance it with other elements, and be sure it is appropriate to the public placement of your poster?

Choose your typefaces carefully, remembering to stick to just a couple and to go decorative only when appropriate. And don't forget the personality of your type and how it works within your overall composition scheme. Will it engage audiences young and old? Will it give the festival the appropriate tone? Is the hierarchy clear?

6. Review Your Work

Make any final tweaks that you feel are appropriate, and then take a step back and look at your work.

How do the shapes relate to each other? Is your design unified and balanced? Do you feel a sense of rhythm? Is there a clear focal point? Good; now you are ready to present your work to the client!

If you want to go one step further, why not adapt your composition to a horizontal format? Suppose it will be used for advertisement on the side of a bus. The dimensions should be 12" by 4" for this optional project.

Student Work

Here are some sample posters from Sessions students with a similar music project:

FIGURE 8.28: Hammad Iqbal creates a strong balance in his muted, sophisticated composition, and keeps the text simple and clean against the detailed photography.

FIGURE 8.29: Wilbert Reddit makes some great type choices in this poster. Notice the interesting negative space created by the outline of the violin.

FIGURE 8.30: Ulf Finndahl's poster uses a large, simplified photo to balance perfectly with the smaller, more detailed photo and typography. Also notice how the violin itself leads the eye.

9 Logo Design

What's in a name? Everything, if you're a logo designer. An effective logo represents much more than a company, product, or service. From Des Moines to Dubai, logos fly the flag of an increasingly global business world, setting off emotions, triggering desires, creating identities, and (occasionally) sparking riots.

Logo work is a challenging and specialized niche for a graphic designer. Successful logos achieve a balance between clear communication and flexibility. This requires a simplicity that's hard to achieve but essential to the solution of corporate identity.

In the following chapter, you'll explore some important concepts that every logo designer should have under his or her belt. You'll learn about the role of fundamental shapes and symbols, get tips on the professional design process, and explore some typography basics.

FIGURE 9.1: The logo and visual identity design for Menu Pages, an innovative new restaurant search site.

In this chapter you will:

- Learn some of the principles of logo design.

- Discover how the field of logo design evolved.

- Learn how to identify three classic logo design genres.

- Gain insights into the professional logo design process.

- Explore important typography concepts for logo design.

- Learn how to manipulate text in Illustrator for your logo design projects.

- Tackle a challenging logo project: designing a record label.

Logo Design Fundamentals

A logo is just one element in a corporate identity system, but its importance cannot be underestimated. Everything about a company—its products, people, and place in the market—contributes to our perception of its identity. But ultimately it's the logo, a simple combination of letters or symbols, that has the tough job: to identify a company and express its personality at a glance.

Effective logos, said the late great American designer Paul Rand, are like flags: universal, timeless, and durable. Logos vary greatly in scope and breadth: They can be letters or numbers; circles, squares, or triangles; or suns, moons, or stars. In fact, many fundamental shapes and symbols are the cornerstones of the logos we see every day.

FIGURE 9.2: **See anything familiar? Logo designs tap the underlying properties of letters, numbers, shapes, and symbols and make them memorable.**

What are the design objectives that define a successful logo? While each logo is unique, the best ones share some similar qualities.

THREE CORE PRINCIPLES

First, a logo must be practical. It must work at both large and small sizes, and in black and white as well as full color. It must translate well across a wide range of media, from billboards and newspapers, to Web sites and TV broadcasts. Unlike other representations of a corporation or organization (such as letterheads, business cards, and Web pages), a logo cannot—or at least should not—be hastily updated or modified to fulfill sudden changes in management directives.

Second, a logo must communicate on several levels. Even if a logo is just typography (and many are), it must communicate:

- A company description (who is the company?)

- A simple emotion (what kind of company is this?)

- A business aspiration (what are the company's goals or defining principles?)

Third, and most importantly, a logo must hold a quality of visual appeal that Paul Rand once described as "sheer pleasure." When you see it, a logo should immediately trigger a visceral reaction: communication, identification, and emotion.

▼ note

The late Paul Rand was a great American designer who created visual identities for ABC, IBM, UPS, and many other companies.

FIGURE 9.3: Logo design concept for an Internet service provider. Chunky but stylish typography and illustration reinforce the company's name, its core service (providing bandwidth), and its youthful, fun approach.

FIGURE 9.4: Logo design for a medical services company. As befits the industry, this logo is more sober and restrained, though a nice compositional balance and modern colors help distinguish the company from stodgy competitors.

Ultimate objectives aside, what really makes a logo work? There is no easy or exact answer to this question. A logo is a shorthand signature (sometimes literally) that expresses the company or product it represents. And like a signature, it has the power to impart personality, definition, and dimension.

FIGURE 9.5: A logo is like the signature of a company or organization. In this National Constitution Center logo, the script font and quill image evoke the signing of the Declaration of Independence.

Of course, while a great logo (sometimes called a *logomark* or *mark*) has the power to elicit a desired emotion, it's also true that an ill-conceived or misappropriated design can trigger an unintended negative reaction from its audience. For that reason, logo design projects are intensively critiqued and meticulously researched. It takes passion and precision on the part of the designer to get it right.

A Short History

How did logo design come about? Let's take a trip back through time.

Prehistoric Origins

Nike may be new, but logos are prehistoric. Identifiers have been around since before human history, when early Homo sapiens smeared blue mud on themselves during territorial battles with the Cro-Magnons so that in the heat of conflict they could identify whose brains to bash out. And which identifier won, you might ask? Talk about functional design!

Symbols occupy an important place in the history of human communication. Linguists believe that our languages all started with a need to externalize thoughts and ideas—at first as simple grunts and groans—that eventually evolved into speech. Symbols helped this process along, as they were first used to identify different social groups, and later used to communicate concepts and ideas.

note

Many logo symbols incorporate symbols indicating ownership or status (think of crowns and shields) and have been used for centuries by monarchs and powerful organizations.

FLATIRON RELAY

FLATIRON DESIGN

FLATIRON INDUSTRIES

FIGURE 9.6: Four early iterations of logos for my company Flatiron Industries. These designs explored the potential of various time-honored marks: a globe, architecture (the Flatiron building), shields, and stars.

Simple signs were humanity's first attempt to communicate without sounds. As verbal communication evolved, so too did the need to project our thoughts in a more concrete form. Words and hand signs could easily be misinterpreted or misconstrued, but marks were reliable and definitive. A symbol became something you could trust. Symbol-making itself became a visual form of spoken language that eventually developed into writing.

FIGURE 9.7: The internationally recognized and beautifully realized Canada Dry logo is built on a shield and a crown, symbols of strength and trust.

The fundamental symbols upon which today's logos are based can still be a rich source of inspiration. Shape itself has overtones. A circle, for example, was originally used to signify the endlessness of the universe. It was a symbol for God. A square, on the other side of the design spectrum, signified the earth and physical matter. Squares today are symbols of order and restraint, more rational and less spiritual than circles.

FIGURE 9.8: The Packiderm logo, by DesignKitchen, created a beautiful elephant from a simple square. The square is a very appropriate and efficient symbol for a storage company.

If you look around you, you'll see that ancient symbols such as crosses, keys, shields, and flags are constantly being reused and reinvented in the field of commercial logo design. The term for such identifying symbols is "logo," from the Greek term meaning "the word" or "the way." From the beginning, the word *logo* has meant a visual representation that symbolizes or communicates an idea or meaning. There is no incompatibility between the simple and the complex in this form of visual communication.

Early Logos

How did logo design evolve? Let's look at two early examples of the medium.

Procter and Gamble

By the beginning of the 19th century, trademarks began to play a pivotal role in the establishment of brand recognition. Procter and Gamble was one of the first companies to capitalize on the use of trademarks. In its early days, the company shipped candles to ports along the Ohio and Mississippi Rivers. Wharf men stamped the company's crates of candles with a crude star image to differentiate them from those of other suppliers.

P&G soon noticed that its distributors would recognize the containers as holding their goods. After the company refined the mark, the symbol became, well, a true "symbol" of quality merchandise—and distributors would pay top dollar for the "starred" crates.

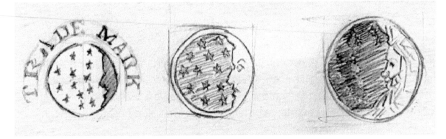

FIGURE 9:9: The early P&G logo looked something like this sketch—it combined a moon and stars representing states.

Aspects of the mark were carried into the 20th century, but its privileged status did not last. In 1982, the Procter and Gamble logo became the focus of a bizarre, potentially damaging rumor that claimed the company was involved in devil worship because of the 13 stars that the designer incorporated into the logo design. (The stars, a reference to states in the union at the time of the logo's creation, were actually intended to be a patriotic gesture.) After trying to find a way to suppress these falsehoods, the company decided to drop the mark from its products for good.

The World's Fair

The 1939 World's Fair provided hope for a United States emerging from the Great Depression. The fair, with its emphasis on product consumption, had as its centerpiece the Perisphere and the Trylon, symbols that were widely applied to the memorabilia sold at the fair. These symbols and how they were marketed truly exemplified the theme of the fair: "The World of Tomorrow."

FIGURE 9.10: The Perisphere and Trylon symbols sketched here were emblazoned on memorabilia sold at the World's Fair.

Today, of course, they represent the past. Logos (like languages) are not immortal. Many of our human languages have died out over time (Sanskrit, anyone?). Logos can perish too, so they must be designed for longevity. Symbols, marks, logos—whatever you'd like to call them—represent value because they can communicate meaning over time.

At the same time, a designer must know that nothing lasts forever. The World's Fair identity is beautiful but unmistakably associated with a specific period. As times change, so does the style of symbols—with more complex levels of information necessitating an innovation in the forms used to communicate new ideas.

Three Logo Categories

The discipline of logo design is boundless in its creative possibilities. A logo designer can choose from a host of different techniques and styles to achieve the desired goal. When you're starting out, though, it's helpful to think about the main categories of logo design that can be used independently or combined within one design.

Typographic Logos

Typographic logos—just type—are the most common logos, since they can be quick to assemble. It's a straightforward way of defining a company. But don't be fooled into thinking that a typographic logo is easy to do well. An expert handling of typography is required to create a readable, memorable, personable mark. Often a typographic logo is a starting point for the addition of descriptive or symbolic elements.

ANGEL™ | LEARNING MANAGEMENT SUITE

FIGURE 9.11: ANGEL Learning developed this balanced typographical identity for its product, an online course management system.

Descriptive Logos

Descriptive logos draw a direct correlation between their visual message and their owner's products or services. The logo can represent a product, demonstrate an area of expertise, and/or define the cause or mission of the organization. Broadly speaking, a descriptive logo says "Here's what we do." It follows that any symbol used to define the purpose of an organization must be handled with care.

FIGURE 9.12: **A descriptive logo for MultiMed Solutions illustrates what the company does.**

FIGURE 9.13: **Without the cell phone icon, would you know that the CareText company provides a phone text service?**

CARETEXT*

Symbolic Logos

Symbolic logos incorporate a figurative element into the overall design. These symbols play off an intangible or abstract theme that relates to the company or organization's overall business or purpose. Broadly speaking, the combination of type and logo says "Here's what we stand for."

FIGURE 9.14: **The Worldwide Studios logo uses a compass to depict a company that navigates global priorities.**

FIGURE 9.15: The I-silver logo uses a circle to represent Earth and file-loading symbols to represent Internet technology.

Inside the Design Process

If you're hoping to take on professional logo design projects, you'll need to develop a design process with latitude for creativity and room for multiple rounds of interaction with and feedback from the client.

Remember, you're designing a logo or visual identity that meets the needs of a company and its customers—not to suit your own creative whims! You must be prepared to set up plenty of client meetings, ask lots of intelligent questions, and steel yourself for a few twists and turns as you present your work at each stage along the way.

This section has some thoughts on the logo designer's approach to projects. The design process is typically structured in three steps, for sanity's sake. I'll also offer some insights on getting your projects off the ground.

FIGURE 9.16: One-of-a-kind product, one-of-a-kind logo. The visual identity for Shawnimals uses off-center typography and an illustration of a handmade stuffed animal to convey the nature of its product.

FIGURE 9.17: This nicely descriptive Sewing Stars logo also looks handmade, as befits an arts and crafts company.

Three Steps to Success

1. Expansion and evolution. Got a client? Then get to know the client's business and determine his or her needs. Evolve your design, brainstorming a wide range of possible design solutions. Schedule your project and price it appropriately.

2. Contraction and definition. Present your visual ideas to the client, and use the client's feedback to narrow options to a few leading designs. Hone the artwork to address such key issues as legibility, simplicity, and typography. Look for a solution that is easy to read, simple enough to grasp at a glance, and supported by appropriate typography.

3. Finalization and presentation. Present your final designs confidently, and handle client feedback in a professional manner that moves the project forward, not backward. Final changes often occur at this stage. Then make a polished presentation of the final work and give the client art specifications for implementing the design.

Tips for Your Design Process

Before beginning any design work, you must look at the logo or visual identity the client's company or organization already has in place. Your first design jobs may be for pro bono clients or small businesses that are starting from scratch. However, very few professional projects are undertaken for clients with no prior visual identity. Evaluate the client's brand as if you were *not* the designer hired to revamp it.

Audit the Existing Identity

One key question is how much brand equity the company's current name and visual identity has established over the years. Visual identities always have a track record with companies and customers. Strengths and weaknesses will emerge from your initial interviews. More than likely, you will want to retain the favorable aspects of a current design.

Your consultation might conclude that the current brand identity doesn't really need to be changed at all, or that a few slight modifications will do the trick. Such honesty may not make you rich, but it will lend you credibility as a professional and establish you as a serious design consultant.

Alternatively, perhaps nothing less than a radical redesign may be required. If so, be honest about that too. Clients need to be told when their identities are ill-conceived, inappropriate, or just plain stuck-in-the-mud ugly! You're there to clarify the issues and save the day.

> **tip**
>
> Many logo design projects require you to refresh an existing design rather than overhaul it. Find out early on which aspects of an existing identity are judged successful by clients and customers.

Research the Company

To create a logo and identity system that will grow with the client's needs, it's important that you get as much background on where your client's company is headed—what it is trying to achieve not just this year but also five years down the road.

FIGURE 9.18: Menu Pages, a New York area online restaurant guide, was a new client with a very specific brief: to evoke the excitement of eating out. The approach was a stylized logo treatment redolent of 1950s diner signs.

If your client has been around for a long time, it will behoove you to examine past marketing efforts to discover some previously used visual resources. You may discover some earlier visual message in an old advertisement, some well-defined mission statement that will set off a visual cue, or even a previous logo buried long ago that could be refined and incorporated into your client's current visual direction.

Never forget that the inspiration for a logo design can come from current or past sources. Keep your mind and eyes open from the outset of a branding project. Recognize the value in any work that was done prior to your involvement—treat it with the respect that you would hope later designers will accord to your work.

Start with a Sketch

The most polished design can start with a sketch. I am not a skilled illustrator by any means, but I find that sketching helps my ability to explore as many design directions as possible.

Many of today's designers immediately start work in their favorite graphics software programs, such as Illustrator, Photoshop, or Freehand. That's not wrong, but it can be limiting. Putting pencil to paper will often give you the freedom to explore initial ideas unencumbered by email distractions, technical glitches, or computer design techniques that (trust me) can look like worn-out design elements.

How many visual ideas can you sketch in a minute? How many can you draw in Illustrator? Now you see why sketching is a great way of opening yourself up to creative possibilities.

Don't be a "safe" designer who concocts ideas only through a computer mouse. You may think you're saving time, since you'll eventually work on most of the design on your computer, but you're really restricting yourself by not at least exploring what you can draw out on paper. (Of course, this is a technique issue, and different designers work differently. But do make sure you explore various options when coming up with your initial creative ideas.)

Think in Black and White

Always take the initial steps of designing in pure black and white. The shape of your design should be refined and established before you even think about adding color. Applying color to an evolving design too early will only mask any flaws in the form of the design.

And since most logos will eventually appear in black and white in some form during their use, it's better to discover any design flaws during the creative process rather than after the logo has been implemented.

FIGURE 9.19: **Print your logo in black and white and at different sizes to make sure it is legible.**

Pricing and Scheduling

Fact: Multinational companies pay tens of thousands of dollars for their logo designs. That's a measure of the importance of logo design to a large corporation.

If you're starting out as a logo designer, you may not be pitching your work to Apple or Microsoft. But you still need to charge an amount that reflects your expertise, your time, and the value of a successful logo design (the end result). Quality design takes time, professional skill, the latest software and hardware, and knowledge of current graphics industry standards. These all cost money.

My approach is to charge a realistic professional rate, and back it up with hourly work estimates if necessary. Prices for developing a logo range from a few hundred dollars to thousands. But—of course—the price you charge should *not* be the only factor when a client is looking for a designer or design firm to develop a brand identity.

> **tip**
>
> Never underestimate the value of well-designed visual identity to a client, who may use it in literally millions of communications.

If a client balks at your professional quote, you have several options. Explain the process in depth. Show the client your previous excellent work. Emphasize the power of branding (positive or negative), perhaps by referring to real-life examples that the client will recognize. If your client is looking for a bargain price rather than skill, service, and technical knowledge, warning lights should go off. Logo design is like any other commodity—you get what you pay for.

Faster Is Not (Necessarily) Better

Thinking takes time. Takes me time, anyway! Logo designers who crank out a logo in a day or two as a standard service are doing just that—cranking 'em out. Quality design takes time. It's as simple as that.

Consider all the steps in the process. Designers must research a company, a market, and a client's needs. They then must create original work that can be trademarked and/or copyrighted. Otherwise the client may run with the logo, printing it on everything in sight, only to find out that the icon that took two days to create came from an obscure clip art CD, and is in fact being used by dozens of other companies—ooof!

Reputable design firms usually charge high premiums for rushed design work, and that's because a team of designers must drop all other projects and concentrate all their energy, time, and equipment on a project that requires overtime salaries to be paid. Time and energy is required for innovative design. Keep in mind that the less distinctive your logo, the more difficult it is to trademark. Three multicolored brushstrokes may be wonderful and all, but the trademark office won't think so.

Meetings and Presentations

The contraction phase is the part of your project in which 20 great ideas get whittled down to 1 or 2. It's time to execute something specific. During this part of the process, it is essential that you as a designer hit your creative brakes and switch gears from being an idea generator to becoming a client advocate. It's a whole new ballgame.

When you meet with clients about identity projects, the process inevitably becomes personal. What a client is really asking you to do is to put a new face on the work he does or the product he creates. It's important to establish trust between yourself and the client, who's counting on you to give his product or service a makeover.

FIGURE 9.20: **The Menu Pages logo ultimately required some additional elements that could be applied in different areas at the company Web site. Typographic, descriptive, and symbolic, all in one logo!**

Presenting a logo to a client can be a daunting task, since you're trying to distill a company's attributes and brand objectives into a unique and memorable mark that will capture the essence of what the company represents. Even though a logo is a single mark, it will always need to be integrated into whatever branding system is already developed. So be sure to define at the outset how and where the new identity system will be applied within the company's existing branding strategy.

Typographic Techniques

What do you need to know about typography to design logos? Here are some design fundamentals to consider.

Selecting a Letterform

Thousands upon thousands of typefaces are available today with a few clicks of your mouse. But that doesn't necessarily mean that your logo design solution will be found within any typeface collection. Type foundries produce high-quality letterforms with style, creativity, and grace, but a specific design problem often requires a specific design solution. Many times a designer will produce a whole new typeface to apply to a client's identity.

Other times you will find that an existing typeface can be used, with modifications to individual characters, to fit a client's personality initially. Establishing an initial look through the selection of typeface is a great starting point for establishing a company's identity. Inventive symbols are often generated from a play on a letterform within the client's name.

 BRETFORD

FIGURE 9.21: The Bretford furniture logo, designed by PlanetPropaganda, exhibits a masterful use of typography. Just look at the many facets of the letter *B*.

Letterforms as a Visual Language

Creativity is the process of seeing limitless possibilities. Most people would feel greatly limited by the idea of using a single letter for a logo. But a designer should be able to see the opportunity to apply one of thousands of typefaces to a particular letter, with the possibility of creating a new typeface for that particular letterform.

FIGURE 9.22: Can a single letter represent a company? This three-dimensional *G* provides an appropriately assertive touch.

Many designers prefer to begin developing a logo that consists entirely of text. By experimenting with fonts, size, and shapes, they seek to find an interesting way to represent the company using the form of letters. Again, simplicity is extremely important—this is not the time to use fancy decorative fonts. Whether alone or combined with graphic elements, the text in a logo must be easily readable at small sizes.

Consider every nuance as you look at letterforms. Being able to explain the background and reasoning for your decisions can be a great benefit in discussions with clients. You must effectively communicate the specialized descriptive terms for professional lettering. A logotype must be legible, particularly if no illustrations are added to make it distinctive.

Kerning Letters

To really make your logo's typography stand out, you'll need to explore the technique of kerning. *Kerning* refers to adjusting the space between two letters. Kerning is usually focused on large type, logos, and headlines—places where such tweaking is the most needed.

Why does kerning often need adjusting? Blame the digital design tools you love. Most people think good type just pops out of the computer by default. On the contrary, graphics programs usually approximate the kerning between digital letters for convenience.

Most of the time, type is set small and the computer does a respectable job of adjusting the kerning by default. But when you are working with large type, you should always take a closer look—more than likely you'll find some inaccuracies in the spacing between letters. Your goal with kerning is to adjust the positive and negative space between the letterforms so that the rhythm appears visually consistent—flowing without gaps or tight spaces.

FLATIRONWORKS

FIGURE 9.23: To illustrate that logo design is indeed a process of evolution, here's how my company logo for Flatiron Industries ultimately turned out. The anvil symbol plays unexpectedly off the theme of ironwork. Hard work, logo design!

Record Label Project

In this chapter's project, we'll roll up our sleeves to create a new logo identity, coming up with three different logos for a record label. It's common in logo design projects to create at least three versions of a logo for a client to review. I would recommend that you begin by creating your logos in black and white. It is important that a logo's design hold up in black-and-white form before it is tested with different color treatments.

FIGURE 9.24: Musical tastes vary greatly. And, as we'll soon find out, so do tastes in logo design.

Case Study: Dinny Bin Records

Here's a case study just for kicks. This is a recent logo I designed for a small record label, Dinny Bin Records. This company has only a few select clients, but it wanted a new logo design for the launch of its latest CD, *This Time* by Eddie Elliott (one of the record label's founders).

The company was named after an imaginary character who lived under the bed of the producer who works for the label. Not much of a background story on the logo's origins, but sometimes a playful, incidental name can give a designer the freedom to invent an original, unique design that does not have to adhere to any strict corporate brand strategy.

FIGURE 9.25: Dinny Bin Records' logo was created for a creature under the bed.

Project Summary

Think up a memorable name for a record label.

Research, brainstorm, and sketch your concepts.

Design three distinct black-and-white logos for the record label in Illustrator.

Project Steps

1. Do Some Research

Before you open up Illustrator and begin designing, do some research. Try to think of a company name that has graphic potential. Remember, logo design is a conceptual challenge as well as an artistic one.

Creating a contact sheet of established logos related to the project can be very helpful to your design process. What's been done? What hasn't? If you take a look at your CD collection, you'll find that record label designs can take many different directions. The freedom of the product (music) affords the designer an infinite amount of creativity to visually define what the record company stands for.

2. Brainstorm and Sketch

Feel free to apply more than one of the three categories (symbolic, typographic, or descriptive) to your designs—or even try to incorporate all three. There are no parameters to the creativity and imagination that you can use for this project. Maybe the label will be named after you! You might want to use an old advertising image of a microphone or a phonograph. The only limit is the edge of your imagination.

3. Select and Modify Font and Character Settings

Manipulating type is a large part of designing in Illustrator, whether you're creating logos, graphics, design layouts, or illustrations. You covered some basic text tools in Chapter 2 of this book. Now it's time to stretch it further.

Type the word **Illustrator** on the Artboard with the Type tool, and then select it. Turn on the Character palette (Window > Type > Character). The overall role of this palette within Illustrator is to provide you greater control over your type.

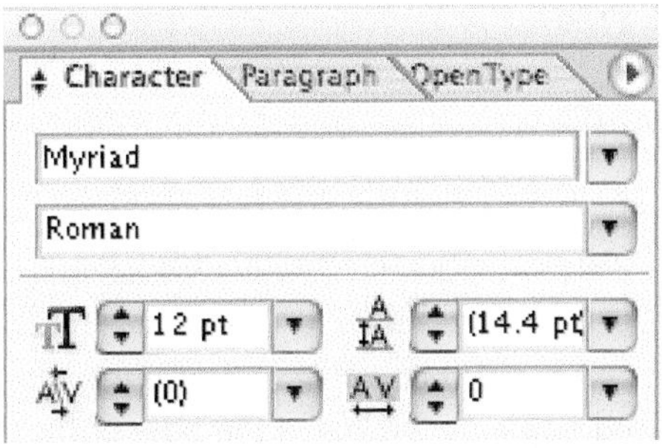

FIGURE 9.26: The Character palette.

The palette displays both the name of the currently selected font and its style (bold, italic, regular, and so on). The name and style each feature a drop-down list of available choices. Make a new choice, if you desire.

Just below the font name is Font Size. Choose a size by using the up and down arrows, selecting predefined sizes from the drop-down list, or entering a value yourself. Type a value of **100** and press Enter/Return to enlarge the word (unless your type size was already set to 100 or more).

4. Adjust Leading and Kerning

To the right of the Font Size box is the Leading function. *Leading* controls the amount of space between individual lines of type. For spacing between individual letters, kerning and tracking controls are available. Most logos have just a single line of type, but this feature is useful if you happen to have more.

Whereas kerning adjusts the spacing between two letters, tracking handles a selection of any number of letters. To change the tracking of characters, click and drag the Type tool I-beam cursor to select the letters you wish to change. Place the I-beam between two letters to use the kerning feature.

You can use the Character palette to make modifications to a letter's scale. Open the palette's option menu and select Show Options. Three new controls appear: Vertical Scale, Horizontal Scale, and Baseline Shift.

FIGURE 9.27: Other options in the Character palette.

Take your pick of either scale box and enter a value of 300 in one of them. You break my heart every time you do this. Moving along…

The Baseline Shift option moves letters or words either above or below the text baseline. Select *Illustrator* on the Artboard and note the line at the base of the text. That's the baseline! Select a letter or two and enter a value (positive or negative) to see its effect. The drop-down list features predefined numbers to select from as well.

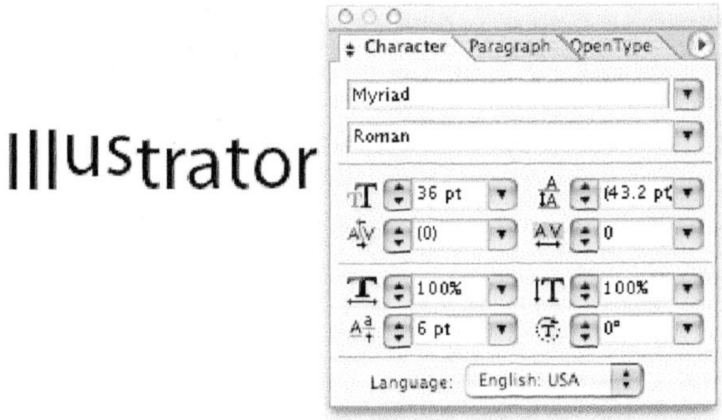

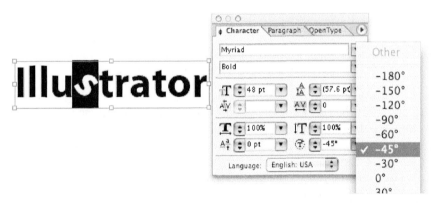

FIGURE 9.28: **Using a baseline shift can move a letter or word off the baseline. Here, the *us* in *Illustrator* was moved up 6 points.**

5. Rotate Characters and Use OpenType

The Character Rotation option can rotate individual letters 360 degrees in a line of type. Give it a spin!

FIGURE 9.29: **Character rotation will angle letters off the vertical axis.**

Rotating a single character in a logo, even slightly, can add something memorable and unusual to the design, as long as it's also still clear and readable. Select a single letter of your word, and enter an angle (or choose one of the presets) in the Character Rotation field of the Character palette. This operation can also be performed on a selected series of letters.

Another new addition to Illustrator CS is the OpenType palette, which provides a wide range of controls and commands when working with this relatively new typeface format. Whereas TrueType and PostScript typefaces were limited in range by the number of characters they could contain within a font file, OpenType allows for vastly more characters such as ligatures, old-style figures, small caps, and so on. Adobe ships Illustrator with a number of OpenType typefaces, which are identified by this icon and/or by the addition of the word *Pro* to the end of the name.

FIGURE 9.30: The OpenType palette.

6. Type in an Area

You may want to create a logo to fit a shape or a path. For this you'll need to try out the other type tools: the Area Type tool and Path Type tool.

Find a clean area on your Artboard, or create a new document to begin this discussion. Select the Polygon tool from the Rectangle tool fly-out, and click the Artboard to display its options. Enter a value of **100** for Radius and **6** for Sides, creating a hexagon. Click OK. Select the Area Type tool 🔟 (note the different I-beam cursor) and click the edge of the hexagon shape. The shape is now an object we can type within. Go ahead, type a few lines. You can use this tool to type within any closed path.

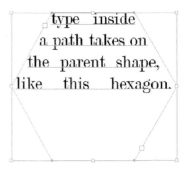

FIGURE 9.31: The Area Type tool.

This tool's cousin is the Vertical Area Type tool ▣. With it, text cascades down a shape's interior. For those of you wondering whether you can use the Vertical Area Type tool to manipulate text you've typed with the regular Area Type tool, wonder no more: The answer is that you cannot. We live in such a cruel world, huh?

7. Type on a Path

Of the type tools, the Path Type tool ▣ (and its vertical cousin) is the most fun. With it, you can type text around the edge of a star or along the contour of a scribble. Anywhere there's a path, you can type on it.

To try this out, set the Fill in the toolbox to None and the Stroke to black ▣. Select the Pencil tool and a draw a simple, continuous path all over the Artboard. Select the Path Type tool and take a close look at the cursor. It changes to the now familiar I-beam and has a small slanted line running through it. The point at which the I-beam intersects with the slanted line is the point you want to click on a path lest you generate one of Illustrator's many errors.

If you click correctly, the path turns into an outline, a simple I-beam cursor appears, and a flashing cursor indicates where to begin typing. So type away and watch as your text follows the twist and turns of your path.

FIGURE 9.32: What's my line? You can draw a line and flow text along it.

To position your text elsewhere on the path, use either the Selection tool or the Direct Selection tool and click and drag the bottom of the I-beam that appears at the beginning of the text. To drag your text to the other side of the path, click and drag the I-beam toward the opposite side of the path until the text reverses direction and turns upside down. This tool is finicky when moving the text about, so be patient. Don't forget to try out the Vertical Path Type tool ▣ as well.

8. Convert Text to Outline

To get to know your text on a more intimate level, convert it to outlines. Doing so turns editable text into a regular object that you can modify as if it were a circle, square, or any other shape. Caution, though—the conversion is permanent. Once you save the type as an outline, you won't be able to convert it back to text. You might want to save an editable version of the text on a separate, hidden layer if you feel you may later want to go back.

FIGURE 9.33: Turn editable text into a regular object that you can modify as if it were a shape.

Set some type on the Artboard with the Type tool, and then select it. To create outlines, press Ctrl+Shift+O/Cmd+Shift+O or select Type > Create Outlines from the menu bar. It may appear that little happened other than the baseline disappearing and the bounding box shrinking. The text, however, is now just as susceptible to the Direct Selection tool as a circle or square—meaning that you can now apply the same modifications and transformations to it.

The Create Outlines command automatically groups your text objects by default. To select individual letters with the Selection tool, you will first need to ungroup them.

Converting text to outlines is useful not only from a design perspective, but also professionally. Doing so ensures that other viewers of your file will see your type as you had intended, even if they don't have the font you used, which is often the case. If you don't convert your text to outlines before sending it to others (such as clients or printers), the fonts you selected may default to other fonts, seriously degrading your design.

Student Work

What have other design students done with this project? Here are some work samples from the Sessions classroom:

FIGURE 9.34: Sean Lynde from New York City developed some very clear and legible sci-fi-influenced designs.

TRANCE RECORDS

FIGURE 9.35: Jeff Jenkins from Seattle came up with this hypnotic design. Great indie subcultural look.

FIGURE 9.36: Asa Iversen from Norway devised these clever typographical and symbolic variations on her company name.

10 Advertising Design

Advertising, it's said, is nothing more than an exquisitely crafted message. That may be true, but when it's done right, it can change minds, set trends, and touch lives.

Want to design ads in a powerful, multibillion-dollar industry? Before you put on your Madison Avenue shoes, you should know that designing ads is not always glamorous. It *is* always interesting, creative, and fun, however. And if you stick with it, you can earn a respectable living.

Success in advertising design requires not only talent, but also a degree of business savvy and an understanding what makes consumers act. The purpose of this chapter is to make you a better ad designer by sensitizing you to business and design principles in the advertising field.

FIGURE 10.1: Funny, timely, targeted, and well designed—this Diamond Trading Company ad has what it takes to persuade consumers and generate sales.

In this chapter you will:

- Learn about the origins of advertising and the evolution of advertising in the United States.

- Learn about the different phases of consumer behavior and how advertisers motivate consumers to buy.

- Learn how to organize your advertising message and design using the "AIDA" formula.

- Explore methods of using context and association to deliver clever, effective ad designs.

- Learn about the four major advertising tones: humorous, dramatic/informative, sexual, and scientific.

- Create a magazine ad design promoting a new reality show based in New York City.

Advertising Design Fundamentals

Let's start by defining just what we're getting into here. The word *advertising* comes from the Latin *ad vertere*, which means "turn the mind toward." A more modern definition would be "impersonal communications through various media by businesses hoping to persuade a targeted audience." Advertising communications come in many guises—magazine ads, posters, billboards—but all have the ultimate goal of motivating an audience to purchase something.

FIGURE 10.2: A little humor goes a long way in making an ad memorable. The skinny gingerbread man in this Oregon Chai ad conveys the flavor of the product and its sugar-free nature, along with a few laughs.

FIGURE 10.3: This striking ad for the Museum of Latin American Art conveys the experience of seeing an amazing piece of artwork in person.

When did advertising begin? No one knows exactly, but as long as civilization and commerce have existed, it has been around. It has simply become more sophisticated as human societies and methods of communication have advanced. One of the earliest pieces of advertising known to historians is a Babylonian clay tablet circa 3000 B.C. containing inscriptions for an ointment dealer, a scribe, and a shoemaker.

Ancient Greece had its town criers, who called out to passersby about the goods coming into port on arriving ships. The Romans had ads too—evidence of them was found in the ruins of Pompeii.

Symbolic Origins

In our modern world we take literacy for granted, but in earlier times, signs and ads consisted mainly of symbols—some of which are still used to this day. A good example of a pre-modern symbol is the traditional red and white barber pole. In the Middle Ages, hair was not the only thing that barbers cut. They also performed surgery, tooth extractions, and bloodletting (Ouch!).

Every barber provided a staff for the patient to grasp (so that the veins on the arm would stand out sharply), a basin to hold leeches and catch blood, and a supply of linen bandages. After the bloodletting was completed, the bandages were hung on the staff and placed outside as advertisement. Twirled by the wind, the bandages formed a red and white spiral pattern, which was later adopted in the painted pole you see everywhere.

FIGURE 10.4: Early advertising, for a haircut and so much more.

Makes you think twice about getting a haircut, doesn't it? Let's explore a brief history of advertising to establish a foundation for working in the field.

Short History of Advertising Design

The history of advertising can be broken down into three distinct eras defined by technology. In fact, you may be lucky enough to be witnessing a transition into a fourth era. We'll briefly define the three eras and trace how advertising evolved in the United States throughout the 20th century and into the present day.

Three Advertising Eras

Scholars of advertising break down the evolution of the field into three general eras:

- The premarketing era, from prehistory to the 1750s—This era spanned from clay tablets and town criers to barber poles and tavern signs. The tremendous boom in mass printing marks the end of this era.

- The mass communication era, from the 1750s through World War II— This era covers the proliferation of the printed word (newspapers, magazines, and so on) through radio's heyday. With the inception of television in post–World War II society, the next era began.

- The research era, from the end of World War II to the present day— During this era, techniques in advertising have been methodically improved with the goal of finding and targeting various consumer groups using mass communications.

Present-day advertising is beginning a transition from the research era to a new era focused on information technology and new media. It is almost certain that the current "information age" will be retrospectively reclassified with regard to advertising.

Emergence of Advertising in the U.S.

No matter what country you work in, your advertising is undoubtedly influenced by an advertising industry that developed in the United States. So let's take some time to look at the evolution of advertising in America. If you work outside the United States, you may find it interesting to research the history of ads in your country and compare it with the account that follows.

By the time the United States gained independence in 1776, there were 30 newspapers in the country. Advertising had arrived in the New World. Colonial postmasters were the first Americans to act as advertising agents; they accepted advertising copy for publication in newspapers from other locations and made financial arrangements with advertisers and publishers.

The American perspective with regard to the advertising industry is quite unlike any other. The 19th and 20th centuries saw unprecedented growth in industry and technology as well as invention—which has continued into the 21st century. The advertising business grew hand in hand with the country and therefore became deeply ingrained into American society and popular culture.

During the late 19th century, a laissez-faire philosophy of government pervaded the United States—there was very little government regulation or intervention in the affairs of business. Advertising became flamboyant and contributed to the unethical practices of many corrupt businesses by communicating false claims about dubious products. Medical products were among the most notorious for this practice, and the most dangerous.

Eventually there was a backlash. *Ladies Home Journal* was the first among several publications to completely ban medical advertising from its pages. In 1906, the Pure Food and Drug Act was passed to protect the consumer, and the pendulum began to swing toward official reform. The Federal Trade Commission expanded its duties to protect the public against unscrupulous advertising. Just as important, many advertisers wanted no part in the "flimflam" that was running rampant—they not only believed it was immoral, but also felt that this type of practice would put the ad industry out of business by creating public distrust. So in 1905, a group of advertising professionals got together and founded a professional association complete with guidelines and bylaws; it eventually evolved into the American Advertising Federation.

By 1911, a national campaign was under way for truth in advertising, and in 1916, an advertising vigilance committee became the Better Business Bureau. Circulation audits began so that publishers could no longer make unsubstantiated claims as to how many people would see ads in their newspapers and magazines.

The Impact of War

When the United States entered World War I, some advertising professionals offered their creative services to U.S. government officials. The admen's expertise was dismissed as irrelevant, and their offer rejected. These professionals then turned around and offered their services to the National Council of Defense, which immediately recognized their value and gave them their first assignment: to motivate young men to register for the draft. Their efforts resulted in 13 million registrations in a single day. This proves the old saying that it pays to advertise! After World War I, a boom in industrial production brought more products than ever to the public. There were more stores and better roads, and consumers listened to radio broadcasts in their homes. All of these changes created an opportunity for more advertising.

During World War II, goods manufacturers had to shift their focus away from the consumer and toward the war effort. Many companies therefore stopped advertising. Those that were intent on staying in the mind of the consumer wisely invested in product branding. They simply switched from a sales pitch to a public service or educational message tagged with the company name. For example, a tire maker might run an ad entitled "How to take care of your tires."

FIGURE 10.5: During wartime, food was rationed and it was important not to waste it. Skinless brand frankfurters offered tips on how to use leftovers—including their product, of course.

The War Advertising Council was formed in 1942 to enlist civilian help in the war effort. Again, ad agencies were enlisted for purposes including stopping careless talk among wartime workers ("The enemy is listening"), selling war bonds, and recruiting. This group created such icons of American popular culture as Rosie the Riveter and Smokey the Bear.

After World War II, a baby boom, a pent-up demand for products, and an expanding economy fueled ad spending. In 1952, the first nationwide network television broadcasts were launched. These developments revolutionized the ad business once again. With more competition for larger markets than ever before, the eyes and ears (and voice) of the consumer became even more important. Gradually, consumer protection groups lobbied successfully for much greater government regulation of ads. During this era, the discipline of market research first showed signs of developing into a systematic, almost scientific field of analysis.

FIGURE 10.6: Life wasn't quite as fast-paced in the 1940s as it is today. Magazine ads like this one contained a lot of text, which consumers actually took the time to read. Fast-forward to today's ads, and you'll see that minimal text and direct images get the message across in seconds.

Fast-forward to now. In the past decade, the Internet has changed not only the advertising industry, but also the fundamental manner in which business is being conducted. The emergence of new goods on the market always accompanies a message encouraging consumption—inciting, enticing, persuading, and pushing us to buy, and often to pay later! It will be interesting to see how history documents the informational and technological developments of today. While the Internet is called a superhighway for information, it is arguably even more of a vehicle for promotion.

FIGURE 10.7: Designs with bright colors and clear representations of the product and brand, like this 1947 Curtiss ad, command attention—and that sure hasn't changed in the 21st century.

In the 21st century, everything has changed: the complexity of ads, the education of consumers, and the proliferation of ways to do business. But the general principles of good advertising are timeless. Your job as an advertising designer is to turn the consumer's mind (and money) toward the product.

Basics of Effective Ads

Form and Function

It's time to start exploring some principles of effective advertising. One basic tenet of design is that form follows function. Selling the product or service is always the function of your ad, and how you achieve this visually (in form) is secondary.

To function effectively, advertising must:

- Take the customer's point of view. The ad must focus on meeting the customer's needs—not those of the seller or designer.

- Deliver a sales message. If not to persuade, the ad must inform or remind. Advertising is never art for art's sake.

- Communicate in terms of product benefits. The ad must showcase how the product will benefit the customer, as opposed to showing mere product attributes.

While function is essential, form is still important. Creative design can draw attention to ads, making the most important selling features stand out and creating a positive association with the product.

While you must take pride in your work and endeavor to create outstanding ads, don't be too quick to judge other designers' ads as "good" or "bad." Advertising is ultimately about generating sales, and the only way to accurately appraise the quality of an ad is to find out how well it performed. Some ads you may dislike from a design standpoint might well be astoundingly effective when it comes to consumer response. For example, even the most plain-Jane newspaper ad in terms of design might have a strong call-to-action that readers just can't deny.

Consumer Behavior

Effective advertising targets the behavior of its audience—not simply who the customer is, but what he reads, where he works, his level of education, and how he responds to ads. The designer must understand the different typical stages of consumer behavior and apply these concepts to the anticipated viewership of the ad being created.

The four stages in consumer behavior are:

1. Pre-contemplation—Lack of awareness of the product becomes awareness.

2. Contemplation—Awareness of the product becomes a notion of buying that product.

3. Action—The product is bought.

4. Maintenance—The product is bought again (and again, and again).

If a product or service is brand-new to the target audience, the ad must aim at stage 1, pre-contemplation. The goal of such an ad is ultimately to persuade the audience to buy a product, but first the audience must be made aware of the product. That will set the scene for contemplation, in which repeated exposure to the product leads the consumer to think about buying it.

Ads for products that have already gained recognition in the target market (like Mountain Dew for teenagers and diamonds for men planning engagement) can skip the pre-contemplation stage altogether. These can be highly effective because they can answer questions already in the consumer's mind about buying the product: "Can I afford that?" "What do I do with one of those?" or "Won't I be cheating on my diet if I eat one of those?" Answer the question successfully, and your campaign is well on its way.

> ▼ **note**
>
> **Ads must foster trust in the product and brand to effectively maintain sales and make customers loyal. It's why you see ads for brands that are already ubiquitous (like a favorite drink or restaurant)—loyalty must be maintained.**

FIGURE10.8: Excellent copywriting and a focus on the product are hallmarks of this Diamond Trading Company campaign. What sentient man doesn't already know that his wife wants diamonds for Christmas? The ad designers used a familiar concept—that diamonds are a desirable gift—to deliver an ad with punch

Motivation and Appeal

Leo Burnett, the founder of Leo Burnett Worldwide, a Chicago-based ad agency, said, "Make it simple. Make it memorable. Make it inviting to look at. Make it fun to read." The fun and the challenge of advertising design is that it is both utilitarian and aesthetic. As a designer you must try to get the most impact through the simplest means. You are not merely working to get noticed, but also competing for the mind of the consumer through persuasion. A good ad must attract attention and then hold that attention long enough to persuade the viewer. That's where the aesthetic aspect comes in. In advertising, the quality of the design always takes precedence over realism.

FIGURE 10.9: This subway ad gets attention with an unrealistic situation, asking consumers "What's missing from this picture?" and reminding them of a reason to drink milk.

Persuasion involves the motivation, attitudes, and perceptions behind a person's choices. The power of persuasion is so great that people who are known for their persuasive genius are sometimes mistrusted.

Cultural anthropologists, psychologists, and sociologists all have theories about a phenomenon called the *emotional buy*. The founders of the London-based Saatchi and Saatchi simply refer to it as "that leap from logic to magic." People buy a product because of the benefits that they expect from it. Most products have many benefits—and many angles that could be used to promote them. The trick is to find which approach, or appeal, will best work for the client and consumer. The underlying premise is that consumers are often motivated by emotions they might not be consciously aware of.

Organizing Your Message

Some commonsense rules apply to the use of persuasion in advertising. First of all, people are more easily persuaded when they are primed or prepared for a message. You wouldn't run an airline commercial during a TV movie about a plane crash, or place an ad for men's suits in a kids' educational magazine. The airline commercial would go well with a travel show, though, and the suit ad would fit nicely in a finance magazine.

If the ad is placed where there is no priming available (like a billboard or the side of a bus), the ad must be a bit more conservative and also clearer because the audience is not narrowed in any way.

Second, a well-organized message is infinitely more persuasive than an unorganized one. The message and audience must be clearly identified. The most effective ads follow a standard formula, "AIDA":

A = (attract) attention
I = (hold) interest
D = (arouse) desire
A = (motivate toward) action

The last step of AIDA is arguably the most important. The ad must make the viewer want to perform an action suggested by the ad. To persuade a consumer, an ad must not merely promise a benefit, but also spell it out, amplify it, and make it obvious which action (usually "buy the product") must be taken.

> **tip**
>
> Ads for broad audiences require a more conventional design approach than targeted ones. Viewers outside your target audience must still be able to understand the message and gain a positive impression of the product.

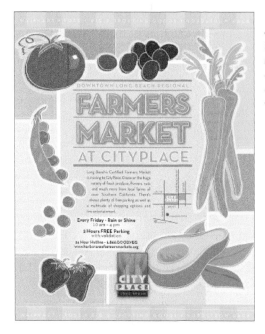

FIGURE 10.10: With illustrations and colors that suggest the offerings of the advertised farmers' market, and details on how to get there, this design presents an organized message that compels viewers to visit.

A designer can use many approaches to accomplish this. These include identification, the appeal that if others are doing it, you should too ("4 out of 5 bakers choose brand *x* sugar"); a factual approach ("kills 99 percent of bacteria"); and an appeal to ethics or values ("less harmful to the environment"). Ads can also take imaginative or emotional tacks—or combine two or more approaches to develop the total concept. Visually speaking, photos tend to get more response than illustrations; and before/after photos, though overdone, are good persuaders.

Connotations and Context

Connotations are the mental connections between the abstract and the tangible. Every message can have at least two meanings—a literal one and a suggestive one. The ability to make associations on both a conscious and unconscious level is a remarkable phenomenon in the human imagination. We have both emotional and environmental thoughts about what we see. We don't just "think" about things; we feel and remember them as well.

Psychologist and philosopher William James once said, "Whilst part of what we perceive comes through our senses from the object before us, another part (and it may be the larger part) always comes from our own mind."

Words and images with similar meanings can evoke responses that are quite different. For example, consider the words *fat* and *plump*. Words like *plump* feel jolly when applied to people, or juicy and ripe when applied to food. *Fat*, on the other hand, can feel much more negative, even though its definition is quite similar to that of *plump*.

Just like words, visual images have different connotations. Generally speaking, when something is left to the imagination it has more impact than when all the details are made evident. This also makes your audience feel more intelligent and flattered. So rather than spell things out entirely, we rely on connotation. Things seem more "fun," "healthy," "masculine," "feminine," "young," or "old" not because of what they intrinsically are but because of how they are presented.

FIGURE 10.11: Jumping over buildings, wearing sneakers. The images in the Steve Madden ad series create an association with a dynamic youthful lifestyle.

Because the human mind is an association machine—that is, we link new information with familiar knowledge—certain concepts can be represented or suggested by other elements. This effect is often more subconscious than conscious—it's known as *associative recall*, which is closely tied into the working of memory. Thinking one thing gets a person thinking related thoughts. If those related thoughts are positive, that's good news for your product.

Among the first forays into artificial intelligence was a 1960s computer called the Perceptron. Using this device, a response to a stimulus triggered another response, which triggered still more until the computer "recognized" the stimulus. Human psychology works in a similar manner, as people associate ideas, emotions, and objects with the things they see and read.

Association is one reason that endorsements are often used in advertising. The public "knows" celebrities and associates them with various attributes and qualities. Also, people are more likely to do what's requested when they like the person making the request, just as they're more likely to listen when they feel they are hearing the voice of an authority such as a doctor or dentist.

The context in which we see things also shapes our overall impression. An ad can reflect certain specific objects or events—historical, sociological, cultural, political, seasonal, and so on—that color our perceptions.

Context can be expressed by a very subtle image. For example, have you ever noticed that on a sapling, the leaves are really about the same size as those on a full-grown tree? It's their relative size to the branch and trunk that lets us know whether we are seeing part of a young tree or an old one. Be aware of context as you design, and remember that your audience will see only what you show them—not the "big picture" in your head.

Making use of context can be a wonderful exercise in subtlety or a bold and daring statement. Sometimes throwing something unexpected into a layout will attract attention. However, if you want to employ this technique, you must understand what you are doing and what you wish to achieve. Unless it is to make a particular point, don't treat something in an "artistic" manner that deprives it of its true character. The viewer won't understand how to interpret it, and it will merely serve to distract and confuse. As Thomas Jefferson once said, "If there is not a good reason for doing something, you have one good reason not to do it."

Tone in Advertising

Humorous

Humorous ads play on the desire to laugh and have fun. They can comprise a play on words, a cute photo that gives a quick chuckle, a gag out of left field, intelligent "thinker" jokes, and irreverent humor best suited to highly targeted audiences.

FIGURE 10.12: This Playland poster uses humor to encourage (or dare!) thrill seekers to visit.

Humorous ads grab attention better than almost any type, and they get a lot of word-of-mouth recognition—when you see a hilarious ad, you're bound to tell someone about it. But often they can be misused. Humor can be applied to situations that many people wouldn't find funny, or used purely for attention with no connection to the product itself.

To use humor well, make it appropriate to the intended audience (consider where the ad will be placed). Tie the joke in to the product, but be careful— never cast the product in a negative light by making it the butt of the joke.

FIGURE 10.13: Creative, funny copy in this ad for Wick Fowler's 2-Alarm Chili makes the product sound macho, persuading the viewer to accept their dare.

Dramatic/Informative

Dramatic ads tell a story or set a scene. They typically avoid direct humor in their delivery and stick to a matter-of-fact method of conveying the product and brand. A dramatic ad can simply present a product in a clear and informative manner, or adopt a lighthearted but not comic tone. A somber approach may even be used for a public service campaign.

Dramatic ads do not need to be disturbing or painful to view, unless the desired effect is to prove a difficult point, and they do not need to be overly plain. Dramatic and informative advertising can be just as vibrant and pleasant to look at as any other type of ad, as well as persuasive—the only difference is that it is delivered in a more straightforward way.

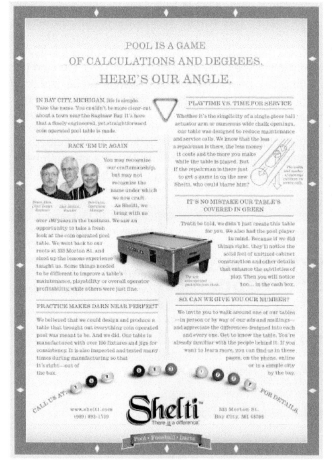

FIGURE 10.14: Even with some humorous touches, this Shelti ad is all about information. By honestly detailing the company's history and craftsmanship, this ad persuades and builds trust without the need for bells and whistles that would cloud the message.

Sexual

Many contemporary ads have sexual overtones, particularly in the use of imagery of attractive women to present a product. Sexual ads can be very tasteful and subtle to make a product more alluring, or overt and potentially offensive.

Sexuality is handled best when it's presented in situations that are expected and when it accentuates positive features of the product. For example, a seductive woman using a soap product in the shower places the sexuality in context and may present the soap as feminine, clean, fresh, or having an alluring fragrance.

If creating a sexually driven ad campaign, it is important to take local laws and customs into account. (For example, it is not customary to show breasts in U.S. advertising, but it's common in western Europe.) Also take the medium into account, as these campaigns are most effective in very targeted media rather than presented to the general public. Overall, if using sex in an ad, use it with taste so as not to offend but instead to project your product in a positive light. Remember that a negative reaction will make your product seem negative as well.

FIGURE 10.15: This model suggestively presents one "flavor" of Gelati shoes; this ad is a great example of touching on sexuality just enough to get the message across, rather than being overt.

Scientific

Scientific ads are often used for innovative products or those that the public might find confusing without explanation (for example, a high-tech device that has no equal on the market). These ads typically involve statistics, before-and-after images, or other methods of measuring product effectiveness—telling the consumer that the product does what it claims to do.

FIGURE 10.16: This Syngenta ad grabs your attention, using an arresting and impossible image to convey the idea of a threat to cotton crops. In this case, presenting a visual concept for the product may be more effective than spelling out all the scientific details.

When using comparisons, data, or other scientific methods in advertising, be sure to observe some basic ethical rules. First, be sure that you're using accurate information. If you cannot fact-check yourself, be sure that you really trust what the client has given you before proceeding. If you feel the ad will make false claims, do not take on the project—this can hurt your reputation as a designer. Also, don't distort before-and-after photos or make any other manipulations that may falsify claims that are initially accurate. Finally, treat your audience intelligently. Do not talk down to readers when presenting facts and figures, or appear so overly scientific that people cannot relate to the ad.

> **note**
>
> **Ethical rules apply to any type of ad—not just scientific ones. Persuading with false or misleading information hurts the product and brand in addition to your reputation as a designer. Take the high road and use your creativity to deliver honest messages that respect the audience.**

Reality Show Advertising

Every ad has the goal of communicating a brand, and it can be done in a number of creative and effective ways that depend on the medium, existing brand familiarity, viewing environment, and other variables.

Your goal in this exercise will be to develop an ad to announce a new TV show in a men's magazine. That's the primary goal; the secondary goal is to communicate a brand in your magazine ad. Your client requires his company's logo and product's logo in the ad, and he expects you to follow his style guidelines.

Project Brief: Stranded in New York

The latest reality TV show to hit the airwaves is *Stranded in New York*, airing this fall on RTN, the Reality Television Network. The premise of the show is that seven strangers will be dropped off in New York City with just $100 between them. With that $100, they'll have to figure out how to manage for one full week. They're not allowed to leave the city in that week, and they may not use any money other than the $100 they've been given. Doesn't sound too bad—except that certain people they meet will be TV executives in disguise, attempting to sabotage their mission with scare tactics and other surprises. Any contestant who can't take it can quit, but any contestant who makes it through the full week will win $25,000.

The network wants this show to be a megahit so they can try it in additional cities every season, and they expect it to be most successful with men ages 18 to 30. They'd like their campaign to begin with a full-page ad in the summer issues of various upscale and mass-market men's magazines around the country.

FIGURE 10.17: The client has provided these logos for you along with specifications on how they can be used.

The client will provide you with an RTN logo and the following strict style requirements for its use (common when working with any established brand):

- You may change the colors of the circle and the lettering. The circle may be partially transparent over other imagery, but the lettering must be 100 percent opaque.

- Each letter must be the same color—you cannot make one letter red, one yellow, and so on.

- No imagery may obscure the circle shape or the lettering.

- The design of the logo may not be altered except to proportionally resize. No effects may be added to the logo, including but not limited to shadows, glows, and bevels.

You will also be supplied with a logo for the TV program with the following style requirements:

- You may change the colors of all lettering. However, the word *Stranded* must always be a single color, and the words *in New York* must always be a single color. The words *in New York* must always be darker than the word *Stranded* unless the entire logo is the same color.

- No imagery may obscure the lettering.

- The design may not be altered except to proportionally resize. No effects may be added to the logo, including but not limited to shadows, glows, and bevels.

- As a variation, you may move the *in New York* text to another location, such as to the right of *Stranded*.

You may use any imagery you choose to accompany your design—photos of New York City, people, illustrations, and so on.

Project Summary

Research and brainstorm a magazine advertisement for a reality show.

Follow the client's guidelines for usage of the company and show logos.

Choose an appropriate tone and attitude for the ad design.

Create an advertisement layout that would persuade the target audience to watch the show.

Project Steps

Before you begin, open the RTN logo and *Stranded in New York* logo from the Images CD.

1. Research the Audience

The client gave you some brief but important information about the demographic that should be targeted in the ad you're creating. You know the age and sex that you should design for, and where the ad will be placed.

With this information, you should do some research on the audience. Learn what colors and images trigger a response from this group. Identify trends by researching ads in similar locations. In men's magazines, is there a trend toward black-and-white photos, stark simplicity, humorous copy, bold colors and patterns, or dramatic statements? Look at how print ads promoting TV shows differ from ads for tangible products like coffee or MP3 players, and pay attention to how company and product brands are communicated in the ads you see.

2. Conceptualize the Design

Sketch out some design ideas for your full-page magazine ad based on your own research and creative ideas. The client has left the design open to you—you could do a very minimal, text-only design, or add complexity with various images and detailed copy.

As you plan your ad, consider some of the following questions:

- What tone do you think will best convey the message and attract the audience—humorous, dramatic/informative, sexual, scientific? Why?
- What type of image, if you choose to use any, would work best? Should you use a literal, direct image such as a city shot, or should you let your audience make an association with an indirect image? Would a photo or an illustration work best?
- How will the main image appear in the ad; for example, will it take up the whole page? How will any secondary images work in the layout?
- How much copy must the ad have to be effective? What exactly should it say?
- What style(s) of typography will work best to make your copy attractive to the audience? How large will the copy need to be, and where on the page will you place it?
- Which of the two logos should have the most importance? How will you modify the logos provided, and where will you place them?

3. Begin the Ad Layout

The software you choose to work with for this project will depend on your preferences and the type of imagery you plan to have in your ad. If you will be using only type, or type and illustrations, you may want to work solely in Illustrator. If you are including photographs, you might work on those in Photoshop and bring them into Illustrator when they are the way you like them, or work solely in Photoshop.

Start with a document 8.5 inches wide by 11 inches high in CMYK color mode in the program you plan to complete your layout in. If using only Photoshop, the document resolution (set in Image > Image Size) should be 300 dots per inch. (Remember, Illustrator is vector-based and therefore independent of resolution issues.)

To help in your composition, show the rulers on your document (View > Show Rulers in Illustrator, View > Rulers in Photoshop) and drag guides from the rulers to represent your margins and other areas you want to block out for your design.

Fill your document with the background color you want, or use another background like a pattern or gradient. If you've planned any geometric background elements such as circles or lines, add them now. If you're using only Photoshop for your layout, work carefully with your drawing tools to make sure those geometric items are the right size; resizing them later will reduce their quality. In Illustrator, you don't have to worry about this—resize your vector shapes at will!

FIGURE 10.18: Those composition rules you learned for poster design should come in handy as you plan your layout. Here, I'm balancing the large white area with a smaller orange bar. Though I'll be adding images and text, a balanced start is the best strategy for a balanced end.

4. Edit and Place the Main Image

Unless you're dealing with a type-only design, your next step is to prepare your design's main image. If this is a photograph, open it in Photoshop and apply any edits needed. For example, you'll probably want to crop the image to the size and shape you want, and accentuate the point of interest. Then you may need to retouch problem spots, apply color modifications, and use a filter or special effect to get the desired appearance.

Now's a good time to revisit the notion of form following function. As fun as special photo effects can be, they are best used only when they suit the goal of the ad—helping to draw attention to the message, deliver it, and persuade the viewer to perform an action (in this case, watch the show). If you're considering an effect just for art's sake, it's probably not the best approach.

Save a .psd copy of your edited photo in case you want to go back and make changes later. If you're laying out your ad in Photoshop, use the Move tool to drag your photo onto your ad document, and rearrange your layers as needed.

FIGURE 10.19: I'm going for a mostly dramatic ad, though in a moment it will have a touch of humor, so I went with a photo that sets up the city as a gritty, rough place to be.

If you are laying out your ad in Illustrator, use File > Place to bring the .psd file into your Illustrator document. If it overlaps other elements, send it back using Object > Arrange, or move the layer down in the Layers palette.

If your main image is an illustration, work in Illustrator to create it, and then save a copy and simply copy and paste it onto your layout document.

5. Place the Branding

Regardless of what program you're using for your layout, open the RTN and *Stranded in New York* logos in Illustrator. Here you can make any color and sizing changes you'd like, easily and without fear of losing quality.

Remembering the client's guidelines for the use of type, apply your chosen colors to the logos and make any other changes necessary for your design. To make color changes, select the elements you'd like to modify with the Selection tool (holding down Shift to select multiple items), and adjust the fill color in the Color palette.

Save a copy of each logo as an .eps or .ai file in case you'd like to go back and make changes later.

Now you can copy and paste your logos into your layout document in either Illustrator or Photoshop. Select and move them to the appropriate place in the hierarchy of your design.

FIGURE 10.20: I felt that the show logo was more important than the RTN logo in my design, so I gave it top billing and colors that match my orange bar and photo. The RTN logo is smaller but still carries plenty of weight.

6. Set the Type and Additional Images

Now that the background, main image, and branding is in place, you can apply the remaining (but very important) components of your ad.

If you have additional photos or illustrations to place in your design, add them to your layout now and follow the same process for working with them as above.

FIGURE 10.21: Here's my final design, where that touch of humor is finally added with text. Now the viewer has a good sense of what the show is about—and hopefully plans to watch!

Many successful ads have just one image or none at all, but compositions using multiple images can work well too, as long as they help communicate and persuade without making the layout too confusing.

The final step is to set the type. You should already have come up with the copy and thought about where it will go on the page, but presenting it isn't always as simple as it sounds. Keep the following in mind as you make your typography decisions:

- Choose the size and color of type based on the copy's importance and place in the hierarchy. If your main image is more important than your main copy, make sure they aren't competing for attention.

- Be sure there is enough contrast between the type and the elements behind it so that it's easy to read when flipping through a magazine.

- A special type effect such as a filter, warping, or an interesting perspective is an option, but it should not detract from the readability and should help convey the message or attitude.

- If you have trouble placing your copy and making it fit, don't just squeeze it all in—consider rewording to shorten it. This will result in a message that is even quicker to read and absorb. Keep in mind that in a real project situation, you might need to run such a change by your client first.

Review your layout carefully and make any final tweaks you think are necessary for it to be effective. Try printing it out and tucking it into a magazine to see how it looks in its final destination.

Student Work

What *Stranded in New York* ads have other designers created? Here are some work samples from Sessions students:

FIGURE 10.22: Dominic Guadiz made a gritty photo the center-piece of the ad and provided text that works perfectly against it. In addition to the use of branding at the bottom, notice that *Stranded* was repeated over the photo for added impact.

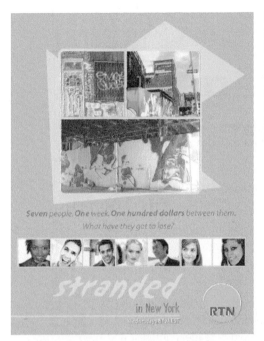

FIGURE 10.23: This design by Krista Olsen uses many different images but puts them in two cohesive groups so the layout doesn't feel too busy. There is a nice balance between the edginess of the main photo group and the lighter, more pleasant colors.

FIGURE 10.24: Michael Wrigley uses minimal color to give the layout drama, and presents a strong hierarchy of branding, imagery, and typography. The images give an air of suspense that persuades viewers to watch.

11 Magazine Design

Whether you stack them up or fan them out, magazines are an enduring and visible feature of the modern home. In fact, your coffee table is most likely groaning under the weight of a few right now.

Is it content that absorbs us? These days, there's a magazine to suit any interest, passion, or pursuit. But while readers will always seek information, it's good design that makes that information clear and attractive.

In this chapter, we'll explore some of the challenges of magazine design. We'll analyze the process of creating a layout, examining how text and images are combined on magazine covers and inner spreads to pique readers' interest and keep them reading.

FIGURE 11.1: The aged, European feel and unexpected use of imagery perfectly convey *Zoetrope All Story*'s foreign affairs issue and set it apart from related magazines on the rack.

In this chapter you will:

Explore what makes magazine covers and spreads eye-catching.

Learn key questions to ask when conducting magazine design research.

Analyze the creation of a successful magazine article layout.

Learn how and why designers use grid systems for magazine spread designs.

Learn how images are framed, cropped, and placed to support a layout.

Explore common types of magazine text styles and how to handle them on covers and spreads.

Learn how contrast, alignment, repetition, and proximity are used to create effective covers and spreads.

Design a magazine cover and an introductory spread for a new fashion magazine.

Magazine Design Fundamentals

We've all spent a few minutes admiring a beautiful magazine cover or spread. Whether it's a home decorating feature, a *National Geographic* special on Alaska, or a dreamy picture of a favorite model, the magazine has the power to draw us in.

Why is this so? Magazines inspire us through the marriage of content and design. Every aspect of a magazine, from its cover to its inner pages and ads, is handled with precision. Beautifully written and carefully edited text is integrated with expertly handled photos and illustrations. Magazine design attracts people who have a flair for design and a love of storytelling; a successful magazine designer must be accurate and eagle-eyed on top of being creative and technically skilled.

FIGURE 11.2: These covers created by Cyclone Design for *Seattle Weekly*'s 25th anniversary issue leap from the newsstands with their strong composition and angelic/devilish illustration.

Let's explore some of the fundamentals that make magazines tick.

Layout and Content

What makes a magazine cover or page so visually compelling? Partly it's the magic of layout: the artful arrangement of text and images on a page.

Designers use a grid system to determine the placement and alignment of all page elements (text and graphics), particularly on inner pages and across facing pages called *two-page spreads*. Invisible to the reader, the grid provides a structure of lines or guides that determines where all the content goes on the page. The grid helps the layout artist balance the information to create an intriguing logic. This creates continuity and visual interest, which is especially important if a story has multiple pages.

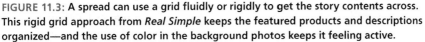

FIGURE 11.3: A spread can use a grid fluidly or rigidly to get the story contents across. This rigid grid approach from *Real Simple* keeps the featured products and descriptions organized—and the use of color in the background photos keeps it feeling active.

How is the layout decided? Every magazine has a set of general guidelines for design and layout that are consistent but revamped every few years or so. The nature of the magazine itself will determine whether the focus is mostly text content or graphic content, or a mixture. A fashion magazine will have a very different set of layout standards than will a newsmagazine or literary journal, for example.

---

note

Within a single magazine, you might first notice a variety of design styles—one for each article, with images and layouts based on the article content. But on closer inspection, you'll see that certain elements are repeated among all of the articles—the body text style, the number of columns in the grid, and so on—to give the magazine a consistent feel.

A magazine designer or art director is asked to work creatively within these overall constraints. In a best-case scenario, an art director will begin shaping creative ideas for an article at the early planning stage for the magazine's next issue. At an initial story meeting, an editor will assign writers and photographers to each article and discuss some possible directions for a story, so that writers, photographers, and editors are all working in concert. In the corner of the room, art directors are busy sketching in their notebooks.

Inevitably, however, the unrelenting pressure of publishing deadlines, coupled with the designer's penultimate spot on the production line, means that many decisions about a story's layout are made at the last minute, as copyedited text, new photos, and sets of illustrations make their way in at the eleventh hour.

This is where the magazine designer really earns her stripes. Dozens of subtle or not-so-subtle manipulations to an article's headline, photos, pull quotes, and text columns may be required to add power and punch to the visual message of the page. Done effectively, a page layout doesn't just pull in readers; it also tells a reader where to look and what's important.

Please note that even if you're not dying to work in magazine publishing, the layout concepts in this chapter can applied in many other fields: book publishing, brochure and marketing design, and Web design, to name just a few.

Research

tip

Don't stop at magazines when doing your magazine design research. Look at ads, posters, packages, books, Web sites, and other media targeting your audience. Pick up on trends that attract the audience and the design staples that speak to them.

One of the great things about magazine design is that you're continually asked to take on projects that explore subjects or genres you're not familiar with. An on-staff designer at a magazine will work with graphic and text content that is always changing. And even if the content is well-traveled (what, *another* article about getting rock-hard abs?), the challenge of expressing it anew is all the greater.

Freelance designers experience an even wider range of material. Oftentimes freelancers are called in to assist during a deadline crunch or to assemble special editions. Those folks need to get up to speed fast. Even if you don't know your axle from your elbow, you may suddenly be charged with laying out an article for a car mechanics magazine. Magazine art directors will expect you to be knowledgeable about what their readers are looking for, so it pays to do some research. If you're called, take a trip to the newsstand to gather issues of the magazine and others targeting a similar audience.

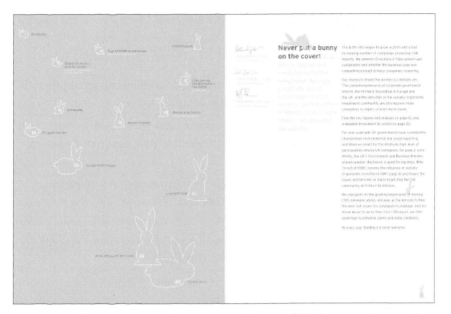

FIGURE 11.4: This report on CSR (corporate social responsibility) put together by salterbaxter and Context illustrates the application of the grid, headline, body text, negative space, and other concepts you'll explore in this chapter. The rabbit motif is a fresh and engaging approach to communicating the proliferation of CSR.

FIGURE 11.5: The introduction to this Zoetrope foreign affairs essay is enigmatic: just a single headline, a powerful color block, and a vintage passport photograph draw the reader into the story.

As you pore over periodicals, here are some questions to ask yourself to prepare for designing:

- Who is the target audience?

- What key colors and words come to mind when thinking about this audience? How are these reflected in the designs you see?

- What colors are typically used for backgrounds? For text? Would deviating from these colors make a positive statement in your design or be jarring for the audience?

- Are the images primarily photographs or illustrations? When are they treated as accents to large amounts of text? When are they the main attraction?

- Does the design appear to be classic? Trendy? Sophisticated? Playful? Edgy? Should your design follow this direction?

- What typefaces are used for the body, headline, pull quotes, and so on? Why do you think they were chosen?

Using the Grid

The idea of using a grid when designing a cover or spread might sound a little limiting to a creative type, but it isn't at all since you, the designer, will set up the grid before you begin applying elements to it. Furthermore, a grid is not an ironclad set of rules; it's a structural tool that opens up many possibilities.

Before you construct a grid, you must take stock of your content. You'll most likely get text and images from other departments at the magazine along with some other rules such as the amount of ad space to be allotted. From here you can sketch out your plans for the text and images, and begin to turn this into your grid framework.

To learn how text and images interact in a layout, we'll explore a design for a *Magnet* article about the innovative musician Tom Waits as we work through this chapter.

FIGURE 11.6: We'll follow the design of this captivating article from *MAGNET* throughout the chapter, learning about the grid, page elements, and overall composition.

Step 1: The Grid Itself

Let's explore the grid concept more closely, looking at *MAGNET*'s article on Tom Waits. The layout began as a tabula rasa: a blank slate. Before any text or images could be added, the designer most likely poured a cup of coffee and mapped out an empty white space with a grid. This can easily be done on paper, in layout software such as Adobe InDesign or QuarkXPress, or in Illustrator and other programs.

The designer opted for a column grid, which is common to many articles and can be approached in a variety of ways. The grid has three columns on each page with some space between them. Text can flow from one column to the next, or the columns can be joined or *spanned* so that they house photos. (Magazine covers, by the way, tend to be based on relatively simple grids that mark out the page margins and logo area.)

▼ note

You'll notice that in most magazines (and newspapers too!), the columns are spanned with images or headlines but almost never with the main body text. That's because narrow areas of text are much easier to read than wide ones, and the columns help the text flow easily.

FIGURE 11.7: The grid system doesn't mean every page will look the same. Notice how some elements span columns to create an interesting but structured layout.

When using a column grid, you'll generally want to place some horizontal guides as well to help position items to visually break up the columns. In the case of this *MAGNET* article, it appears that the designers used guides that divided the pages in thirds horizontally.

On the grid, you'll notice placeholders for images, headings, and body text or copy. These represent just a starting place and are by no means meant to limit creative design ideas.

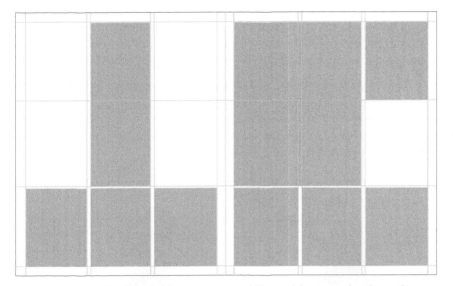

FIGURE 11.8: Popping placeholders onto your grid is a quick way to sketch out the framework for your magazine spread—before going to all the trouble of editing text and images and fitting them in.

You'll also notice some empty space on the grid. What's up here—did the designer forget something? Not at all; like every other part of the layout, the empty space was carefully planned. In graphic design, one of the most important tools for creating contrast is through the relationship between positive and negative space: areas that house content (text and images) and areas that do not (colored backgrounds, empty parts of a photo, white areas, and so on).

Why allot negative space? A strong contrast can attract a viewer's attention and enhance the message that each design element conveys. Providing empty space around a column of text gives the eye a break and lets the text breathe; layouts that are jam-packed can feel constricting. Negative space is the designer's friend—it creates the best possible frame for a design, even if the content is flat and lifeless. Well, that part is up to the editor, after all.

Step 2: Text and Images

Let's continue dissecting how the Tom Waits article was put together. The designer's next step was to assemble the basic design elements—text and images. The magazine article is about a new Tom Waits album, which is a dark and gritty work focused on the world's political woes. The photos are simple and arresting, and their sepia-toned treatment underlines the dark theme. They make the reader focus on the man himself and think about his point of view.

One thing to consider is that a magazine photo is never simply dropped into a layout. Magazine photos are nearly always retouched, corrected, creatively cropped, and positioned so that they span columns and rows of the grid. The empty areas in the photo are viewed as negative space, which must work well in the overall composition of the page.

FIGURE 11.9: The photographs in the second spread of the Tom Waits article flow along the top two horizontal rows of the grid, and the text is easy to read broken over three columns per page.

The framing or cropping of photos or illustrations is also essential for magazine cover design. A cover typically uses just a single image to draw our attention, but that doesn't mean the design is simple.

Should the photo's subject be centered on the cover? Looking off to one side? Can the subject overlap the logo? Is there room for all the story titles? The answers to these questions are decided by the art director and the editor, but there's a lot of flexibility from one issue to the next.

For example, nearly everyone knows when they are looking at a cover of *Vogue*, even if the model partially obscures the logo. You will see a glamorous model wearing unaffordable clothing. She will be dead center and looking straight at the reader. A *National Geographic* cover, on the other hand, grabs readers in a different way. The cover may be a scenic photo with a point of interest off to one side to draw attention to the accompanying headline.

On a magazine article or cover, text is the designer's next hurdle. Some magazines have rigorous typographic standards that are applied throughout the whole magazine (think *The Economist* or *New Yorker*), while others permit the flexibility to innovate from one article to the next. One thing's for sure: Text layout can make or break a magazine design, no matter how effective other elements may be.

A quick reality check for those designers who are reluctant readers. A designer often focuses on the way the text *looks*, which often takes his or her attention away from what the text *says*. This is wonderful, because it means you are attuned to the appeal of text as a graphical object. Still, you should always keep in mind that you are responsible for communicating the whole message. Most of the time, visual layout is there to accommodate and organize the text.

Let's look at some of the key text layout terms a designer needs to know, with examples pulled from the magazine article:

- Heading—A short main message that announces the title of the story. Generally it's the largest and most prominent text on the page ("It's Last Call Somewhere in the World").

- Subheading—Supplementary text that adds information to the heading. Often it appears under the heading and is smaller in size. ("In the midst of a national hangover….")

- Copy or body text—The main portion of the written information that tells the story in detail. This text is typically pretty small, but it must be extremely easy to read.

- Caption—This describes the content of images and illustrations on a page and is generally set in a smaller typeface than body text. It appears right next to (or on top of) an image or refers to the image. They're common in news articles, but they aren't necessary in our sample article since the subject of the photos is clear.

- Quote or pull quote—An interesting portion of the text is repeated in a more prominent part of the page to draw interest to the article. ("It doesn't take much to tick me off. I'm like an old hooker, you know.")

The typeface and size used for the body text are usually dictated by the magazine's style guide, but it is the designer's job to determine the column widths and text breaks for readability. Often an article title leads into a chunk of large text that flows into the beginning of the article. The purpose of introductory pages is to entice readers with smaller chunks of copy before they get into the meat of the article.

In some cases, the positioning and design of headings, subheadings, pull quotes, typefaces, sizes, and even colors may be entirely up to the designer. For consistency, of course, it's best to stick to a single typeface or family throughout an article. In the Tom Waits article, you'll see that an aged-looking font is used in colors that complement the photographs, and the pull quotes are never larger than the heading and subheading.

Step 3: The Final Layout

Back to our Tom Waits article. Next, the designer started placing text and images on the grid and refining the layout. This is an important step. By deciding how information is presented on the page, the designer determines how it will be understood by the reader.

The importance and order of the content on a magazine page (or any designed surface) is often broadly defined by editors before it reaches the design stage. But as a good designer you should take the initiative to investigate and study the material thoroughly, so as to make design decisions that highlight the interesting parts of the content.

The size and placement of text and images is key to creating what is called a *hierarchy of information*. When a reader opens a two-page spread, which element does she look at first? The headline? The image? Or an interesting pull quote? Our featured magazine article tells a story through layout alone.

Where does your eye fall first? On the image and the heading, most likely. The layout creates a visual connection between the photo of Waits and the heading, and your eye shuttles back and forth between the two, trying to interpret the subject of the article. It's not immediately clear, and the ambiguity makes the article compelling. You're intrigued—you want to read more. Before you get to the full article, you check out the subheading, and then proceed from there with a better sense of what you'll be reading about.

FIGURE 11.10: The first three spreads of the *MAGNET* article on Tom Waits. Notice the design of each one as well as the way they flow into a cohesive story.

When you turn the page, you are greeted with a new layout, but the grid and elements are consistent. The photos and the pull quote draw you into the body text. You continue reading to the next spread of pages, and now what you are reading is supported by the images and pull quote, rather than the other way around.

One rule of human nature is that in order to determine the content of an article, readers look at the image first, no matter how descriptive the headings and subheadings may be. A common eye-catching effect is to use an image that does not reveal the story line but rather forces the reader to dig deeper to get what is called the solution to the problem or the answer to the question. Same goes for the headline, which is often a play on words to attract your attention without giving away the details.

Cover designs share the same goal: to intrigue you with snappy copy and a dazzling image and entice you to explore further by buying and reading the magazine. A cover photo must give a general sense of what's inside without giving it all away. A single, bold headline will refer to the most important, must-read article inside or the theme of the issue. Smaller, less critical story titles will bolster the photo and hold your interest without distracting from the main message. You'll explore these concepts more in the project at the end of this chapter.

The Art of the Layout

What makes the *MAGNET* design work? The designer used some classic principles to energize her two-page spreads: contrast, alignment, repetition, and proximity.

In the following section, we'll explore those principles in action on various well-designed magazine covers and articles. Once you've seen the examples, I invite you to reexamine the Tom Waits article and see how well the *MAGNET* designer implemented the ideas.

Contrast

Remember our discussion of negative space? The designer of the Tom Waits article created a strong contrast by using photographs that had large areas of empty space. Sometimes magazine pages are quite barren places—negative space can be crucial to a well-designed page. At other times, the designer will use empty space for a heading or pull quote, breaking the conventional separation between text and image.

How else can a designer add contrast? Think of all the ways you experience contrast in your life. When something happens that is not a part of the daily routine, it creates contrast. Cold, gray days make you appreciate the warmth of summer. The same goes for layouts. The empty spaces in the photos may contrast with the detailed text below them. Photographic detail may contrast with the simplicity of text. Large elements contrast with small ones, loud elements with quiet ones, and so on.

Keep in mind that contrast is also about the content of the information that you are designing, not just the visual aspects of the material. An article about erupting volcanoes might appear alongside a witty heading and a nonchalant pull quote: "10,000 tons of lava was not that surprising, really." Like any good designer, a magazine designer will play with the reader's expectations.

▼ | **tip**

Space is seemingly at a premium in magazine design—how do you cram all the text and images into the given page layout and still leave some space empty? Take a tip from our MAGNET example and try using nearly blank areas of a photo or illustration as your negative areas.

FIGURE 11.11: In this cover of *Bust* magazine, the details in the upper two-thirds contrast with the more stark lower section, and the black-and-white photo contrasts with the colors of the logo and text—as well as the common convention for full-color photos on magazine covers!

FIGURE 11.12: Contrast makes this entire spread from *Azure* magazine bold and intriguing. The black and white lettering on the left is severe compared to the serene, colorful picture on the right—and yet they work together perfectly. Notice how the white of the left page continues into the building, and how the blocks of text are balanced.

Alignment

In our analysis of the Tom Waits spreads, we saw that while the grid provides a good deal of organization, none of the pages look exactly alike. The columns make the body text easy to read, photos are made bolder by stretching them over several columns, and horizontal guides keep photos and pull quotes aligned consistently with other page elements throughout the article.

The alignment of elements on an introductory spread creates a synergy between photo and text, with the goal of making it compelling and clear. Alignment keeps a balance throughout the composition so that the reader is psychologically comfortable. The images or text of articles might be used to cause a stir, but in most cases the layout should not aggravate—or readers will not have the patience to delve further into the article.

FIGURE 11.13: In this introductory spread, a horizontal line is used to emphasize the relation between the text on the left and the frog photo on the right. Also notice how the clever treatment of the text mimics the frog's webbed feet. The result is a beautifully unified design.

Repetition and Proximity

The repetition of design elements imparts a subtle consistency to the *MAGNET* layout. Body text always flows neatly through all of the columns, photos all share a similar treatment, the same grid is used on all pages, and the special text areas are handled in the same style. This is no accident, and was not done to save design time—it was all to make the reader feel comfortable as he or she continues reading through several pages of the article.

Such internal consistency helps make the article a neat little package that is separate from all of the other articles in the magazine, and yet part of the whole.

You can create order by putting similar items together: captions with photos, heading with subheadings, and so on. Using proximity helps readers quickly see the relationships between elements rather than have to search for them.

FIGURE 11.14: Throughout this *ReadyMade* spread, proximity helps readers connect the descriptions to the photos quickly, forming a number of pockets of content.

Some Rules of Thumb

Newspapers and newsletters or other media that convey current information are mostly too packed and dense to give the designer any breathing room. Designing for these media is considered difficult and requires years of experience, even though it may look simpler and less creative on the surface.

However, the layout and design of magazines (both spreads and covers), as well as posters, advertisements, and brochures, allows you to play with drama and contrast in terms of content and spatial relationships. Here are some rules of thumb that designers find useful:

- Keep it simple. The number of main messages should be at a minimum. One large main image and one major headline normally work best, especially on a cover.

- Leave 30 to 40 percent of the opening page empty. This refers to multipage designs such as spreads and brochures. The more information you need to put on a page, the more space you should leave empty. Note that the continuation of a story on subsequent pages can be in a denser layout because the reader's attention is already there.

- Keep elements in as few groups as possible. Avoid a busy page by tying the elements together according to their relevance to one another.

- Maximize the contrast. Contrast is the basic foundation of all design and art. Commonly perceived as the relationship between black and white, contrast involves much more than just opposites. It appears whenever there is a tension created between two design elements.

The style or visual language of layout is always changing, perhaps because it makes an identity statement. Anything relating to fashion, for example, must live in flux. Thousands of magazines are currently published, and new ones are created every day. Who knows—as a designer, you may be tasked with creating a visual language for the next generation of readers.

FIGURE 11.15: The logo and the headline of this *Venus* cover stand out thanks to contrast, and the headline and photo are grouped to make the main story clear. Secondary stories are listed in a separate grouping, and there is lots of negative space used for balance.

Designing a Cover and Spread

This next project will tap all of the design skills you've learned in this book so far. You're going to create a magazine cover and two-page spread from scratch. The client is looking for something cutting-edge but also clear to readers— something that will really jump off the newsstand and keep readers interested when they start reading.

To kick it off, you'll hit the newsstand yourself for some research, and then get to the challenging task of preparing images and text and laying them out.

Project Brief: Phashion Magazine

A Chicago-based publishing house is planning to launch a brand-new magazine called *Phashion*. As the name suggests, this print magazine will cover the latest news and creations in the fashion industry worldwide and will focus on the Internet as a global marketplace for trendy clothing. It targets retail consumers more than industry insiders; readers will find stories covering online fashion events and where to buy clothing on the Web. The magazine will also include guides to related Internet resources, as well as hot topics such as the need for new international size standards in Web merchandise.

The target audience is fashion-savvy cosmopolitan types and interested suburbanites, both male and female. They're typically well-paid professionals between their mid-20s and late 40s.

The execs over at *Phashion* are looking to you to help them determine the design direction for their future spreads and covers. You'll work on a cover and a two-page spread based on your own article and image choices, and then present it to them.

Project Summary

Research the client's target audience and collect appropriate images and stories for use in the cover and spread designs.

Create a simple, type-based logo for the magazine.

Design a compelling cover for the magazine that follows the "one-message rule" and includes the logo and a main image.

Design a two-page introductory spread for an article utilizing a three-column grid system, at least one image, a headline and subheading, and other text or image elements if needed.

Project Steps

Unlike many large-scale design jobs, this project puts you in charge of every facet. You have lots of creative freedom, but you must still communicate to your audience clearly and effectively.

1. Collect Images and Ideas

In the magazine industry, the editorial department will generally provide text and images. But *Phashion* just doesn't have any yet, so to nail this design job, it's time to go to the nearest newsstand and check the Web for images and possible titles and topics that are relevant to this magazine. You can scan or download images as necessary since they are for mock-up purposes—but remember that for any real-world professional design, all images must be original.

You should come up with at least 15 small and large images for the project. You won't use them all, but they'll give you a good starting point. Try to find shots of catwalks, photo shoots, famous designers, celebrities in designer wear, geographic locations where fashion events take place (such as Paris, New York, and Milan), and other fashion-related images. Also, try to grab groups of photos that have the same theme, since they may be used in a spread for the same article later.

If you're not sure of the style and quality of images typically found in classy fashion magazines, spend some additional research time on this before choosing your images. Find out about the target audience as well, and learn what these readers will find appealing.

To keep yourself on track, describe in short sentences the visual content of the images you have collected.

2. Collect Topics and Story Ideas

Jot down at least five topics, articles, or stories that could accompany the images you've found. Here are a couple of examples:

- Any article about the Global Garment Association's attempt to standardize the clothing and shoe sizes around the world. Headline: "Size 9 or 43?"

- Guide to the Internet's fashion malls, covering prices, shipping, and competition. Headline: "Internet Fashion Guide"

- Article on how to find the hottest skirts from Tokyo online. Headline: "Skirting Tokyo"

You may wonder why you, as the designer and not a writer, have to come up with stories and ideas for a magazine cover. For draft purposes, you'll often have to give a client a polished sample that incorporates some believable *dummy text* as a placeholder. Also, inventing the stories and searching for the images helps you to understand the audience and learn the best way to convey the magazine's themes.

3. Create a Simple Logo

Did we mention that *Phashion* doesn't even have a logo yet? If you've already finished Chapter 7, "Logo Design," you should be able to tackle this step more easily.

Magazine logos are typically type-based with no supporting graphics. And the typeface is usually just a simple one. Why? Overly decorative elements and ornate text can distract readers from the cover image and headlines. Since the most common use of the logo is on the busy cover itself, the logo doesn't need supporting elements to explain what the brand is all about.

That's why magazine logos are usually just one color as well. When you create your logo, just work with black on white. Then, when you add it to the cover in the next step, you can choose a color that coordinates or contrasts with the cover image.

The logo should be simple, but take your time with each letter and experiment with things like spacing, upper- and lowercase, and other elements to make it clean, cohesive, and unique.

FIGURE 11.16: Experiment with logo designs—come up with lots of them, and narrow them down to theone you think does the best job of conveying the *Phashion* theme simply.

Work on your logo in Illustrator and save it as an .eps file to use later.

4. Plan Your Cover

After you've identified your source images and story ideas, narrowed them down to the best ones, and finished the logo, you're ready to work on a cover. But where do you begin? Here are some ideas to get you going.

First, do your research. Yes, again! If you're not familiar with fashion magazines by now, go back to the newsstand. Especially if you are not a member of the magazine's target audience, you'll need to look long and hard at comparable cover designs. Ask yourself questions such as:

- What do the photos on the covers have in common? How many photos are generally found on a cover?

- How much room does the logo take up on the cover?

- How is negative space utilized?

- How is typography handled in terms of color, spacing, size, and placement?

Next, you'll need to be compelling. The cover will need to compete with hundreds of other magazines sending hundreds of other messages. The combination of text and image will need to intrigue the viewer. Speaking of images, please be tasteful when making your image selections.

The cover should call attention to specific articles in addition to expressing what the whole magazine and brand is about. The audience will likely be giving the news rack a quick scan. Since this is a fashion magazine with an Internet twist, the cover needs to scream "fashion magazine."

Stick to the "one-message rule." If you take a closer look at most (good) magazines, you will find that they feature one main message on the cover. Even if the cover hints at several storylines, one image and heading will generally be linked to create an effective message.

FIGURE 11.17: One bold image, with an unexpected pose, ties in with the largest headline on this *Budget Living* cover—"Dive In! 201 Splashy Steals and Dazzling Deals." Like most popular magazines, Budget Living lists several secondary stories but presents them with less emphasis than the lead story.

FIGURE 11.18: The "50 gifts under $50" headline on this *Real Simple* cover ties right into the bold gift box imagery to form a single main message. Less important stories are listed with less emphasis so you notice them after the first one attracts your attention.

5. Design the Cover

Most magazine covers are around 8 by 11 inches or larger and created in CMYK color mode in a high resolution for printing. They're often created in layout software such as QuarkXPress or InDesign, but you can get a good feel for layout with your trusty friend Photoshop.

To begin, create a new document in Photoshop that is 8 inches wide by 11 inches tall, in CMYK color mode, and 300 dpi resolution. Remember to save often as an editable .psd file as you work.

Locate and open the .eps file of your final magazine logo. When opening this in Photoshop, you will be asked what size and resolution you would like to use. Choose 300 dpi and a size that spans most of the width of your cover. If you don't like the size you select, close the logo file and try again—this will give you much better quality than if you try to scale the logo later. When you have it the size you like, drag it to your cover and position it.

When positioning the logo, think about the magazine examples you've seen in the lesson and the ones you found in your research. At this stage, you'll most likely want to change the color of your logo to fit your planned design.

Now, select the most intriguing of your stories and choose one image as the main eye-catcher. Keep in mind what you learned earlier and your other research. Bring your image onto your cover file and position as needed. You may also want to do some tweaking to the image, such as retouching, cropping, or modifying the background.

Take close notice of the negative space around the image and how the image interacts with the logo at the top. Make any changes you need to.

Use the Type tool in Photoshop to place the dominant headline for this topic/image as well as any subheading that accompanies it. Make sure that it, along with the image, dominates the cover. Consider the headline's placement (around the image? over the image?) and its font and color.

If you choose to present other, secondary story titles on the cover, make sure that you give them minimal visual attention while still handling them tastefully. You may also like to add other standard magazine elements to the cover, like the month or price.

6. Plan Your Spread

With the cover finished, you'll create a two-page spread that will introduce your cover story. Take some time to review the spreads in this chapter as well as from the magazines you researched, and consider the various successful approaches you can take in presenting an article.

Recall that in the opening spread of the *MAGNET* story, the designer used very little copy in order to create good contrast and impact before entering the text-dense area on the following pages. The *Popular Science* spread uses a similar approach but includes some of the body text as well to draw readers in.

Regardless of whether you choose to include some of the body copy, the goal is not to overwhelm the reader with text but rather to get her interested enough in the idea of the story to turn the page.

Take inventory of the elements that you could use in the spread—various images you've collected and text you've come up with. Narrow it down to what you think is necessary to get the point across, and then start sketching some ideas for placement with a grid.

The number of images is up to you, but typically one main image and perhaps a smaller image or two works well. Don't reuse the image on your cover, but a related image works great.

7. Design the Spread

Like the cover, you'll create a CMYK, 300 dpi Photoshop file. This time, make it 16 inches wide (representing two pages side-by-side) and 11 inches tall. Save your editable .psd file often as you work.

Though your text and image placement will certainly be different from the examples we've seen so far, the grid may be similar and should start with three columns. Go to View > Rulers to get started with the grid.

Click your pointer in the left ruler and drag to the right until you reach the center of the document. This guide divides the two pages. Then measure and drag guides to create three columns on each page with an equal amount of spacing between them. You may also want to drag horizontal guides from the top ruler, though these don't have to be in thirds like in the *MAGNET* example—use your judgment based on your design ideas and page elements.

Retouch your images as necessary before bringing them onto your grid. You can apply an interesting graphic treatment as well if you feel it contributes to the article—like the sepia treatment in the Tom Waits article. Bring your images to the grid, and size and position them considering the alignment, proximity, and negative space.

Add at least the headline and a subheading, carefully working to maintain the appropriate hierarchy on the page. It is up to you how much text you want beyond that, such as body text, pull quotes, or captions.

Step back from your spread and see if it needs additional elements such as background colors, decorative lines, and so on that help draw attention to the right parts of the page and provide appropriate contrast and interest. Add these last, and be sure they are not a dominant part of your design.

Student Work

What icons have other designers created? Here are some work samples from Sessions students:

FIGURE 11.19: This cover by Rollo Girando is fresh and feminine with strong photo composition and a clear main message.

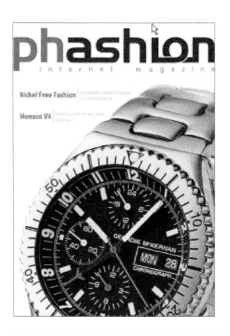

FIGURE 11.20: Geordie McKernan built his cover around this illustration of a watch and used a three column grid in his spread to flow the text and present an interesting take on the main article image and pull quote. The far-left column is blank aside from a spanning heading and subheading for negative space.

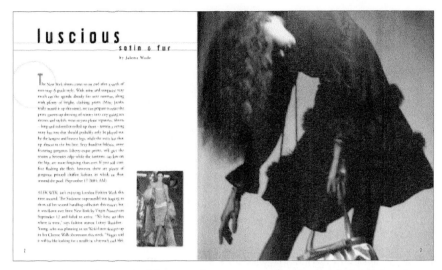

FIGURE 11.21: In Lauren Bzdak's spread, some geometric accents add interest and balance, and lots of negative space keeps the spread clean and sophisticated.

Packaging Design

Ready to create some three-dimensional designs? Packaging design is a fascinating and challenging niche for a graphic designer. What makes a product stand out on a crowded shelf? What makes it attract the eye—exciting customers, informing them, and motivating them to buy?

Packaging designers understand how to visualize a carton design in three dimensions and make it stand out on the store shelf. They are adept in the differences between mass-market and prestige products and know how to use the visual language of a product category to reach a target audience.

In this chapter, we'll explore some important concepts of packaging design. Focusing primarily on carton design, you'll learn concepts for visualizing a package in three dimensions, designing for the mass market and prestige audiences, and working within an existing brand or product line.

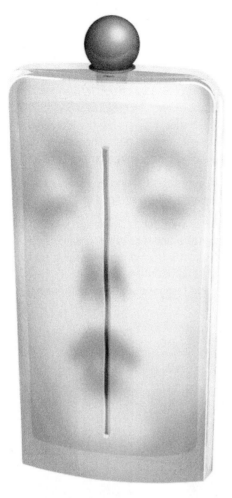

FIGURE 12.1: A conceptual design for a fragrance bottle explores sensual shapes and lighting effects.

In this chapter you will:

- Learn some general principles for designing three-dimensional packages.

- Examine the major types of 3D packages a designer may be asked to create: cartons, bags, and bottles.

- Learn about the principle of counter animation.

- Learn how a product's category, target audience, and placement affects the design process.

- Learn the important roles of visibility and consistency in packaging design.

- Explore the differences between mass-market and prestige packaging design.

- Redesign a mass-market package as a prestige brand.

Entering the Third Dimension

What's in your brimming design portfolio so far? If you're like many graphic design students, you doubtless have a stack of two-dimensional work: logos, posters, print layouts, and maybe a few Web sites. Projects like these are just great for developing your design skills. Concentrating on one page, one canvas, can help you focus on the fundamentals—color, typography, composition, and so on.

Now while these projects are all very essential and no doubt excellent, they all have one thing in common: they are two-dimensional.

Packaging design adds the dimension of depth. To design product packaging properly, you must learn to visualize a package in three dimensions. You must be able to see how a package will look from different angles, up close and at a distance, and stacked alongside its competitors. You must discover in yourself a knack for handling materials, and target your audience like a laser.

FIGURE 12.2: An initial design for Aveda Blue Oil, by Steam Design Group, shows the challenge: designing each panel and visualizing how it will look in three dimensions. A high-end cosmetics package must convey affordable luxury in its design.

Compared with two-dimensional design, packaging design affords more room for creativity (good) and more challenges (also good). Every design technique you've learned designing for pages can be applied to each surface on a product package. But your work must also pass a very powerful test. It must attract the eye in a sea of products, create a perception of value and/or quality, and, ultimately, persuade the customer to purchase the product.

Phew! We're designing the little carton that could.

Types of 3D Packages

Each manufacturing industry has its own traditional and legal requirements for the display of information. For the most part, product information must be shown on the front of your container. But the rest is total design freedom, limited only by the client's budget. In most professional situations, you are given the container dimensions up front, so you are free to concentrate only on design.

Let's begin by examining some of the types of packaging you might be asked to work on as a packaging designer and discuss how best to visualize them from a design perspective.

Folding Cartons

The folding carton is the most common and versatile form of packaging. A basic carton is constructed from a flat art design with six panels that fold together into a box. Designing some six-sided pieces is a great way to begin your packaging portfolio. It might appear simple, but it's actually a challenge, and it will give you a good foundation for pitching a packaging design project to a client or designing for some more esoteric shapes later on.

Two aspects of a carton design require very careful attention: the design of each individual panel, and the interaction of the different panels in the overall carton design. You can see both areas beautifully executed in these folding cartons created by Landor Associates for the Coleman Company.

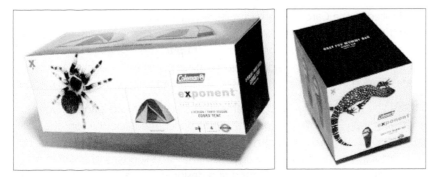

FIGURE 12.3: Eeek! With this Coleman Exponent package, the eye is drawn by photos of bugs then seduced by the clever use of each panel.

What did you notice? Your eye is immediately drawn to the box by pictures of the kind of creepy-crawlies you might encounter while using the company's camping and outdoor gear and equipment. The contrasting panels draw attention to the clear text treatment. Nice photos and detailing of product features make the product stand out. What *could* otherwise be a mundane product is positioned as high-tech gear for committed outdoors types.

To see an example from the cosmetics industry, go to www.CarolinaHerrera.com and view the Classics line of products. You'll see that the designer kept the look very simple, yet added some fun elements—dots. The dots are smaller for the more sophisticated and mature Carolina customers, and larger on the *Carolina* product for the younger customers. There is a whole graphics story told here just by the dots. All hail to the power of strong graphics!

Look closely at the Carolina Herrera cartons and you'll also notice that the designer wrapped the edges with a gold border. The gold is continued onto the back, top, and sides of the carton. It's an extremely effective use of all six sides. An added detail that contributes subtly to the carton design is the *deboss* of the dots—the slight recess of the graphics into the carton material.

If you get a chance, take a look at the packaging at your local fine department store. Packaging design is very tactile; to appreciate the fine details, it's best to have these things in your hands.

Counter Animation

You might not think packaging designers get to do a lot of animation. Well, think again.

If you looked at the Carolina Herrera carton, you'll have noticed it sported an enlarged dot pattern wrapped around the sides. Now imagine seeing several of those cartons arranged on a store counter, set up to show side, front, side—or stacked, showing alternating sides. This effect—the powerful visual impact of repeated design elements in a retail display—is referred to as *counter animation*.

Suppose you've made your design elements work well on one panel of your carton, and then applied them onto the next panel, the back, the top, the bottom, and so on until you are finished. Then you stack the finished carton or put a few cartons together in a stylish arrangement—and suddenly the whole is greater than the parts. It's a very intriguing design detail, almost a design freebie. Nice, right? I always love the surprise of that part—it's one of my favorite aspects of packaging design.

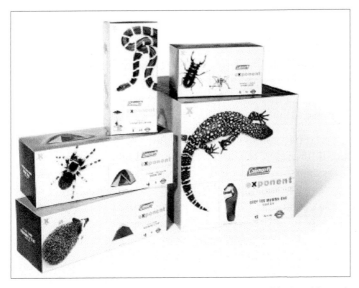

FIGURE 12.4: Stack the Coleman Exponent packages side-by-side and the cumulative effect is fun and quite powerful.

The moral of this story is not to leave any panel, flap, or tuck unloved. Note: Leaving a certain package component undecorated is *not* synonymous with leaving it unloved, for you have may love a panel and decide that in the overall design scheme it's best to leave it *un*decorated. Take great care of each part of your carton—panels, flaps, tucks—and the overall effect will reward you in turn.

▼ note

Packaging designs are contextual—you must think about how a package will look stacked along-side comrades and competitors, in good light and poor.

FIGURE 12.5: This subtle cosmetics package design by Sabine Welty draws attention to her logo and creates an interesting counter animation.

As well as cartons, an experienced packaging designer may be asked to develop related product designs such as bags and bottles. Let's look at those now.

Bags

All along the city streets or in the parking lot behind the mall, shopping bags are fighting for your attention. Shopping bags are a joy to design, especially for high-end stores, which use bags as both a status symbol and a branding opportunity. If you've got a premium shopping bag in your closet, pull it out sometime for closer inspection.

The front and back of a bag command attention. And yet, though consumers don't usually notice it, the sides, top, and bottom of the bag are also ripe for exploitation by a designer. In addition to a front and a back, bags also usually have a side, called a *gusset*. The gusset is not flat like the side of a carton— it's creased down the center and at the bottom. This unusual shape gives the designer an added opportunity to consider. What happens in the shadows? What happens within the folds? What happens when the bag is filled, or when it is empty? Do the gussets need graphics and text, or would a blast of color suffice?

FIGURE 12.6: **The gusset, the inside, and even the bottom of a shopping bag are all opportunities for a designer.**

▼ note

A shopping bag design speak for itself, projecting a clear brand message outside the store.

These are great opportunities for designers to get creative. And don't forget to consider the extras. The bag's handle—what is it made of? Does the bag even need a handle? Should the top be turned over and glued down for a clean edge, or left raw and serrated for a rougher look? Handles are an added detail that completes the graphic story of your bag design.

It should be noted that most bag design projects require working with a printer to identify production options that match your budget. Special manually applied handles, for example, can add to the cost of the bag. Rope, raffia, string—anything that requires that extra step—means you'll be paying extra for the labor, and that drives up the production cost.

Bottles

Once you've explored the delights of designing cartons and bags, other many-sided product containers such as bottles and cans will surely beckon. The tremendous variety in container shapes can add challenge and opportunity to the design process. Say you are assigned a gnarly bottle design for a Bavarian beer company. How will your graphics wrap? How can you make that wrap interesting? What color or finish will you use for the bottle top and foil?

FIGURE 12.7: This Aramis Surface collection, by Steam Design Group, illustrates the challenge of dealing with different shapes and surfaces when designing containers for a product line.

The design and labeling of bottles and cans is a challenging project usually only given to experienced packaging design professionals. A great way to begin exploring this area is by experimenting with label designs (or redesigns) for existing bottles or cans that you own.

Product, Audience, and Placement

Every design must communicate something to the viewer, and in packaging design the communication is particularly urgent. Packaging can make or break the sale of a product, so it must speak to the customer instantly. What are some of the design considerations that inform this visual language? Let's look at some of the issues that packaging designers must think about.

Product Category

Most importantly, always remember that the type of product will drive your design decisions. The Carolina Herrera example we looked at earlier shows that a high-end product such as a subtle and sophisticated fragrance requires a specific design solution: simple graphics, elegant colors, and quiet and subtle color schemes. A bottle of bleach or a chocolate wrapper would require a completely different treatment.

One important variable is color. Every product has its own visual rules and conventions. Bleach bottles, for example, are always white, with some clean blue text or red highlights. Who'd buy bleach in a dirty brown bottle? Chocolate bar wrappers, on the other hand, use shades of brown and purple to create to communicate the product and inspire indulgence. As a designer, it's your job to thoroughly research these established conventions before you begin your work.

FIGURE 12.8: **What color should a bleach bottle be? Check out the visual conventions of the product category before you go too wild.**

The food packaging industry shows why such "color rules" are paramount. Proper color choices are essential to making food packaging appealing and appetizing. The color of a food is generally represented in its brightest and liveliest colors and alongside complementary color combinations (think of yellow pasta peeking out of a blue box). Nothing can or should be more appetizing than the food itself.

FIGURE 12.9: Candidas chocolate packaging, designed by PlanetPropaganda. A bold, modern design anchored by colors that unmistakably evoke the luxury of chocolate.

It's also worth noting that colors are used to evoke specific feelings about a food product. Reds and oranges make food seem warm or hot (think frozen entrees or spicy chips). Brown or muted oranges make it appear wholesome, as seen in many bread and rice products. A few years back, green signified vegetables, but now this color is used to represent a healthy food choice. Blues, purples, and other vibrant colors are used on snack foods to make them appear more fun and eye-catching—witness that oh-so-tempting Oreo cookies packet.

One color that is rarely seen in food packaging is black. In the 1960s, the Screaming Yellow Zonkers brand broke this unspoken rule and used a mainly black box for its popcorn product. Hysterical—great packaging for a zany product. Who would have thought to put food in a black carton? The designers made it work because it was not your usual party snack food. As the name implies, it was over the top, funky, and different.

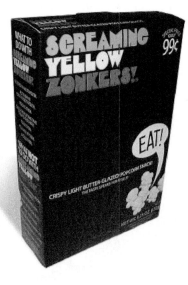

FIGURE 12.10: Screaming Yellow Zonkers broke the mold in food packaging when the company's black-colored bag was first introduced in the 1960s.

Target Audience

Just as important as the type of product in packaging design is the *target audience*. That's right, you are designing pieces to be picked up, purchased, and possessed. As packaging designers, we must be sensitive to what we are packaging and whom we are targeting. It's not just design for design's sake.

Most of the time, you will get information about your target audience from someone who has done extensive market research—*marketeers*, I call them. In any large company, it is a marketing group's job to study a product's target audience, using marketing surveys, focus groups, studies of purchasing patterns, and so on. Market analysis results in customer profiles that can be astonishingly detailed, indicating a whole set of characteristics and preferences about the ideal customer.

Once these bold marketeers' research is compiled, it is generally handed to the design team at a start-up meeting to help everyone focus on creating the best product and packaging designs for the customer. Some quite granular marketing data can become part of your design process. But while such data is important to your design, you should not pander to it. Designers must always supplement it with their own visual instincts and knowledge of styles.

Placement

You will not be responsible for the actual placement of your items on store shelves (good thing, too, because this generally happens in the middle of the night), and in fact, you generally won't even know how or where your package eventually will be placed. This makes it more important that you consider all sides of your carton design.

FIGURE 12.11: **There's no missing this Archer Farms product line by Templin Brink Design: Bold, vivid colors and a nice use of contrast ensure that these products stand out.**

I know you were thinking that your carton would be front and center on the very best shelf. That would be nice. Those decisions are complicated and have to do with financial bartering for "in-store real estate." Store placement is a tough arena in which companies compete for the best location, often actually paying retailers for prime positioning.

Next time you are in your supermarket, notice how foods are placed for the consumer. Where are those sugary cereals whose cartons are covered in popular cartoon characters? At a kid's eye level. There is no escape for the unknowing parent. The lesson is to make sure you evaluate each panel as you design in terms of its potential placement. Will it work on the very top shelf? How about the very bottom one? In shadows or in bright light? Try out your designs in best- and worst-case scenarios.

Package Composition

When working with 3D designs, a designer has both the benefit and the challenge of using many surfaces to communicate. A standard rectangular carton has six sides, each of which is your responsibility. Approach this with care, because the placement of information and graphic elements is essential to your carton's visibility and branding. Let's discover how.

Visibility

The store shelf is a crowded and competitive place, and you must always remember that when coming up with a new design. A too-modest package can easily be overshadowed by its neighbors.

There's one way to prevent this: Research! The simple secret to standing out is to conduct thorough research into competitors of your package. Take a trip to the store and see how competitive brands have addressed the composition of their packages. What design elements have the designers used, and how strong is their counter animation?

Take note of what works and what doesn't, then design something better than (not similar to!) what you've seen. You are creating a design that will lead your customer to your product, not to its competitor.

FIGURE 12.12: For a brand breakout, look no further than this award-winning Mrs. Meyers cleaning kit design from Werner Works Design. A no-fuss, no-frills product is given serious distinction through some great copy, retro illustrations, and fantastic attention to detail.

How do you decide what information goes on which panels? Primary information stands out and identifies the product. Secondary information, such as ingredients and instructions, can be less prominent and visible. In most cases, any decisions about the placement of information will have already been made by the client prior to your meeting. The client will provide not just the text you need but also any legal specifications on its size and appearance. If the client doesn't give you this information initially, you must ask. Sometimes the client will be flexible and give you some leeway as to where it goes—a design opportunity for you.

It is also important to consider how your packaging looks when it viewed in isolation. A shopping bag, for example, must work as a stand-alone piece because it is intended to be carried out of the store by a customer. When it stands alone, it must clearly advertise the product or store. To do this, the information must be prominent and visible at a glance. Out on the street, passersby will get only the briefest glimpse of the name of the store, product, or designer (oooh, Prada), so the graphics should reinforce an already established look.

Once again, it is generally the client who will dictate how prominently the secondary information should appear. I'm sure you've seen store addresses printed in the bag gusset or artfully placed beneath the store name. Secondary information can be displayed in subtle ways to reward the curious.

Consistency

Print and packaging designs created for a particular product or store must observe an ever so important design principle: consistency. Otherwise, the marketing opportunity created by recognition and repetition is wasted.

If you stack up items from any good product line, you will see that while the different products vary in shape, they will be consistent within the product line in terms of logo size, spacing, fonts, and so on. They will also be *internally consistent*: using the same fonts, colors, and other elements on all sides of the package to create an appearance of cohesion.

tip

It sounds obvious, but you need to figure out any informational or legal constraints at the outset of your project.

FIGURE 12.13: In this Maxwell's Apothecary line, many careful adjustments to the positioning of elements (but not their size and proportion) were required to impart visual consistency.

Here are some basic rules to keep your designs consistent within a product line:

- Use the exact logo and/or product logo called for by the client (it's branding, remember?).

- Use the same size of logo. Where this becomes impossible, make it visually feel the same based on the spatial relationships with your other elements.

- Keep your spatial relationships consistent. The placement of the logo, the measure of where the copy begins after the logo, where the weight claims sit, and so on should be consistent across products.

- Align your graphics as precisely as you can. Where this is impossible, make it visually appear to align. This will happen automatically if you keep your spacing consistent.

- Keep your graphics reading in the same direction (generally left to right or top to bottom).

- Maintain your color palette.

- Use the same fonts.

Mass vs. Prestige Design

A packaging designer's life is never dull, because the target audiences for products are many and diverse. Someone once said there are as many target audiences as marketers (and that's saying something). Every project you take on will involve thinking about a different group of people.

One thing you'll have to figure out about every packaging design project: Are you designing for a mass market or a prestige market? Depending on your answer, there is a big difference in what your packaging design should communicate about the price of the product and, interestingly, about the people who buy it. In this section, I want to talk about these differences to help you make better design decisions for your clients.

Some definitions before we begin:

- Mass-market design—Of or relating to the majority of people. Familiar and accessible. Think drugstores, supermarkets, Kmart, Target, and so on.

- Prestige market design—Commanding status in people's minds. Exclusive and expensive. Think boutiques, specialty shops, and upscale department stores.

What you would design for Porsche would look very different from what you would design for Hyundai. What you would design for a supermarket-brand springwater would look very different than your project for Evian. Zest soap versus Aveda cleansing bars, Lipton bags versus Tazo fine teas, and so on. If you understand the difference between mass-market items and premium brands (and oh, how keenly the pain can be felt!), then you get the picture.

The Mass Audience

When designing for a mass audience, the key to remember is that the product must sell to the masses. Sounds obvious, right? But it can be tough. The design must feel familiar and inclusive—it must appeal to a broad range of people without excluding any major customer group.

Please note that this doesn't mean bad or cheap-looking design—it simply means a more approachable design. In most cases, a mass-market carton design requires a very restricted budget, which usually results in using inexpensive materials and production processes. But these constraints are balanced by the challenge of achieving a high level of graphic design.

FIGURE 12.14: **A mass-market brand package such as Canada Dry is immediately recognizable and always accessible.**

The mass audience demands clarity and approachability in design: friendly colors, clear fonts, readable illustrations, and understandable graphics—nothing to rock the boat. Your audience is interested in price and value too, so if your carton production cost raises the overall cost of the product, chances are your audience will avoid your item. The design itself must convey the value of the product—value for money, that is.

▼ tip

Mass-market products should never look cheap—instead, they should convey affordable value.

One of the challenges in the mass-market package design is how to arrange primary and secondary information so that each carries the proper weight for the audience. The mass audience must get the gist at a glance and quickly understand the cost of the product. That's a significant issue—just think about how *you* shop for staple items. Conveying the product's price may require a call-out or another emphasis that says "new," "special," or "natural," in addition to all of the other text on the package.

Case Study: Garnier Hair Color

Here's an effective illustration of mass packaging design: a hair color package produced by Garnier. By definition, it's a mass-market product, and the designers are generally required to communicate a lot of information all over the carton.

The Garnier hair products company does a very nice job on its carton designs, which appear in drugstores and other mass retailers. The designers manage to arrange everything in a pleasing composition, while giving the customers all of the practical, product-related information they need. And as anyone who has dyed their hair will tell you, hair color boxes require a *lot* of information.

FIGURE 12.15: Prestige or mass-market? This Garnier package combines some expensive production values with clear, accessible design and pizzazz.

For this product, the designers created an effective text layout that makes the most important content stand out. The main focus on the carton is the hair color itself—the box must have a great shot of a woman with fabulous-looking hair color and an expression of joyous self-expression. The next focus is "100% color," a statistic that shouts out the product's competitive edge in the hair color market. Next comes the brand name and hair color number and name. Then, the "new" flag is added along with the technical bit in the circle. Finally, you'll see some more technical information at the bottom left: "permanent color, one application."

Compare the Garnier box above with similar products at different price points. You will see that the designers of the Garnier package used all sides of the carton to convey an incredible amount of information. Other brands will handle that information differently depending on the price of the product and the skill of the designers. Put yourself in the designer's shoes; it's challenging to compose all of the information and still end up with a carton design that looks and feels inviting.

The production on the Garnier carton was very expensive. Yes, I know, I just contradicted myself. A little while back I told you that mass-market packaging must convey inexpensive production values. That's true, but as a packaging designer, you sometimes have the goal of conveying affordable luxury.

The hair market is special. Yes, it's a mass product and its packaging design is for the masses, but the goal of the product to create natural-looking hair color. Every man or woman who is shopping for hair color has some reservations about the purchase, and so expensive production processes are required. The printing of the actual hair color and color swatches on the carton must match the dye inside the carton. This requires intensive print proofing and an incredibly accurate printing processes—it cannot be subjective. On press, the designer may have signed-off color proofs, production dyes, actual hair samples, a hair color expert, and a hair color technician all on hand to check the final color.

No-Frills Marketing

Let's look at another drugstore product on a much tighter budget. Pretty carton design, right? This product packaging design isn't going to win any awards, but I guarantee it's a huge seller. It's simple and approachable, it has in-your-face information, and it's printed on a very inexpensive board stock (a type of card) with cheap colors.

No-frills packaging is the extreme logical extension of conveying value for money in a mass-market product. Every expense is spared, including the design!

FIGURE 12.16: Every expense was spared for this fictitious no-frills product—including design.

Look at that photo. Do you think they spent any money on a photo shoot? No; this is a very inexpensive job, so the designers probably didn't even use a professional hand model. Odds are they used a neighbor or friend who had nice-looking fingers.

The logo is extremely large and garish—the client probably wanted it that way. But this generic, no-frills carton design has all the information in the right order; it's bold enough for the customer to grab; and the design matches the low price. To me, this carton has some potential. If you just changed the fonts, the colors, and the composition, this could still work, even using that terrible photograph.

The Prestige Audience

OK, now that we're done looking at the drugstore generic brand, let's hop in an uptown cab. Madison Avenue, here we come. When designing for a prestige audience, always remember that less is more. Less is *always* more in good design, but it's particularly important in the packaging for prestige brands. Prestige brands must look exclusive—a quality that is conveyed by subtle details.

Research, restraint, and refinement are required when designing for prestige audiences. Graphics must be exquisitely chosen and impeccably placed. Unusual or fashionable colors are de rigueur, as are clear, interesting (often hand-drawn) fonts. Rock the boat here with the details and your choices. In most cases, a prestige carton design will have a higher budget than a mass-market one. This permits relatively expensive materials and finishing. You can't put a $45 cleanser in a 2-cent carton.

One challenge with prestige brands is how to arrange minimal information in an interesting way—more editing of the layout is involved than with mass-market products. It is often hard for designers who are not used to designing for prestige brands to hold back.

tip

Prestige packaging design involves finding out about expensive and esoteric production techniques, a topic that most printers are happy to discuss with you!

FIGURE 12.17: **A hot chocolate carton designed for New York emporium MarieBelle. All of MarieBelle's packaging exhibits a luxurious and appetizing use of color and finishes.**

For a cosmetics industry example, seek out the Ralph Lauren Polo Blue fragrance package online at www.polo.com. It uses only the essential elements: logo, texture, finish, and color. When you look closer or, better yet, take a look at a real carton, you'll notice a hand-drawn pony; simple, straightforward, wonderfully kerned type; and beautiful blue printing.

If you get this product in your hands, you'll find that the matte blue ink is entirely saturated into the fiberboard of the carton. A subtle overall pattern emboss gives the carton a texture. Next, you'll see the gloss silver foil stamping and embossed pony and frame line. All design elements work together to create a seemingly simple, clean design. The genius is in the details as well as in the editing. No unnecessary design geegaws.

Mass to Prestige Carton Design

Ah, the marketeers, our friends and foes. Our next project springs fresh from the fertile imagination of one of those marketing experts I mentioned earlier. This project will enable you to tackle a 3D carton design and explore some of the differences between mass-market and prestige packaging. You'll be given a generic carton for a nail polish remover and asked to give it a prestige makeover.

FIGURE 12.18: Hmm, this humble package needs to go uptown. What colors and details will you add to prepare it for the spa?

Project Brief: Anaf Spa and Salon

The marketing executive at a major drugstore chain has developed a brief to reposition an existing generic product package as a prestige brand. The client wants a designer to take its popular but design-challenged nail polish remover upmarket. Read through the brief, and then we'll talk about how to approach the project.

We at Mass Market Drugs want to upgrade the packaging graphics for our Nail Polish Remover Pads.

The exclusive Anaf Spa and Salon wants to use our product in its salon. We need to give the carton a face-lift—to transform it from a mass-market box to a prestige package. The new carton should look completely different from the existing one. There should be no similarities. We also need this carton to work for us on the salon shelves, as the product will be offered for sale to convey that "at-home salon" feel. The product will be the first in a product line called Anaf Salon.

Please present your final redesign to our marketing director and explain how you see its counter animation working. Good luck with your presentation.

A few things to note about Anaf Spa and Salon. It's a Zen-inspired salon that isn't overly Zen or overly New Age. The decor uses lots of wood, metal, and deep earth tones. A visitor will see plenty of beautiful, imported tiles in deep, rich colors. The mood is very peaceful, private, and serene. It's a full-service salon, very exclusive with the finest amenities.

I think we need to spend a week at the salon in order to get "the feel" right, don't you?

Project Summary

- Research the product type by doing a store tour to look at mass-market and prestige products.

- Take careful note of the product specifications.

- Research, brainstorm, and sketch your concepts.

- Create a flat package, 3D presentation, and counter animation for your revitalized product.

Project Steps

1. Do Some Product Research

Store tour No. 1—Go to a local drugstore and find an example of a beauty product carton that is displayed on a shelf or in a counter. Briefly register what you saw. Ask to take notes or photos if you need to. Then try to answer the following questions.

- How many sides of the carton are used to display the product?

- How much space on the shelf or counter does the carton take up?

- Are any merchandising elements provided with the carton (such as posters, bags, displays, table setups, banners, and so on)? If so, what are they, and what design elements do you find consistent throughout the "family" of merchandising?

- How much of the front of the carton is decorated with graphics?

- How many colors are used in the printing? Any special finishes?

- Is the shape interesting or unusual? Does it work?

- Do you see any good design approaches to remember for your own work?

- Are any interesting materials or finishes used? Stickers? Die-cuts? Emboss/ deboss? Foils? Tints?

- Does the overall design work? If not, identify why not—and remember not to do those things!

Store tour No. 2—Now repeat the process at a fine department store. Find an example of a beauty product carton displayed on a shelf or counter. Try to answer the same questions as above. For an added bonus, try comparing mass-market and prestige packages in another genre, such as toys (try a large discount store and a higher-end toy "boutique") or food products (your super-market versus a small gourmet shop).

Remember that there are always designs that challenge the notions of mass-market and prestige and try to be all things to all people—a prestigelike mass-market product, or a mass market–like prestige product (Target pronounced "Tar-zhay," if you will).

2. Note the Product Specifications

Carton dimensions: 3" wide by 1.25" deep by 3" high

Counter animation presentation should show flat panels side by side in a horizontal line as if on a real shelf—showing front, side, front, side, and so on, five cartons long.

Front of carton:
One to four colors, possibly six (full color plus two "spot colors") if the design merits.

Anaf logo

Anaf Salon

Nail Polish Remover Pads

Non-acetone for artificial and natural nails

6 individual pads

Back of carton:
6 individually wrapped pads

Non-acetone for artificial and natural nails

Directions: Use saturated pad to gently rub polish from all nails. Pad will absorb color while special formula conditions cuticles and nails.

CAUTION: Flammable. Keep away from heat or flame. Keep away from children. Exposed pad may damage furniture or clothing.

Ingredients: Ethyl Acetate, SDA35, Water, CDP Conditioner, Fragrance, Denatonium Benzoate, D&C red #33

Distributed by Mass Market Drugs, New York, NY 10001

3. Create the Design

Go to the Images CD and save the Anaf logo as an .eps file. You will need it to create the flat package, the 3D presentation, and the counter animation. Let's break down the necessary design elements before we get into the design.

FIGURE 12.19: Different packaging of the same information, with a different brand—a true challenge for the packaging designer.

First let's look at the original, decidedly mass market–oriented box. This packaging serves its purpose, but it needs an upgrade for the spa and salon audience. Consider colors relevant to the company's story to create a mood. Think about the fine elements used in the Anaf salon decor so that your carton design fits right in.

Remember, we want to tell the story but we don't want to overcrowd the message. If you choose to leave a panel blank or just use a color field, that's a valid decision. Editing is very important—if something feels like too much, take it out. Listen to your gut, and if an element starts to irk you, remove it—no second thoughts.

Ready to start designing? Use these steps to plan your attack.

1. Plan and select your images or illustrations.

2. Edit your images in Photoshop.

3. Make a flat carton template in Illustrator.

4. Import Photoshop images into Illustrator, add text, and save the flat package file.

5. Create a 3D mock-up showing the carton panels in perspective.

6. Create a counter animation by showing several examples of your 3D mock-up side by side (in either Photoshop or Illustrator).

Good luck—and remember to read and reread the brief, research, follow your gut, relax, and have fun.

Student Work

What have other design students done with this project? Here are some work samples from the Sessions classroom:

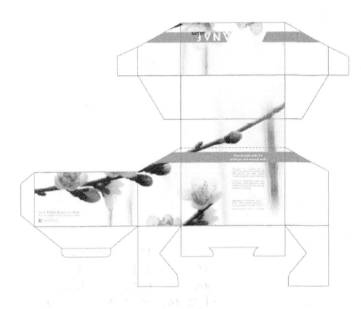

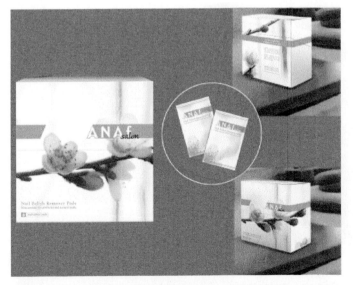

FIGURE 12.20: Sahar Shawa created an airy and refined floral design that wraps invitingly around her carton.

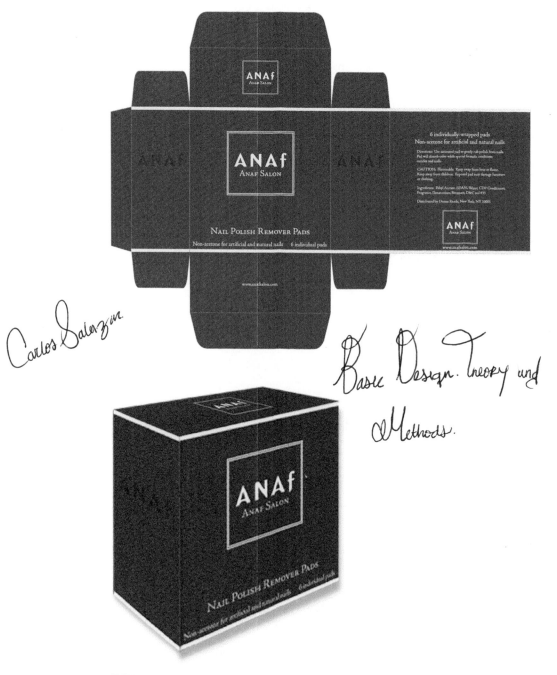

FIGURE 12.21: Erin Dorholt put together an understated package that luxuriates in the color brown.

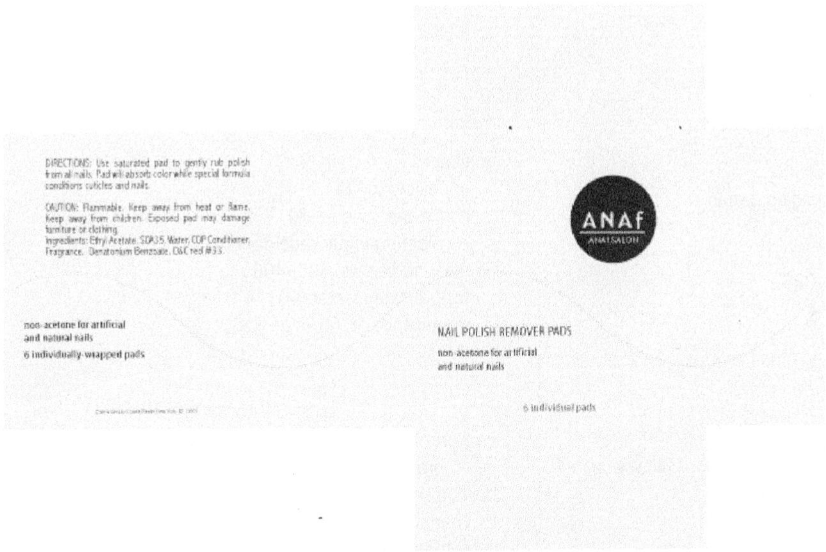

DIRECTIONS: Use saturated pad to gently rub polish from all nails. Pad will absorb color while special formula conditions cuticles and nails.

CAUTION: Flammable. Keep away from heat or flame. Keep away from children. Exposed pad may damage furniture or clothing.
Ingredients: Ethyl Acetate, SDA35 Water, COP Conditioner, Fragrance, Denatonium Benzoate, D&C red #33.

non-acetone for artificial
and natural nails

6 individually-wrapped pads

NAIL POLISH REMOVER PADS

non-acetone for artificial
and natural nails

6 individual pads

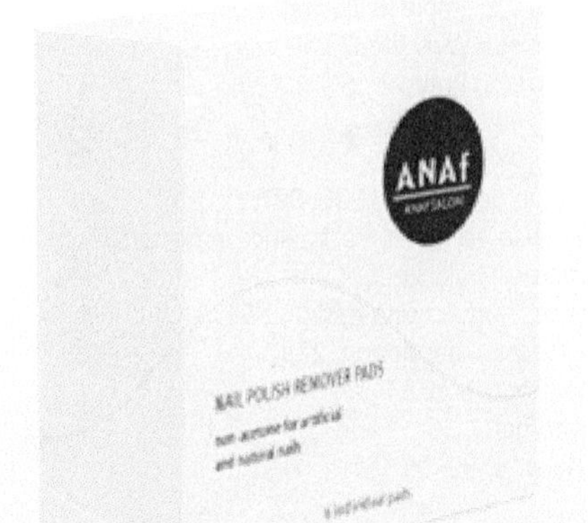

FIGURE 12.22: Sabine Welty developed this minimal upscale design that has an interesting counter animation and is a wonderful showcase for her logo.

Index